D1606063

ITALIAN AMERICAN

DAVID A. J. RICHARDS

ITALIAN AMERICAN

The Racializing of an Ethnic Identity

New York University Press • *New York and London*

NEW YORK UNIVERSITY PRESS
New York and London

© 1999 by New York University

Library of Congress Cataloging-in-Publication Data
Richards, David A.J.
Italian American : the racializing of an ethnic identity / David
A.J. Richards.
p.   cm.
Includes bibliographical references and index.
ISBN 0–8147–7520–9 (cloth : alk. paper)
1. Italian Americans—Cultural assimilation. 2. Italian
Americans—Ethnic identity. 3. Immigrants—United States—Cultural
assimilation. 4. Racism—Political aspects—United States—
History—19th century. 5. Racism—Political aspects—United
States—History—20th century. 6. United States—Emigration and
immigration—History. 7. Italy, Southern—Emigration and
immigration—History. 8. Constitutional history—United States.
9. Constitutional history—Italy. 10. Constitutional history—
Europe.   I. Title.
E184.I8R52   1999
305.851073—dc21   98–53611
                    CIP

New York University Press books are printed on acid-free paper,
and their binding materials are chosen for strength and durability.

Manufactured in the United States of America

10 9 8 7 6 5 4 3 2 1

For Diane Rita Richards

Hitherto they had thought of me as a sort of man from Mars, the only one of my species, and the discovery that I had blood connections here on earth seemed somehow to fill in their picture of me in a manner that pleased them. The sight of me with my sister tapped one of their deepest feelings: that of blood relationship, which was all the more intense since they had so little attachment to either religion or the State.

—Carlo Levi, *Christ Stopped at Eboli*, at 88–9

Liberalism is being reconstructed from the foundations: its foundation is the personality of man, which has been more oppressed and flouted than any other social and political value. The energy which the Italians will in the future bring to their reaffirmation of human personality will be the measure of their ability to share in the entire life of modern Liberalism.

—Guido de Ruggiero, *The History of European Liberalism*, at 342–3

Contents

Acknowledgments

This book was researched and written during a sabbatical leave taken from the New York University School of Law during the academic year 1997–98. Work during both the sabbatical leave and the associated summer was made possible by generous research grants from the New York University School of Law Filomen D'Agostino and Max E. Greenberg Faculty Research Fund. I am grateful as well to my colleagues and to my dean, John Sexton, for forging an academic culture of learning at the School of Law so hospitable to scholarly work.

My thinking about issues of race has been stimulated over the years by conversations with my colleagues Anthony Amsterdam, Jerome Bruner, Peggy Davis, and Ronald Dworkin and my understanding of comparative public law deepened by teaching several seminars with my colleague and friend Thomas M. Franck.

Work on this project was aided by the excellent research assistance of Yuval Merin; my secretary, Lynn Gilbert, ably assisted me in gathering the research materials used in writing this book and preparing the manuscript for publication.

My work was also greatly assisted by the enthusiastic support for this project of Niko Pfund, director of the New York University Press, including the helpful reader's comments he secured so promptly.

I am grateful, now as always, for the love, conversation, advice, and support of Donald Levy.

My sister, Diane Rita Richards, has conversed with me about the issues raised in this book over many years, and has given me illuminating criticism and comments on its argument; the book is dedicated, with love, to her.

New York, N.Y.
August 16, 1998

I

Introduction

THE NATURE AND the role of the politics of identity have become increasingly important issues in both American political and constitutional argument, involving assertions of rights by, among others, Jews, African Americans, women, gays and lesbians, Native Americans, Asian Americans, and Latinos.[1] I myself have examined many of these issues in recent works, combining interpretive history, political philosophy, and constitutional argument in order to make sense of the role of a politics of identity in expanding the inclusive legitimacy of American revolutionary constitutionalism.[2] I have not, however, discussed nor does the rich contemporary literature of the past decade discuss these general issues of identity politics in a way that self-consciously arises from the perspective of my own Italian American ethnic identity, a silence that is itself quite remarkable.[3] For example, Ronald Takaki has recently offered an overview of the history of multiculturalism in Amer-

---

[1] See, for important recent studies along these lines, Martha Minow, *Not Only for Myself: Identity, Politics and the Law* (New York: New Press, 1997); Joseph Tilden Rhea, *Race Pride and the American Identity* (Cambridge, Mass.: Harvard University Press, 1997).

[2] See David A. J. Richards, *Toleration and the Constitution* (New York: Oxford University Press, 1986); *Foundations of American Constitutionalism* (New York: Oxford University Press, 1989); *Conscience and the Constitution: History, Theory, and Law of the Reconstruction Amendments* (Princeton: Princeton University Press, 1993); *Women, Gays, and the Constitution: The Grounds for Feminism and Gay Rights in Culture and Law* (Chicago: University of Chicago Press, 1998).

[3] There is an older literature dating from the 1970s that does deal with these issues, which I have found useful in developing the argument of this book. See, for example, Alexander DeConde, *Half Bitter, Half Sweet: An Excursion into Italian American History* (New York: Charles Scribner's Sons, 1971); Richard Gambino, *Blood of My Blood: The Dilemma of the Italian Americans* (Garden City, N.Y.: Doubleday, 1974). For more recent studies, see Jerre Mangione and Ben Morreale, *La Storia: Five Centuries of Italian American Experience* (New York: HarperCollins, 1992); Lydio F. Tomasi, Piero Gastaldo and Thomas Row, *The Columbus People: Perspectives in Italian Immigration to the Americas and Australia* (New York: Center for Migration Studies, 1994).

ica in which he assesses the experience of the supposedly non-Anglo peoples of the United States, including sustained studies of Native Americans, African Americans, Jews, Irish Americans, Asian Americans, and Latinos, but he offers no study of Italian Americans except by way of quite cursory comparison to these other groups.[4] The omission of any sustained discussion of an important non-Anglo immigrant group, one that included the nearly four million immigrants who arrived from Southern Italy between 1890 and 1920 alone,[5] let alone such an omission by a scholar of stature who is usually sensitive to the silencing of alternative narratives, suggested to me the existence of a major disciplinary problem in the methodology of ethnic studies—the uncritical perpetuation of the silencing that such studies usually so rightly condemn. We need to understand how and why this could happen in order to preserve the very integrity of the antiracist discourse such studies advance. The problem may raise important general issues about how such antiracist discourse should be theorized, issues that are of pressing contemporary concern. I want, in this work, to suggest good reasons for breaking this silence about Italian American identity in order better to understand the impact of these issues on the role of the politics of identity in American political and constitutional argument.

In particular, the book examines both the durability and the continuing power of American racism in terms of how that racism has targeted immigrant groups regarded as nonvisibly black and suppressed or tried to suppress multicultural traditions that might protest such racism. My thesis is that American racism could not have had the durability or the political power it has had, either in the popular understanding of American culture or in the corruption of constitutional ideals of universal human rights, unless new immigrants, themselves often regarded as racially inferior, had been drawn into accepting and supporting many of the terms of American racism. A reasonable historical understanding of American political and constitutional culture reveals two inconsistent themes: first, basic constitutional principles

---

[4] See Ronald Takaki, *A Different Mirror: A History of Multicultural America* (Boston: Little, Brown, 1993).

[5] Nearly four million Italians immigrated during this period. See Humbert S. Nelli, "Italians," in Stephan Thernstrom, ed., *Harvard Encyclopedia of American Ethnic Groups* (Cambridge, Mass.: Belknap Press of Harvard University Press, 1980), 545–60, at pp. 547–8.

that limit the exercise of political power to respect for universal human rights on fair terms to all, and, second, traditions of entrenched cultural subordination (which I call moral slavery, including racism, sexism, and homophobia) that rest on the structural injustice of depriving whole groups of respect for such basic human rights.[6] In fact, in periods in the history of American constitutional law when the universalistic theme has appeared clearly in the ascendant (for example, after the Civil War, when the Reconstruction Amendments were ratified), the theme of unjust cultural subordination has, if anything, become even more politically powerful nationwide, resulting in blatant corruptions of constitutional principles (including judicial interpretations of the Reconstruction Amendments).[7] American racism, an important expression of this tradition of moral slavery, could not, I believe, have had this kind of continuing political power had it not extended its power well beyond the American South and into the hearts and minds of Americans nationwide, including those of the waves of new immigrants to the United States, many of whom had been and were themselves targets of American racism. We cannot begin to understand or protest the unjust terms of American racism unless all Americans, whatever their ethnicity, have some sense of how their multicultural identity has been importantly deformed or even suppressed in service of this injustice. The book investigates one variation on this larger American theme. If the Italian American experience is as illuminating an example of this injustice as I argue it is, failure to discuss it suggests a conception of ethnic studies that is insufficiently critical about the nature and depth of American racism. If plausible, both this study's methodology and its substance should have important interpretive and normative implications for the investigation of American ethnic identity in general and be useful in the study of other national identities, such as the work of Octavio Paz on Mexicans,[8] in similarly humanistic, interdisciplinary, cross-cultural terms.

---

[6] For further discussion and defense of moral slavery as a normative concept of constitutional jurisprudence, see, in general, Richards, *Women, Gays, and the Constitution*.

[7] See, for general studies of these points, Rogers M. Smith, *Civic Ideals: Conflicting Visions of Citizenship in U.S. History* (New Haven: Yale University Press, 1997); Richards, *Conscience and the Constitution*; Richards, *Women, Gays, and the Constitution*.

[8] See Octavio Paz, *The Labyrinth of Solitude*, trans. Lysander Kemp, Yaro Milos, and Rachel Phillips Belash. (New York: Grove Press, 1985).

This story, of course, was in place well before the massive European immigrations from Southern and Eastern Europe in the period 1880–1920. Well before this time, it had importantly shaped Irish American identity; the Catholic Irish, in particular the million peasants who came to the United States after the Irish potato blight of 1845,[9] were unjustly regarded by Americans, as they had long been regarded by the British, as racially inferior, but many Irish immigrants adapted to that injustice by themselves becoming virulently racist toward African Americans.[10] The study of the impact of this mechanism on each immigrant group (including the resistance of some groups to it) must be different, contextualized both to the history and culture of their countries of origin and to the period in the development of American culture when they came. For example, the narrative and background of the group of Italian Americans on which I focus here may be quite different from those of Italian Americans who came during other periods and from other parts of Italy;[11] such groups require their own separate study and examination. To resist the distorting stereotypical power of American racism, we must cultivate our moral powers to tell all these stories truthfully in their variegated and nuanced interpretive complexity and to see them as valuable demonstrations of ethnic variety, despite the efforts of American racism to reduce them to a racist fantasy of a monolithic, ahistorical American identity based on racial privilege.[12] Here, I tell one such story. In this work, I offer and use a new interpretive methodology to explore these issues, one that combines arguments of political philosophy, history, and law, to make possible illuminating interpretive comparisons of the sources and devel-

[9] See, on this point,. Patrick J. Blessing, "Irish," in Thernstrom, *Harvard Encyclopedia of American Ethnic Groups*, 524–45, at 529.

[10] See, for an illuminating study of this development, Noel Ignatiev, *How the Irish Became White* (New York: Routledge, 1995); on the racialization of the Irish immigrants and their racist response thereto, see David R. Roediger, *The Wages of Whiteness: Race and the Making of the American Working Class* (London: Verso, 1991), at 107, 110, 133–56. See also Lawrence J. McCaffrey, *The Irish Catholic Diaspora in America* (Washington, D.C.: Catholic University of America Press, 1997).

[11] See, on this point, Nelli, "Italians," in Thernstrom, ed., *Harvard Encyclopedia of American Ethnic Groups*, at 547.

[12] On the unjust consequences of such a sense of white racial privilege, see Barbara J. Flagg, *Was Blind, But Now I See: White Race Consciousness and the Law* (New York: New York University Press, 1998).

opment of multicultural identity, of variant interpretations of liberal nationalism, and of the role the political evil of racism has pervasively played in corrupting such nationalisms.

The attraction in the study of the Italian American immigrants is both the fascinating period of Italian culture and history that provided the background of their emigration and the extraordinarily racist moment in American constitutional development at which they arrived in the United States. Both Italy and America were in this period in the midst of revolutionary struggles over the meaning of nationalism. One alternative interpretation was liberal nationalism, a normative conception of national identity defined in terms of protection of the universal human rights of all people on fair terms. In both nations, the liberal interpretation was marked by appeals to universalistic principles of justice and by traditions of moral slavery that corrupted public understanding of such ideals; in both cases, the people of Southern Italy were, I argue, among the victims of such injustice. Accordingly, our interpretive project requires us to investigate and compare the terms of such defective liberal nationalism in both Italy and the United States. For this reason, the methodology of this book importantly calls for and forges the development and elaboration of a conception of comparative public law that makes such a comparison a better tool of both interpretive understanding and critical evaluation. Both the Italians and the Americans, who espoused the liberal interpretation of nationalism, conceived nationalism as a struggle for univeralistic political values of justice in which all peoples are, as equals, participants. Both the Italian emigration and the formation of Italian American identity expressed aspects of that struggle; to do them justice, we must forge a conception of comparative public law adequate to understanding the cultural background both in Italy and in the United States. We must interpretively understand both if we are to make sense of the formation of Italian American identity, in particular, what I call its privatization (its silencing of protest against the injustice inflicted on Italian Americans) as a response to the group's finding itself the nonvisibly black target of American racism. We must also take seriously the later development of antiracist constitutional principles, and the ways that appeal to such principles may and should affect a sense of Italian American identity that may now reasonably understand and protest the unjust impact of American racism on its public and private life and redefine its sense of ethical responsibility accordingly. On this basis, we may understand how and why multicultural identity, properly understood, may be the basis for a morally independent standpoint on critical issues of liberal nationalism that are, today more than ever, the concern of all nations and peoples.

The interpretive methodology proposed here takes seriously what may be the real challenge of the study of American ethnic identity, namely, to do justice to both components of a multicultural identity. The thesis of my study is that much of the power of American racism has derived from its uncritical suppression of the putatively non-American component of multicultural identity, as if the component could have no intrinsic cultural value, let alone instrumental value to American culture and identity. The approach I take arises from the search for an alternative viewpoint, one that takes seriously the aspirations of all peoples to a legitimate form of constitutional politics. Accordingly, the long initial discussion of variant interpretations of what I call revolutionary constitutionalism (chapter 2) indispensably sets the stage of such an alternative viewpoint. Certainly, this approach does not exhaust the range of inquiries that illuminate the immigrant experience, but it does take seriously one of the most important and attractive achievements of American civilization, its constitutionalism, and the interpretive role it played in the immigrant experience and the formation of multicultural identity. Such a viewpoint makes possible fruitful comparisons of variant interpretations of revolutionary constitutionalism (American, British, French, German, and Italian) that are nonrelativistic, yet appropriately contextualized to quite different historical experiences and opportunities. We thus may offer criticisms of variant interpretations (including the American), and yet also better understand why one flawed tradition was reasonably preferred to another (as it was by many immigrants to the United States). We can then both better understand and dignify the multicultural experience of immigrants like the Italian Americans. At the same time, however, we place a flawed tradition of American constitutionalism in its appropriate perspective, subjecting it to criticism, where appropriate, for having placed unjust racist burdens on new immigrants. Such a viewpoint, by taking seriously both components of multicultural identity, suggests how and why such an identity, appropriately understood, valued, and elaborated, may reasonably reshape American identity into a more defensible and legitimate constitutionalism (chapter 5).

That a story of this kind needs to be told at all shows the power American racism has had in cutting Italian Americans off from an understanding of both their own traditions in Italy and the very real struggles of their grandparents against injustice in both Italy and the United States. There is a sense in which Italian Americans do not know who they are, either as Italians or as Americans. Accordingly, such an account must, in its nature, be a recovery of historical memory, an attempt to do justice to the experience of multiple identity under unjust circumstances hostile to self-respecting assertions of identity, a feature of American life brilliantly described by W. E. B. Du Bois as "this double-consciousness" of African Americans under American racism[13] and earlier by Sarah Grimke in characterizing women's consciousness under American sexism.[14] Such a claim of self-respecting identity transforms what it studies both personally and politically by the reasonable force of its rights-based protest of the unjust burdens placed on its dual identity.[15]

I write as a third-generation Italian American. My grandparents on both sides were born in Italy but immigrated to the United States during the great wave of Italian immigration in the period 1890–1920.[16] Their families came from the hill towns of Campania outside Naples (my mother's family was from Santa Paolina, my father's from Torella dei Lombardi), and probably descended genetically from members of the large Greek settlements in Magna Graecia in pre-Roman times.[17] Both my grandfathers worked in construction, one in road building in White Plains, New York, the other in shipbuilding (dying in an accident that left my maternal grandmother to raise the seven children who survived to adulthood, six of whom attended college). My parents both understood and spoke Italian but did not speak the language to us in our home; in consequence, neither my sister nor I (both of whom have advanced degrees) speak or read the language. Our family name (orig-

[13] For citations and commentary, see Richards, *Women, Gays, and the Constitution,* 99–100.

[14] For citation and commentary, see ibid., 100.

[15] I develop this theme at some length in *Women, Gays, and the Constitution.*

[16] Nearly four million Italians immigrated during this period. See Nelli, "Italians," in Thernstrom, *Harvard Encyclopedia of American Ethnic Groups,* at 547–8.

[17] See, on this point, Alberto Piazza, "Migration and Genetic Differentiation in Italy," in Julian Adams, David A. Lam, Albert I. Hermalin, and Peter E. Smouse, *Convergent Issues in Genetics and Demography* (New York: Oxford University Press, 1990), at 81–93. Cf. L. Luca Cavalli-Sforza, Paolo Menozzi, and Alberto Piazza, *The History and Geography of Human Genes* (Princeton: Princeton University Press, 1994), at 277–80.

inally Ricciardelli) was changed by my paternal grandfather to avoid the nativist prejudice of this period (of which my father told me "You could have no idea"); my father was a gifted tenor, who chose not to follow a promising career in opera and worked instead as a civil engineer for the Army Corps of Engineers in order to lead the private family life he so loved and so graced; my mother worked as a hospital pharmacist during a period when women in her position, including the two of her sisters with working husbands, usually did not work outside the home; both parents actively supported and encouraged higher education for their children at national American universities where there were few Italian Americans, including, in my case, further graduate study abroad at Oxford University in Great Britain. Both parents were pious, practicing Catholics in the tradition of Manzoni (our family church was even run by the Capuchin order idealized by Manzoni as model of Christian tolerance and humane charity);[18] consistent with that tolerant tradition, both parents were quite independent-minded on issues like contraception and abortion. My parents were business-oriented Republicans (my sister and I are independent-minded Democrats); both my parents came to accept my gay sexual orientation, and my Jewish companion of over twenty years was very much part of our family until each of my parents' deaths; our life together remains and is lovingly familial in ways my parents came to understand, appreciate, and value.

I offer these brief biographical remarks to situate my own perspective, as an Italian American, on these issues. Italian Americans are, in the contemporary American public mind, more homogeneous than the facts justify, although certainly they are more homogeneous (under the impact of cultural Americanization) than they were as immigrants, given the highly diverse and localized traditions of life (including variant dialects) found in the diverse areas of late-nineteenth-century Italy, including the South (the Mezzogiorno), from which most of them came.[19] What Italian Americans shared was a wrenching experience both of massive migration that removed them from a certain way of life and acculturation to a very

[18] See Alessandro Manzoni, *The Betrothed*, trans., Bruce Penman (London: Penguin, 1972).

[19] See Joseph Lopreato, *Italian Americans* (New York: Random House, 1970), at 21–55.

different way of life.[20] The Italian American experience is, to this extent, one example (among many others) of multicultural identity in American politics and constitutionalism and should be understood and evaluated as yet another variation on the American theme of union and diversity.

To do full justice to the Italian American experience, however, I believe and argue that we must understand that experience through both the American and the Italian perspective on a common theme in their respective struggles for national identity: revolutionary constitutionalism. The relationship between the United States and Italy has usually been studied from the perspective of their foreign relations, focusing on American responses to immigration, the rise of Italian fascism, its role in World War II and in postwar Italian republican reconstruction and European integration.[21] But, there is another, more interpretive aspect of the relationship between these nations that must be brought into play in order to come to terms with the Italian American experience, which is, after all, the most culturally intimate relationship between these two peoples. In this work, I call for and develop such an interpretive approach in two stages. The first stage addresses what it was in the Italian experience that made emigration to America, despite all its difficulties, even injustices, so worthwhile a risk and so acceptable a trade-off for this historically risk-averse people; the second examines what it was in the general American experience that made immigration at first so appealing and then, as time passed, so threatening to Americans (a threat that culminated in the immigration restrictions, growing out of racist and nativist sentiment, incorporated in the National Origins Quota system, passed in 1924 and repealed only in 1965).[22] Both the American and the Italian narratives of revolutionary constitutionalism were cultural narratives of political promise and betrayal, but in different ways and with different bal-

---

[20] See, in general, Robert F. Foerster, *The Italian Emigration of Our Times* (New York: Arno Press and New York Times, 1969); Leonard Covello, *The Social Background of the Italo-American School Child: A Study of the Southern Italian Family Mores and Their Effect on the School Situation in Italy and America* (Leiden: E. J. Brill, 1967); DeConde, *Half Bitter, Half Sweet*; Gambino, *Blood of My Blood*; Lopreato, *Italian Americans*.

[21] See, for an exemplary study along these lines, H. Stuart Hughes, *The United States and Italy*, 3d ed. (Cambridge, Mass.: Harvard University Press, 1979).

[22] See, on this point, Smith, *Civic Ideals: Conflicting Visions of Citizenship in U.S. History*, 442–3.

ances of justice and injustice. For Italian Americans, the promise of justice outweighed the risk of injustice in the United States (in contrast to the increasingly empty promises of an Italy finally united under the terms of constitutional monarchy by 1870) to justify the disruptive cultural burdens of emigration; even America's increasingly blatant racist injustices were sufficiently familiar and arguably not as bad, from Italians' perspective, as those prevalent in Italy (in particular, as we shall see, the racist degradation of Southern Italians) that Italians could decide that the United States afforded a better balance between justice and injustice.[23]

I take the genre of revolutionary constitutionalism as a useful basis for my approach precisely because it is transnational, resting on a universalistic moral conception and associated principles that are, in their nature, the exclusive property of no people or peoples but an enduring vision of just political governance available, on terms of equality, to all peoples. The Founders of the American republic, including Thomas Jefferson and John Adams as well as Alexander Hamilton and James Madison, certainly thought this way, conceiving the American situation in 1776–1787 as an historically fortunate opportunity to not only learn from republican and federal experiments in the past but also to experiment with new constitutional forms more adequate to the underlying moral vision of the revolutionary constitutionalism that had led the colonists to revolt against Great Britain.[24] Among the republican experiments thus consulted were, in the ancient world, the Athenian democracy[25] and the Roman republic[26] and, during the Renaissance, the Florentine and the Venetian republics.[27] More fundamentally, constitutional reflection on these and other such experiments was conducted in the terms of the science of politics of Machiavelli[28] and, for the Founders, in terms of later developments of this science by James

[23] On the flaws in Italy's monarchs, including their complicity in the rise of fascism, see Denis Mack Smith, *Italy and Its Monarchy* (New Haven: Yale University Press, 1989).

[24] For discussion and support of this thesis at length, see Richards, *Foundations*.

[25] On references to the Athenian democracy, see ibid., at 30, 40, 41, 46, 109, 145.

[26] On relevant references to the Roman republic, see ibid., at 20, 22, 25, 30, 31, 57, 71, 97, 109, 145, 289.

[27] See, on this point, ibid., at 20, 30.

[28] 28. See, on Machiavelli's influence on the American Founders, ibid., at 147, 287, 289, 295.

Harrington,[29] Montesquieu,[30] and David Hume[31] (for example, Madison's theory of faction).[32] Like the American Founders, Machiavelli, as Gramsci observed,[33] thought of political science as a way of thinking about political psychology anywhere, and thus as a general contribution to bringing reason to politics as a human activity. His political thought was no more parochially Italian than that of the American Founders was narrowly American. Both, rather, addressed what they took to be universal principles of political life, in terms of which political choices could be reasonably conducted (including the choice of constitutional forms like separation of powers and representative government).[34] This universalism in both American and Italian thought is, I believe, an important interpretive presupposition of Italian American identity, and it suggests that this form of multicultural identity may, like other such forms, bring its universalistic multicultural resources to bear on efforts to better hold America to its promises of liberal nationalism.

Both the American Revolution and the subsequent French Revolution, like the English Civil War before them, justified their claims of liberal nationalism in terms of revolutionary constitutionalism, namely, testing the legitimacy of political power (including constitutional law as a higher-order organization of political power) in terms of respect for inalienable human rights.[35] The genre of revolutionary constitutionalism is, however, interpretively contestable,[36] as a comparison of American and French revolutionary constitutionalism makes quite clear. These two variant traditions proved to be decisively important in

[29] See, on this point, ibid., 100–2, 124, 132, 147, 282, 289, 295.

[30] See, on this point, ibid., 101–2, 111, 120–1, 123, 125, 129–30, 147, 287, 289, 295.

[31] See, on this point, ibid., 129–30, 147, 287, 289, 295.

[32] See, on this point, ibid., 36–9, 43, 47, 52, 55, 103, 107–8, 113, 115, 125, 161, 250–1, 259–60, 288, 290.

[33] On Machiavelli's European cast of thought, see Antonio Gramsci, *Selections from the Prison Notebooks*, ed. and trans. Quintin Hoare and Geoffrey Nowell Smith (New York: International Publishers, 1971), at 117–8, 173.

[34] On Machiavelli's suggestion of such structures, see Gramsci, *Prison Notebooks*, at 140.

[35] See, in general, David A. J. Richards, "Comparative Revolutionary Constitutionalism: A Research Agenda for Comparative Law," 26 *N.Y.U. J. Int'l Law and Pol.* 1 (1993).

[36] See W. B. Gallie, "Essentially Contested Concepts," in his *Philosophy and the Historical Understanding*, 2d ed. (New York: Schocken Books, 1968), chap. 8.

framing the options for the Italian Risorgimento and for Italian emigrants later (a form of French revolutionary constitutionalism, for example, crucially influenced the shape and the trajectory of Italian post-Risorgimento constitutionalism into increasingly illegitimate forms). Accordingly, we need to be clear on what the elements of revolutionary constitutionalism are, starting with America and then turning to the different French interpretation of these elements; we need, as well, to understand the reactionary challenge to these traditions importantly reflected not only in Italian fascism but in German constitutional thought, culminating in Nazism.

The interpretive framework of this book is a discussion of the various promises and betrayals of liberal nationalism in Italy and the United States (including the racism targeted at the people of the South in both countries) that formed the hermeneutic background for both the emigration from Southern Italy in the years between 1890 and 1920 and the experience of these immigrants and their children and grandchildren in America. To do justice to this interpretive background, the book examines the formation of Italian liberal nationalism (the Risorgimento) largely on the basis of French revolutionary constitutionalism, comparing this tradition to that of the United States and to the later development of an antiliberal tradition in Germany and Italy (chapter 2). Fundamental defects in both the French and the Italian constitutional traditions are then examined as the context for the growing sense of a legitimation crisis in Italian constitutionalism as the people of the South not only found themselves economically worse off under the ostensibly liberal terms of a reunited Italy but suffered the indignity of racist degradation (condemned by the Neapolitan liberal philosopher Benedetto Croce), which emerged as the rationale for such treatment (chapter 3). The massive emigration to the United States is examined as a reasonable choice, one combining economic and ideological components and seen as the lesser evil of two flawed forms of liberal nationalism. In particular, resurgent American racism, aimed at the new immigrants (Southern Italians and Jews) as nonvisibly black, is examined as the background of the formation of Italian American identity. The Italian and the Jewish responses to this indignity, including the withdrawal of Italian Americans from American public discourse and thus their silencing about the terms of their identity (the privatization of Italian American identity), are contrasted and explained (chapter 4). This privatized sense of identity is itself increasingly challenged by some Italian Americans in the wake of the civil rights movement. The book both explains this development and normatively urges that it should be further elaborated as one aspect of the larger value to American constitutional discourse of multicultural identity. Such multicultural discourse will enable Italian Americans, as it has enabled others, both better to understand and value their heritage and responsibly to bring the cultural resources of multicultural identity to bear on the rights-based criticism of American racism (chapter 5). Such racism, unjustly constructed on the basis of a confusion of culture with nature, is thus subjected to the culture-creating protest and ethical criticism that reveal its ideological naturalization of injustice.

2

Revolutionary Constitutionalism

IN THIS CHAPTER I consider various influential interpretations of revolutionary constitutionalism as the background to subsequent discussions of the impact of these interpretations on the formation of Italian American identity; by revolutionary constitutionalism in all its forms I mean the aspiration, by legitimate revolutionary force if necessary, to replace one set of constitutional forms with others in order better to realize a liberal nationalism (one in which the nation is based on respect for liberal principles, including equal respect for basic human rights).[1] My discussion focuses on a comparison of American and French revolutionary constitutionalism and the German political reaction thereto. I will draw on many of these themes in subsequent discussions.

THE SIX INGREDIENTS OF AMERICAN
REVOLUTIONARY CONSTITUTIONALISM

It is fundamental to the American experience that its revolutionary and constitutional project were conceived as a common enterprise.[2] Leading advocates of the American Revolution, including John Adams and Thomas Jefferson, clearly saw constitutionalism at both the state and the national levels as the test of the very legitimacy of the revolution; accordingly, Jefferson wrote no fewer than three constitutions for Virginia, and Adams was the main author of the Massachusetts constitu-

---

[1] See, in general, Yael Tamir, *Liberal Nationalism* (Princeton: Princeton University Press, 1993).

[2] The following discussion of American revolutionary and constitutional thought is the subject of Richards, *Foundations of American Constitutionalism*. For pertinent supporting arguments and citations, I refer the reader, in the text that follows, to the discussions in *Foundations*, and do not repeat here the citations contained in that work.

tion of 1780, which was consulted by the Founders in 1787.[3] The success of American constitutionalism was, for Adams and Jefferson, literally the test of the legitimacy of the revolution. In order to understand this attitude, we must examine with care (1) the political principles of the revolution, (2) the relationship of those principles to what
the Americans regarded as the pathological misinterpretation of the
British Constitution by the British parliament, (3) the analysis of that
pathology in light of the history of British constitutionalism and the
larger practice of republican and federal experiments over time, (4) the
use of such comparative political science in the construction of new
structures of government free of the mistakes both of the British Constitution and of past republican and federal experiments, (5) the weight
placed on the experiments in the American states and in the nation
between 1776 and 1787 in thinking about institutional alternatives, and
(6) the historically unique opportunity, self-consciously recognized
and seized by Americans in 1787, to develop a new republican experiment that established a new kind of argument more politically legitimate than the arguments of ordinary politics.

Revolutionary Principles

Americans, following John Locke, accepted the truth that persons
have inalienable human rights, tested the legitimacy of political power
against respect for these rights, and justified their revolution against
Great Britain on the ground of its failure to respect these rights.[4]
Locke's argument for human rights and for associated limits on political power must be understood within the framework of his central
defense of an inalienable right to conscience.[5] That defense—the argument for religious toleration—took objection, as a matter of principle,
to the political imposition of sectarian religious views as the measure
of all reasonable religious and moral views. Such imposition illegitimately used political power to entrench systems of religious and political hierarchy that deprived people at large of their reasonable moral
freedom as democratic equals. Locke's political theory generalized
this insight into a general theory of political legitimacy, which con-

---

[3] See Richards, *Foundations*, pp. 19–20, 95, 106, 123, 124, 141.
[4] Ibid., ch. 2.
[5] Ibid., 26–32.

strained political power to respect, not trammel, the equal rights of free people.[6] American religion gave strong support to these political convictions; its Protestant emphasis on the right to conscience naturally took objection to uses of political power that were inconsistent with respect for equal rights for all people, such as the right to conscience.[7]

Constitutional Principles of the British Constitution

Americans importantly believed that their revolutionary principles were also fundamental not only to the legitimacy but also to the proper interpretation of the British Constitution.[8] Americans took pride in being participants in the British common-law tradition of dissent that had fired the English Civil War and triumphed in the Glorious Revolution of 1688. When the British parliament sought to tax them, the Americans rejected this not only as a violation of their rights but also as violations of the common-law principles they took to be fundamental to both the legitimacy and the proper interpretation of the British Constitution. Americans anachronistically appealed to Lord Coke's conception of British constitutionalism, which he had urged against the tyranny of James I, and appealed to common-law principles (no taxation without representation) that applied not only to the monarchy (the gravamen of Coke's argument) but to the parliament. For Americans like Adams, Jefferson, Wilson, Hamilton, and Dickinson,[9] the British Constitution of parliamentary supremacy had betrayed its own basic principles of legitimacy; the Americans needed an alternative form of government that could use the bitter lessons of British constitutional corruption to establish a government more adequate to the true principles of the British Constitution. In that sense, American revolutionary thought was based as much on a view of the true nature of British-style constitutionalism as it was on the inalienable rights of persons, and it would be the natural test of the legitimacy of the American Revolution, thus understood, that it would produce a

[6] Ibid., 32, 51, 52, 82, 83, 88, 146, 148.

[7] For a useful general study, see Alan Heimert, *Religion and the American Mind: From the Great Awakening to the Revolution* (Cambridge, Mass.: Harvard University Press, 1966).

[8] For fuller discussion, see Richards, *Foundations*, at 65–77.

[9] See ibid., 65.

more adequate conception of constitutionalism than the British understanding of these matters in 1776.

Analysis of Political Pathologies

For Americans, the betrayal by the British of their own constitution required an analysis of political power and its corruptibilities, and they brought to bear on this question complex historical reflections. These reflections included not only their own oppression by the British, but a larger inquiry into the pathologies of political power under other forms of government, including classical republicanism (e.g., ancient Athens, Sparta, Rome; the Florentine and the Venetian republics).[10] These investigations led to the pivotal role in American constitutional thought of James Madison's theory of faction[11] and John Adams's theory of fame.[12] The theory of faction identified as a permanent fact of group political psychology that it tends to ignore or denigrate both the rights and the interests of those external to the group; the theory of fame analyzed the psychology of leadership as often motivated by drives of comparative emulation, rather than by more ultimate aims of justice and the public good. Neither Madison nor Adams was a moral skeptic, and neither doubted what each of them had demonstrated to an astonishing degree in his own life, namely, people's capacity for a sense of justice and the public good. As constitutional architects, they strove to point out not the need for moral skepticism but the permanent tendencies of political power over time that, it was reasonable to assume, an acceptable form of constitutionalism must take seriously as among the facts of humankind's political nature. The evolving political thought of James Madison—in a memorandum prepared for his use at the Constitutional Convention, in speeches at the Convention, in his correspondence with Jefferson after the Convention, and finally in the now classic argument of No. 10 of *The Federalist*—exemplifies how this perspective framed the American project of drafting, debating, criticizing, and ratifying the Constitution.

---

[10] See, for fuller discussion, ibid., ch. 2.

[11] See ibid., 32–39.

[12] See ibid., 49–55.

In his important memorandum "Vices of the Political System of the United States,"[13] Madison analyzed defects not only in the Articles of Confederation but in the state constitutions; in particular, Madison was alarmed not only by the bad policies pursued by state laws but by their unjust failure to respect rights; such laws brought "into question the fundamental principle of republican Government, that the majority who rule in such Governments, are the safest Guardians both of public Good and of private rights."[14] The difficulty was not only in the representative bodies but, more fundamentally, in the political psychology of the people themselves. The mistake of American republicanism prior to the time of Madison's writing was that it had, consistent with much Whig opposition thought, focused on the political corruptibility of government officials, not on the corruptibility of the people themselves. But the facts of political psychology applied, Madison had come to see, to all political actors; republican government was distinguished by the power it gave the people to be political actors, but it could claim no legitimate exemption from the laws of political psychology; the political power of the people was as subject to these laws as the power of a hereditary monarch or aristocracy. American constitutionalism, he asserted, must, consistent with its commitment to the uses of emancipated religious and political intelligence in service of the rights of human nature, take account of these facts, and frame its task accordingly.

Madison characterized the facts of political psychology pertinent to the American situation in Humean terms:[15]

> All civilized societies are divided into different interests and factions, as they happen to be creditors or debtors—Rich or poor—husbandmen, merchants or manufacturers—members of different religious sects—followers of different political leaders—inhabitants of different districts—owners of different kinds of property &c &c.[16]

Such factions, by definition, pursue their own private interests at the expense of any fair weight to the interests and rights of others, and the

---

[13] Robert A. Rutland et al., eds., *The Papers of James Madison, 1786–1787*, vol. 9 (Chicago: University of Chicago Press, 1975), 345–358.

[14] Ibid., 354.

[15] For discussion of the Humean influence on Madison's thought, see Richards, *Foundations*, 34–35.

[16] Rutland et al.,*Papers of James Madison*, 355.

commitment of republican government to majority rule allows majority factions untrammeled power to achieve their ends at the expense of the public interest and the rights of minorities.

Madison considered three motives as possible limits on the oppressive power of such majority factions: interest, character, and religion. But, the political psychology of faction was such, especially in a republican government, that none of them was constitutionally adequate. The ugly truth about faction was that people's critically independent judgment, as persons of conscience, about their long-term interests and about justice to others were distorted and even subverted by their group identifications:

> However strong this motive [respect for character] may be in individuals, it is considered as very insufficient to restrain them from injustice. In a multitude its efficacy is diminished in proportion to the number which is to share the praise or the blame.[17]

Indeed, Madison underscored the special ferocity of this type of factionalized injustice in republics: the sense of justice in a republican community reflects public opinion, but public opinion "is the opinion of the majority" so "the standard [of critical public opinion] is fixed by those whose conduct is to be measured by it."[18] And religion, far from being a constraint on majority factions, is often its worst expression:

> The conduct of every popular assembly acting on oath, the strongest of religious Ties, proves that individuals join without remorse in acts, against which their consciences would revolt if proposed to them under the like sanction, separately in their closets.[19]

Madison reproduced and elaborated this argument in his addresses to the Constitutional Convention on June 6[20] and June 26, 1787,[21] and in

---

[17] Ibid., 355.

[18] Ibid., 355.

[19] Ibid., 356.

[20] Max Farrand, ed., *The Records of the Federal Convention of 1787*, vol. 1 (New Haven: Yale University Press, 1966), 134–6, 138–9.

[21] Ibid., pp. 421–3.

his letter of October 24, 1787, to Jefferson that both explained and criticized the work of the Convention.[22] At the Convention Madison argued that it was not enough that new powers be given the federal government; it must provide

> more effectually for the security of private rights, and the steady dispensation of Justice. Interferences with these were evils which had more perhaps than any thing else, produced this convention.[23]

The oppressive force of faction was well supported by history and by contemporary examples in America, one example of which Madison acidly brought to stage center:

> We have seen the mere distinction of colour made in the most enlightened period of time, a ground of the most oppressive dominion ever exercised by man over man.[24]

An important task of the Constitution was to take seriously the corruptive force of many such factions and "to protect [the people] agst. the transient impressions into which they themselves might be led."[25] Madison later wrote to Jefferson in no uncertain terms about the felt need to address the problem of the oppression by majority factions of minority rights at the state level:

> The injustice of them has been so frequent and so flagrant as to alarm the most stedfast [sic] friends of Republicanism. I am persuaded I do not err in saying that the evils issuing from these sources contributed more to that uneasiness which produced the Convention, and prepared the public mind for a general reform, than those which accrued to our national character and interest from the inadequacy of the Confederation to its immediate objects.[26]

---

[22] See Robert A. Rutland et al., eds., *The Papers of James Madison, 1787–1788*, vol. 10 (Chicago: University of Chicago Press, 1977), 206–219.

[23] Farrand, *Records*, vol. 1, 134 (speech of June 6, 1787).

[24] Ibid., 135.

[25] Ibid., 421 (Madison's speech of June 26, 1787).

[26] Rutland, *Papers of James Madison* vol. 10, at 212.

Indeed, Madison's main criticism of the Constitution was conceptualized in similar terms: it had not gone far enough in imposing strong institutional constraints on majority factions.[27]

In *The Federalist* No. 10, Madison defended the Constitution to the nation at large on the basis of the constraints it imposed on "the violence of faction."[28] Madison defined a faction as follows:

> By a faction I understand a number of citizens, whether amounting to a majority or minority of the whole, who are united and actuated by some common impulse of passion, or of interest, adverse to the rights of other citizens, or to the permanent and aggregate interests of the community.[29]

In his memorandum prepared for the Convention, Madison had earlier pointed to the especially malign force of faction under republican government, namely, its erosion of citizens' capacity for critical moral independence by a public opinion that often is the self-serving opinion of majority factions. The argument of No. 10 of *The Federalist* generalized this theme.

Republicans valued liberty above all. We know that liberty for Madison[30] crucially included the inalienable right to conscience that made possible religious and political emancipation (see my earlier discussion), including the exercise of public judgment in drafting and ratifying a constitution. But such liberty "is to faction, what air is to fire, an aliment without which it instantly expires."[31] The argument of No. 10 has often been interpreted in light of the special emphasis it gives to "the most common and durable source of factions,. . . the various and

---

[27] Madison had unsuccessfully defended at the Convention and defends to Jefferson the need for a Congressional negative on the laws of the states. See Rutland, *Papers of James Madison* vol. 10, at 209–214.

[28] Jacob E. Cooke, ed., *The Federalist* (Middletown, Conn.: Wesleyan University Press, 1961), 56.

[29] Ibid., 57.

[30] For the primacy of the right of conscience in Madison's thought about rights, see his 1785 "Memorial and Remonstrance against Religious Assessments," Robert A. Rutland, ed., *Papers of James Madison*, vol. 8 (Chicago: University of Chicago Press, 1973), 295–306, and his 1792 essay, "Property," Robert A. Rutland et al., eds., *The Papers of James Madison, 1791–1793*, vol. 14 (Charlottesville: University Press of Virginia, 1983), 266–68.

[31] Cooke, *The Federalist*, 58.

unequal distribution of property."[32] Its pivotal argument, however, turns on why the uncompromisable republican value placed on liberty of judgment is inconsistent with the kind of uniformity of judgment and action that would preclude faction:

> As long as the reason of man continues fallible, and he is at liberty to exercise it, different opinions will be formed. As long as the connection subsists between his reason and his self-love, his opinions and passions will have a reciprocal influence on each other; and the former will be objects to which the latter will attach themselves.[33]

In effect, sectarian disagreements (whether religious, economic, or political) will be unleashed by the republican commitment to protection of the liberty of judgment in exercising human faculties ("the first object of government"),[34] and the disagreements thus unleashed will, under majority rule, lead to sectarian oppression. The argument amplified Madison's earlier theme about the self-subverting character of the unqualified majoritarianism Americans had associated with republican rule: the subversion of the moral independence of free people by a factionalized public opinion was generalized to the subversion of republican liberties by the factions that those liberties necessarily unleashed. Some constructive alternatives had to be defined that might resolve this republican dilemma.

Use of Comparative Political Science

American reflection on the pathologies of political power exemplified a larger feature of the American constitutional mind, to wit, its absorption in the best available comparative political science (Machiavelli of the *Discourses*, Harrington, Montesquieu, Hume, and the Scottish social and economist theorists—Smith, Ferguson, and

---

[32] Ibid., 59. See, e.g., Charles A. Beard, *An Economic Interpretation of the Constitution of the United States* (New York: Free Press, 1941), 14–15, 153–4. For cogent criticism of Beard's interpretation, see Morton White, *Philosophy, The Federalist, and the Constitution* (New York: Oxford University Press, 1987), 74–81.

[33] Cooke, *The Federalist*, 58.

[34] Ibid., 58.

Millar).[35] The Americans of 1787 identified themselves—in the sense made familiar by Machiavelli and Harrington[36]—as founders, concerned to use the best political science available to learn from the history of past institutional mistakes in order to construct a better order; indeed, perhaps more than any other people before or since, they took seriously Harrington's project of designing a written constitution that, in light of such political science, could be an immortal commonwealth for posterity. But, unlike Machiavelli and Harrington, Americans had—in light of the later development of political science in Montesquieu, Hume, and the Scottish theorists—become conspicuously skeptical about the continuing utility of the classical republican models (in particular, Rome and Sparta) that Machiavelli and Harrington so admired.

The American skepticism about the classical republics rested, in part, on their basis in militaristic and imperialistic aims no longer suited to the commercial stage of civilization (like the one that existed in America), in which commerce could supply a basis for peaceful and mutually advantageous relations among diverse peoples. The normative heart of the American objection was that the classical republics had blatantly violated the fundamental conditions of legitimate government as such, namely, respect for inalienable human rights. Madison, in particular, expressed this skepticism in terms of distrust of mass political assemblies like the Athenian assembly; such assemblies, lacking any appropriate constraints on political power, give maximum expression to the ferocities of faction, subverting—through the unrestrained political force of group psychology—the moral independence that was, for Madison, fundamental to respect for human rights. Madison puts the point starkly:

> Had every Athenian citizen been a Socrates; every Athenian assembly would still have been a mob.[37]

---

[35] On Machiavelli's influence on American thought, see Richards, *Foundations*, 147, 287, 289, 295; on Harrington, see *id.*, pp. 100, 101, 102, 115, 124, 132, 147, 287, 289, 295; on Montesquieu, see ibid., 101, 102, 111, 120, 121, 112, 125, 127, 128, 129, 130, 147, 287, 289, 295; on Hume, see ibid., 129, 130, 147, 287, 289, 295; on the Scottish social theorists, see ibid., 56–59.

[36] Ibid., 97–101.

[37] Cooke, *The Federalist*, 374.

Whereas Montesquieu and Hume had used similar examples to defend the British Constitution as a preferable form of constitutional government for a large commercial nation in modern circumstances, the American revolutionary and constitutional project was precisely to show that a more legitimate form of constitutionalism than the British was practicable; accordingly, the American Founders defined their task as constructing a new kind of republican government that could learn from the excesses of the classical republics without accepting the antirepublican premises of the British Constitution, with its hereditary class-based institutions (the monarchy, the House of Lords). The use of comparative political science was fundamental to the American enterprise because it enabled them to take a remarkably intellectually independent stance on the issue before them; it enabled them, for example, to take up the thread lost when the English Civil War was aborted by the Stuart restoration, recapturing the Harringtonian dream of an immortal republican commonwealth that the British had forgotten; on the other hand, the Americans gave a quite independent interpretation to how that project should—in light of Montesquieu and Hume—be understood in contemporary circumstances, but one itself not hostage to Montesquieu's and Hume's own preferences for the British Constitution.[38]

American Political Experience

Americans tested their constitutional minds not only against past political history but against their own democratic political experience both before and after the revolution. Americans had working democracies as colonies and, after the revolution, had engaged in a wide range of constitutional experiments at the state level and, via the Articles of Confederation, at the national level. The drive to the 1787 Constitution was the conviction that these experiments, both state and national, had not respected the principles of political legitimacy they had invoked against the British Constitution.[39] Jefferson objected, for

[38] Hume's utopian republican essay, "Idea of a Perfect Commonwealth," did, however, play an important role in shaping Madison's thought. For fuller discussion, see Richards, *Foundations*, 111–114. For Hume's essay, see David Hume, *Essays Moral, Political, and Literary* (Oxford: Oxford University Press, 1963), 499–515.

[39] See Richards, *Foundations*, 19–20.

example, to the Virginia Constitution on the ground that it rested on a legislative despotism as bad as that of parliamentary supremacy,[40] and the Articles of Confederation had been discredited by their failures both to limit the states' power to suppress human rights and to develop a coherent and effective conception of the national interest.[41] The 1787 Convention critically invoked the lessons of the now discredited state and federal constitutions, and looked hopefully to those state constitutions (notably, John Adams's Massachusetts structures as well as those of New York and Maryland) that appeared, by comparison, to afford effective constitutional constraints.[42]

American Constitutionalism as a Self-Conscious Work of Political Reason

Americans thought of their constitutional responsibility in terms of using their remarkable political opportunity in 1787 to bring to bear the lessons of political experience on the self-conscious design of a new experiment in republicanism: an enduring commercial republic in a large territory that would respect human rights. Both James Wilson and Alexander Hamilton celebrated America as enjoying a unique historical opportunity[43] and offered their arguments to one of the most free and democratic processes of constitutional reflection that the world had yet seen. Importantly, Americans resisted the Machiavellian picture of political ruthless founders, favoring instead a process of deliberative reflection about constitutional construction whose legitimacy ultimately depended on deliberative ratification.[44] Americans innovated a new kind of political structure, namely, conventions called for the sole purpose of constitutional construction and special procedures created to permit the democratic ratification of the work of those conventions.[45] This structure was sharply distinguished from ordinary

[40] See Thomas Jefferson, *Notes on the State of Virginia*, ed. William Peden (New York: W. W. Norton, 1954), 120.

[41] See, in general, Jack N. Rakove, *The Beginnings of National Politics* (Baltimore: Johns Hopkins University Press, 1979).

[42] See Richards, *Foundations*, 106.

[43] See ibid., 23.

[44] See ibid., 97–105.

[45] See ibid., 92–97.

politics by the nature and subject of its reflections, in particular, by the kind of deliberative ratification to which it was subjected. These special procedures crucially marked for Americans the special status of constitutional argument that distinguished it from arguments of ordinary politics. In effect, the ratification procedures appropriate to constitutional argument gave institutional expression to the Lockean political legitimacy of the constitution itself: because the Constitution had been subjected to such deliberative ratification, it could be reasonably regarded as having satisfied the ultimate test for the legitimacy of political power, namely, that political power could be reasonably justified to all those subject to that power as consistent with respect for their human rights and the use of that power to pursue the common interests of all alike.[46] Constitutional argument was for Americans supreme over ordinary political argument because it was reasonably regarded as expressive of this kind of authoritative collective democratic deliberation on permanent issues of the legitimate use of political power.

From this abstract deliberative perspective, Americans accepted the justifiability of the three great structural innovations of American constitutionalism (federalism, the separation of powers, and judicial review)[47] on the ground that they reasonably respond to the republican dilemma; that is, they divide and limit corruptible political power (including the exercise of majority rule) in the service of using political power in ways that are more likely over all to respect human rights and serve the public good. Understandably, Americans also required that interpretation of issues of constitutional design must call for a kind of deliberation institutionally distinguished from ordinary politics.[48] Americans gravitated to judicial review as an institution more likely to secure such deliberation,[49] and to a demanding amendment procedure more likely to secure such reflection over time. The American Constitution has, in fact, been rarely amended, and some of its most important amendments (notably, the Reconstruction Amendments) addressed defects in the original Constitution of which the founders were often all too painfully aware (in particular, the legitimacy of slavery).[50]

---

[46] See ibid., 131–157.
[47] See ibid., 105–130.
[48] See ibid., ch. 4.
[49] See ibid., 126–30.
[50] See ibid., ch. 7.

THE CIVIL WAR AMENDMENTS AS AN EXPRESSION OF
AMERICAN REVOLUTIONARY CONSTITUTIONALISM

The genre of revolutionary constitutionalism, understood within the framework of these six ingredients, clarifies not only the founding of the American Constitution, but pivotally important controversies over its proper interpretation such as those that occurred in the antebellum period and their constitutional resolution, the Reconstruction Amendments.[51]

The appropriate framework for the analysis of these matters must be the growing sense of a crisis in constitutional legitimacy during the antebellum period, marked initially by the claims of Calhoun's proslavery constitutionalism[52] and then by its cumulative political successes (first in Congress's repeal of the Missouri Compromise in the Kansas-Nebraska Act of 1854 in accordance with Stephen Douglas's theory of popular sovereignty,[53] and then in the Supreme Court's adoption of central claims of Calhoun's constitutionalism in *Dred Scott v. Sanford*).[54] The narrow issue of constitutional interpretation in dispute in both these matters was the power or lack of power of Congress to forbid slavery in the territories. But the deeper question of constitutional legitimacy, posed by Lincoln among others,[55] was the interpretive attitude taken by Douglas and Chief Justice Roger B. Taney toward the text of the Constitution of the United States, one that disengaged its interpretation from the Lockean political theory of the Declaration of Independence, namely, that all persons subject to political power have inalienable human rights. Calhoun, in contrast to other Southern constitutionalists such as John

---

[51] See, in general, Richards, *Conscience and the Constitution*.

[52] See John C. Calhoun, *A Disquisition on Government*, ed. Richard K. Cralle (orig. pub., 1853; repr. ed. New York: Peter Smith, 1943). For useful commentary, see August O. Spain, *The Political Theory of John C. Calhoun* (New York: Bookman Associates, 1951).

[53] See David M. Potter, *The Impending Crisis 1848–1861* (New York: Harper & Row, 1976), at 145–76.

[54] 19 How. 393 (1857); for commentary, see Potter, *The Impending Crisis 1848–1861*, at 267–96; Don E. Fehrenbacher, *The Dred Scott Case: Its Significance in American Law and Politics* (New York: Oxford University Press, 1978).

[55] See, for example, Lincoln's October 7, 1858, address at Galesburg, in Robert W. Johannsen, ed., *The Lincoln-Douglas Debates* (New York: Oxford University Press, 1865), at 219–20.

Taylor of Caroline,[56] had radically defended his positivistic reading of the Constitution on grounds of a self-conscious repudiation of the very idea of inalienable human rights and thus consistently argued that the Constitution should not be interpreted, either at the state or federal level, as in service of such a vision of equal human rights.[57] Lincoln and others granted that the best interpretation of the history and text of the Constitution protected slavery in the states that had it; they distinguished, however, this short-term political compromise from the more long-term ambition of the Constitution to protect human rights—by requiring federal power to protect human rights (forbidding slavery in the federal territories) and thus over time encouraging slavery's gradual abolition by the states that retained it;[58] such an interpretation would put slavery, as Lincoln argued that the Founders intended, "in the course of ultimate extinction."[59] Calhoun's rights-skepticism disallowed an interpretive attitude sensitive in this way to the ultimate long-term obligation of constitutional government to respect the equal human rights of all persons subject to political power.

The dispute was ostensibly over a matter of constitutional interpretation but was in substance over the very legitimacy of the Constitution itself as the supreme law of the land. The Constitution, as supreme law, must have a basis that renders respect for its terms more legitimate than the laws over which it is supreme. Rights-based political theory gave a natural and plausible substantive basis for such legitimacy: the Constitution, properly interpreted in a way consistent with

---

[56] Taylor had offered a Jeffersonian rights-based theory of the Constitution that gave a central role to the states in the protection of human rights and a correspondingly narrow role to the federal government. See John Taylor, *Construction Construed and Constitutions Vindicated* (orig. pub., 1820; repr. ed., New York: Da Capo Press, 1970), Taylor, *New Views of the Constitution of the United States* (orig. pub., 1823; repr. ed., New York: De Capo Press, 1971).

[57] For Calhoun's most explicit attack on the Declaration of Independence as embodying "the most dangerous of all political errors," Jefferson's "utterly false view," see John C. Calhoun, "Speech on the Oregon Bill," delivered in the Senate, June 27, 1848, reprinted in Richard K. Cralle, ed., *The Words of John C. Calhoun*, vol. 4 (New York: D. Appleton, 1861), at 511, 512.

[58] See the address of Lincoln at Jonesboro, September 15, 1858, in Johannsen, *The Lincoln-Douglas Debates*, at 132.

[59] See ibid., First Joint Debate, Ottawa, August 21, 1858, at 55.

this political theory, secured the conditions of respect for human rights that alone rendered any exercise of political power legitimate, and thus the claim of constitutional supremacy rested on the background political theory of the circumstances in which any exercise of coercive power was legitimate. The Constitution was supreme law because it enforced a political theory that delegitimated exercises of political power inconsistent with its demands.

But, how could one interpret the text and history of the Constitution of the United States consistent with this political theory in light of its putative toleration of slavery, an institution that rested on the abridgment of basic human rights? One response to this question was common to proslavery radicals like Calhoun and to abolitionist radical disunionists like William Lloyd Garrison[60] and Wendell Phillips;[61] namely, a recommendation to abandon any attempt to interpret the Constitution in terms of rights-based political theory. Calhoun, who was skeptical of rights as defensible political values, did not conclude that the Constitution was illegitimate, but sought its legitimacy on other grounds, namely, a Hobbesian theory of the sovereignty of the states.[62] Garrison and Phillips, however, believed in respect for human rights as ultimate political values and concluded that the Constitution, because it did not rest on human rights, was therefore illegitimate. Could the Constitution be regarded as legitimate on the basis of rights-based political theory?

The aim to give an affirmative answer to this question was the motivation for the complex forms of both internal and external criticism of the Constitution sponsored by various forms of abolitionist political and constitutional theory. By internal criticism I mean the criticism of mistaken interpretations of the Constitution on the ground that they failed properly to elaborate the principles of the Constitution itself; by external criticism I mean criticism of the Constitution, even properly interpreted, as inconsistent with enlightened critically defensible political values such as respect for human rights. Advocates of both moder-

---

[60] See, in general, William Lloyd Garrison, *Selections from the Writings and Speeches of William Lloyd Garrison* (Boston: R. F. Wallcut, 1852).

[61] See Wendell Phillips, *The Constitution: A Proslavery Compact* (orig. pub., 1844; repr. ed., New York: Negro Universities Press, 1969); Phillips, *Can Abolitionists Vote or Take Office Under the United States Constitution?* (New York: American Anti-Slavery Society, 1845).

[62] For a good account of Calhoun's theory of sovereignty, see August O. Spain, *The Political Theory of John C. Calhoun* (New York: Bookman Associates, 1951), at 164–83.

ate and radical antislavery positions thus internally criticized *Dred Scott v. Sanford* as a mistaken interpretation of relevant constitutional principles; moderate (in contrast to radical) antislavery activists did not, however, take the same view of the interpretive claim that slavery was constitutional in the states that had adopted it, though many advocates of the moderate antislavery position externally criticized such slavery as a moral and political wrong.[63] Such forms of both internal and external criticism of the Constitution were grounded in the tension, acutely experienced by all abolitionists, between the Constitution and what they took to be its governing rights-based political theory. On the one hand, the text and history of the Constitution apparently contemplated the legitimacy of slavery at least at the state level; on the other hand, the rights-based theory of the Constitution condemned slavery as a violation of inalienable human rights. Various forms of abolitionist constitutional and political theory relieved this tension in different ways.

Perhaps the most plausible interpretive position was that of the moderate antislavery advocates.[64] Fair interpretive weight was accorded the text and history that legitimated slavery in the states as a reasonable short-term compromise with an already entrenched institution that the states could fairly be expected to abolish in due course; fair interpretive weight was also accorded the background political theory of human rights by forbidding any legitimation of slavery by the federal government in service of the long-term goal of respect for human rights everywhere in the United States (including eventual abolition of slavery by the states). The moderate antislavery theme—liberty national, slavery local or sectional—thus gave full interpretive scope to the political theory of human rights only at the national level; at the state level, the political theory afforded a ground for external criticism and set a long-term national goal of encouraging abolition.[65]

In contrast, advocates of the radical antislavery position (for exam-

---

[63] For a good general study on the diverse forms of political abolitionism, see Richard H. Sewell, *Ballots for Freedom: Antislavery Politics in the United States 1837–1860* (New York: Oxford University Press, 1976).

[64] See, for a seminal statement of the view, Salmon P. Chase, "The Address of the Southern and Western Liberty Convention," orig. pub., 1845, repr. in Salmon Portland Chase and Charles Dexter Cleveland, *Anti-Slavery Addresses of 1844 and 1845* (New York: Negro Universities Press, 1867).

[65] For a statement of this moderate antislavery theme, see Chase and Cleveland, *Anti-Slavery Addresses of 1844 and 1845*, 84–5.

ple, William Goodell,[66] Lysander Spooner,[67] and Joel Tiffany[68]) accorded the political theory of human rights decisive interpretive weight at both the national and the state levels. The interpretive implausibility of the approach was the Constitution it claimed to be interpreting, in particular, the text and history of the Constitution as they bore on the legitimacy of slavery at the state level. The interpretive primacy of political theory was sustained and defended by the most theoretically profound advocate of this position, Lysander Spooner, by denying any weight to the constitutional text or history that was in conflict with the claims of rights-based political theory. The clauses of the Constitution that apparently recognized state-endorsed slavery were to be interpreted as not recognizing slavery, on the theory that no interpretation should be accorded the words, no matter how textually strained, in ways that recognized slavery,[69] and history was to be disowned altogether as a valid ground for interpretation in favor of focus only and exclusively on the text itself—a text to be interpreted antipositivistically in whatever way gave best effect to rights-based political theory.[70] The Constitution was to be interpreted in this way because, otherwise, the Constitution could not be regarded as the supremely legitimate law of the land; if slavery in the states that had it were constitutional, such constitutional claims would be a politically illegitimate abridgment of human rights, indeed, a just ground for the right to revolution; as Joel Tiffany starkly put the radical antislavery point, "give us *change* or *revolution*."[71] To avoid such a crisis in constitutional

[66] William Goodell, *Views of American Constitutional Law in Its Bearing Upon American Slavery* (orig. pub., 1845; repr. ed., Freeport, N.Y.: Books for Libraries Press, 1971).

[67] Lysander Spooner, *The Unconstitutionality of Slavery*, in two parts (New York: Burt Franklin, 1860).

[68] Joel Tiffany, *A Treatise on the Unconstitutionality of American Slavery* (orig. pub., 1849; repr. ed., Miami, Fla.: Mnemosyne Publishing Co., 1969).

[69] Since the word "slave" was never expressly used but rather "three-fifths of all other persons" (see U.S. Constitution, Art. I, sec. 2, cl. 3) or "migration or importation of such persons" (see U.S. Constitution, Art. I, sec. 9, cl. 1) or "persons held to service or labour" (see U.S. Constitution, Art. IV, sec. 2, cl. 3), the radicals ascribed to these texts meanings that did not protect slavery. For example, Spooner argued that the three-fifths clause applied not to Southern slaves but mainly to resident aliens. See Spooner, *Unconstitutionality*, at 73–81.

[70] See ibid., Second Part, at 146.

[71] See Tiffany, *A Treatise on the Unconstitutionality of American Slavery*, at 99.

legitimacy, the Constitution was to be interpreted in the mode called for by the radical antislavery position.

Advocates of the moderate and the radical antislavery positions shared a common interest in the analysis of how the interpretation of the Constitution could have been so decadently unmoored from its basis in the political theory of human rights (a national decadence reflected in the political successes of Calhoun's proslavery constitutionalism). The nerve of their analysis—the slave power conspiracy[72]— was itself an elaboration of the Founders' theory of faction,[73] only now applied to a form of faction that had been fostered by the Constitution itself. The theory of faction had identified the pervasive tendency of group psychology in politics to protect the interests of some political group at the expense of denying fair respect for the rights and interests of outsiders to the group.[74] Madison had argued in *The Federalist* No. 10[75] that the Constitution had structured the exercise of republican political power in order better to ensure that such factions would not achieve their mischievous ends inconsistent with the governing political theory of republican constitutionalism, respect for human rights and pursuit of the public interest.[76] The antislavery analysis of America's constitutional decadence was that the Constitution itself, by augmenting the political power of the slave states via the three-fifths clause,[77] had so constitutionally entrenched the political power of slave-owning interests that their power as an effective political faction had flourished to such an extent that, inconsistent with the aims and theory of Madisonian constitutionalism, they had subverted the Constitution itself.

Proponents of the radical antislavery position offered a distinctively deep moral and constitutional analysis of the sources of the constitutional decadence in the Constitution itself and of what would be required to remedy the underlying constitutional pathology. The

---

[72] For a useful study of this idea, see David Brion Davis, *The Slave Power Conspiracy and the Paranoid Style* (Baton Rouge: Louisiana State University Press, 1969).

[73] For further discussion of the Founders' theory of faction, see Richards, *Foundations of American Constitutionalism*, at 32–39.

[74] See ibid.

[75] Cooke, *The Federalist*, No. 10, at 56–65.

[76] For further discussion, see Richards, *Foundations of American Constitutionalism*, at 105–130.

[77] See U.S. Constitution, Art. I, sec. 2, cl. 3.

premise of their distinctive approach was their view of the proper understanding of the relationship of Lockean political theory to constitutional interpretation. The foundation of this view had been laid earlier by the abolitionist Theodore Weld in his analysis of the wrongness of slavery; Weld's analysis invoked the Lockean political theory that legitimate government must protect equal rights, and he made a similar appeal in explaining why Congress had power to abolish slavery in the District of Columbia:

> It has been shown already that *allegiance* is exacted of the slave. Is the government of the United States unable to grant *protection* where it exacts *allegiance*? It is an axiom of the civilized world, and a maxim even with savages, that allegiance and protection are reciprocal and correlative. Are principles powerless with us which exact homage of barbarians? *Protection is the CONSTITUTIONAL RIGHT of every human being under the exclusive legislation of Congress who has not forfeited it by crime.*[78]

The assumption of this view was that black Americans (slave or free) were working members of the American political community and, as such, were subject to its governing Lockean principles of a fair balance of rights and obligations as a condition of allegiance. But many Americans (Lincoln being one of them) wanted to distinguish the question of abolishing slavery in order to recognize the natural rights of slaves from the question of rights of membership in the American political community.[79] This explains the view of moderate antislavery activists that the best theory of the Constitution would allow the national government to achieve its goals of respect for human rights by the long-term abolition of slavery and colonization of the freedmen abroad (thus excluding them from the American political community). They were able to take this view by ascribing rights of American citizenship to the decisional powers of the states alone; the national government might constitutionally achieve the

---

[78] Theodore Weld, *The Power of Congress over Slavery in the District of Columbia*, (orig. pub., 1838; repr. in Jacobus tenBroek, *Equal under Law*, [New York: Collier, 1969] at 243–80).

[79] See, for example, Lincoln's 1854 Speech on the Kansas-Nebraska Act, reprinted in Don E. Fehrenbacher, *Abraham Lincoln: Speeches and Writings 1832–1858* (New York: Library of America, 1989), 307–348, especially 315–16.

long-term abolition of slavery and colonize the freedmen abroad without violating any nationally guaranteed constitutional rights of the freedmen. But, if one believed, like Weld and many more radical abolitionists, that Lockean political theory guaranteed black Americans (slave and free) both their natural rights and their rights to citizenship, moderate antislavery constitutional theory reconciled the Constitution and its background political theory in an unappealing way. The distinction between national and state power over slavery, fundamental to this view, could sensibly interpret the Constitution as in service of its political theory of respect for equal rights only if national power could be read as achieving these rights by abolition and colonization. But, if Weld and the abolitionists were right, that interpretation of the Constitution would violate the rights of black Americans—earned by years of unremunerated labor in service of the national interest—to be free and to be citizens. Was there an interpretation of the Constitution that might better reconcile it with its background political theory?

Radical antislavery constitutional theory responded to this question, as we have seen, by interpreting the Constitution as forbidding slavery at both the national and the state levels. Radical antislavery theory agreed with moderate antislavery theory that the proper interpretive attitude to the United States Constitution must be Lockean political theory, but it disagreed with the moderate view about the best account of such a theory, in particular, about what rights black Americans in fact had in light of the wrongs inflicted on them by American slavery and racism. Taking the same view of political theory that the radical antislavery theory did, the moderate antislavery reading of the Constitution (in terms of a federal-state dichotomy on the slavery issue) could not reasonably be justified as protecting human rights and the public interest; such an interpretation would allow abolition on terms that violated the rights of black Americans as citizens and thus could not be justified. The better interpretation—the one that over all enabled the Constitution to be read more coherently as in service of its political theory—was one that made all participants in the American political community national citizens and therefore bearers of the equal human rights of such citizenship.[80] The radicals therefore argued that

---

[80] Joel Tiffany generalized these arguments into a general constitutional principle "for the equal protection of all, individually and collectively," *Treatise*, at 87.

the national government—both the judiciary and Congress—had power to achieve the abolition of slavery, but, in stark contrast to holders of the moderate antislavery position, they proposed abolition only on terms that recognized the rights of black Americans to be free and to be equal citizens.

The radical antislavery position was, as we have seen, self-consciously proposed as an interpretive theory, but its real force was its profound criticism of the Constitution itself on the very grounds central to the six ingredients of American revolutionary constitutionalism. In effect, the United States Constitution, itself constructed on the basis of a complex empirical and normative assessment of the genre of republican constitutionalism, was then subjected to a comparably profound criticism by radical antislavery advocates in terms self-consciously inspired by the critical achievement of the founding itself.

The radical antislavery movement brought the same critical ingredients of American revolutionary constitutionalism to bear on the criticism of the Constitution itself in light of its antebellum decadence: (1) The distinctive depth of its analysis derived from the remarkable moral independence of its articulation, on the basis of Lockean political theory, of the basic human and constitutional rights of all persons subject to the political power of the United States.[81] (2) That perspective enabled radical antislavery advocates to interpret the pathological misinterpretations of the Constitution as being grounded not only in the slave power conspiracy[82] but (3) in the pathological construction of American racism that the Constitution had fostered,[83] in effect, legitimating the monstrous faction of white supremacy that Chief Justice Taney had explicitly embraced as the measure of constitutional rights in *Dred Scott v. Sanford*.[84] (4) Comparative reflection on the earlier abolition of slavery by

---

[81] See, in general, Tiffany, *Treatise*.

[82] See Davis, *The Slave Power Conspiracy and the Paranoid Style*.

[83] For the seminal analysis along these lines, see L. Maria Child, *An Appeal in Favor of Americans Called Africans* (orig. pub., 1833; repr. ed., New York: Arno Press and New York Times, 1968). Madison at the Constitutional Convention had himself described racism as one of the worst forms of faction: "We have seen the mere distinction of colour made in the most enlightened period of time, a ground of the most oppressive dominion ever exercised by man over man." Farrand, *Records of the Federal Convention*, vol. 1, 135 (speech of June 6, 1787).

[84] "They [blacks] had . . . no rights which the white man was bound to respect." *Dred Scott v. Sanford*, at 407.

Britain and (5) the growing power of slave-holding interests over American state and national politics led radical antislavery adherents to identify a crucial error of American constitutional design in its failure to take seriously Madison's original constitutional suggestions of a power in the nation to ensure that states could not violate a nationally articulated conception of human rights and the public interest.[85] Madison's theory of faction had focused on local interests at the state level as loci of faction and called for nationally representative institutions as a way of detoxifying the evils of local factions. But precisely the most oppressive of state factions—slavery advocates at the state level—had been constitutionally immunized from national scrutiny in terms of enforceable standards of human rights and the public interest, and this lacuna had, in the view of radical antislavery advocates, over time led to the degradation of the Constitution by the worst form of factionalized insularity and oppression (reflected in the political appeal to Douglas and Taney, among many others, of Calhoun's proslavery constitutionalism, with its denial of the role of rights-based political theory in constitutional interpretation). (6) The appropriate remedy must accordingly be a conception of national institutions with adequate competence and power to ensure that the states, like the national government, respect the human rights of all Americans.

Radical antislavery theory had offered its analysis as internal interpretive criticism of the dominant antebellum views of constitutional interpretation, but the analysis was regarded as a marginal view of constitutional interpretation even by mainstream political abolitionists (most of whom gravitated to the moderate antislavery position as the best theory of constitutional interpretation).[86] In the wake of the Civil War, the analysis of radical antislavery theory occupied stage center in the critical reflection on American constitutionalism that culminated in the Reconstruction Amendments because it afforded the most reasonable analysis and diagnosis of the nation's constitutional crisis and of

[85] Joel Tiffany, for example, sharply posed the crisis of American constitutionalism in terms of the despotic powers of the states at home; see Tiffany, *Treatise*, at 55–6; it was not the states that required protection "but the *individual*, crushed, and overwhelmed by an insolent, and tyranical [sic] majority, that needed such a guaranty [sic]; and to him, as a citizen of the United States, whether in the majority, or minority, is that guaranty given, to secure him, not only from *individual*, but also from *governmental oppression*." (Tiffany, *Treatise*, at 110)

[86] See, for a good general treatment, Sewell, *Ballots for Freedom*.

its solution.[87] By the end of the Civil War, slavery had effectively been ended in the South, and the task was to forge a moral and constitutional vision that would memorialize the fruits of the war in an enduring legacy of constitutional principle for posterity. Both the North and the South had come to interpret the Civil War as a controversy over the meaning of American revolutionary constitutionalism, a controversy ultimately justified by an appeal to the right to revolution when constitutional structures proved radically inadequate to their ultimate normative values. From the perspective of the Reconstruction Congress, Southern secession was based on a perverse interpretation of American revolutionary constitutionalism that appealed to the Constitution to justify the entrenchment of slavery, the ultimate violation of basic human rights, against any possibility of inhibition by the federal government under moderate antislavery's reasonable interpretation of the Constitution of 1787. Proslavery constitutionalism, when carried to this extreme, had become the systematic instrument for the permanent abridgment of basic human rights, and the Civil War was thus justified in the same way that the American Revolution had been justified as a protest against a decadent form of British constitutionalism as necessary to protect human rights and to forge constitutional forms more adequate to this ultimate moral vision of legitimate government.

If the legitimacy of the American Revolution required a form of constitutionalism (in contrast to the corrupt British Constitution) adequate to its normative demands, the legitimacy of the Civil War required a comparably profound reflection on constitutional decadence (the Constitution of 1787) adequate to its demands for a rebirth of rights-based constitutional government. Radical antislavery theory's critical analysis of antebellum constitutional decadence met this need because it was the most profound such reflection culturally available in the genre of American revolutionary constitutionalism forged by the Founders of 1787. Its great appeal for the American constitutional mind was both its radical insistence on the primacy of the revolutionary political theory of human rights central to American constitutionalism and its brilliant reinterpretation of the six ingredients of such constitutionalism in light of that political theory and the events of antebellum constitutional decadence and civil war. In light of its analysis, radical antislavery theory supplied

---

[87] I explore the argument merely sketched in this paragraph at much greater length in Richards, *Conscience and the Constitution.*

the most reasonable interpretation of the Civil War as the second American Revolution, and offered, consistent with the genre of American revolutionary constitutionalism, remedies that plausibly could be and were regarded as the most justifiable way to correct central defects in the Constitution of 1787, defects some of which had been acknowledged by leading Founders such as Madison in 1787.[88] The Reconstruction Amendments, the most radical change in our constitutionalism in our history, could thus plausibly be understood as a wholly reasonable conservative way to preserve the legitimacy of the long-standing project of American revolutionary constitutionalism.

The Reconstruction Amendments contain both negative and positive features: the abolition of slavery and involuntary servitude (Thirteenth Amendment) and the prohibition of racial discrimination in voting (Fifteenth Amendment); the affirmative requirements of citizenship for all Americans and nationally defined and enforceable guarantees, applicable against the states, of equal protection, privileges and immunities, and due process of law (Fourteenth Amendment). The political theory of these prohibitions and requirements was Lockean political theory as it had been articulated and applied in the antebellum period by radical antislavery: all political power (including, now, the power of the states) could be legitimate only if it met the requirements that it extend to all persons subject to that power respect for their inalienable human rights and be used to pursue the public interest. And their constitutional theory was, in light of the critical analysis of antebellum decadence of radical antislavery, what such requirements of politically legitimate power clearly required—nationally articulated, elaborated, and enforceable constitutional principles that would preserve or tend to preserve the required respect for rights and pursuit of the public interest. These guarantees thus textually included the central normative dimensions distinctive of radical antislavery: the demand that all persons subject to the burdens of allegiance to the political power of the United States be accorded both their natural rights as persons and their equal rights as citizens, based on the fundamental egalitarian requirement of politically legitimate government stated by the Equal Protection Clause. If the Constitution of 1787 had made remarkably little textual reference to its background political theory, the Reconstruction Amendments textually affirmed and enforced that

[88] See Richards, *Foundations of American Constitutionalism*, at 37–38.

political theory with notable focus on the forms of political pathology that had motivated antebellum constitutional decadence—the untrammeled state power over human rights that had given rise to their abridgment through the political pathologies of the slave power conspiracy in general and American racism in particular.[89] Both the Thirteenth Amendment's prohibition of slavery and the Equal Protection Clause of the Fourteenth Amendment's prohibition of racist subjugation were thus negative corollaries of the affirmative principle of equal respect for the rights of all persons subject to political power. They thus required the national articulation, elaboration, and enforcement of constitutional principles that defined the supreme law of the land because they secured the politically legitimate terms for the exercise of any political power. The Reconstruction Amendments, thus understood, responded to the gravest crisis of constitutional legitimacy in our history, and are best understood and interpreted as negative and affirmative constitutional principles addressed, as a legacy to posterity, to securing the legitimacy of the Constitution as supreme law.

FRENCH AND AMERICAN REVOLUTIONARY AND CONSTITUTIONAL THOUGHT COMPARED

American and French revolutionary and constitutional thought shared a common vocabulary of human rights but interpreted it in quite different ways and with quite different modes of constitutional analysis. For example, each of the six ingredients of revolutionary constitutionalism that distinguished American constitutionalism at its founding did not exist or did so in radically distinguishable ways in French constitutionalism during its same formative period.[90]

---

[89] For a good statement of this general concern at the time of the introduction of the Thirteenth Amendment on the floor of the House of Representatives, see the speech by Representative Henry Wilson, *Congressional Globe*, 38th Congress, 1st Sess., March 19, 1864, 1199–1206.

[90] My analysis here focuses on a detailed comparison of American and French constitutionalism during their initial formative periods, which were roughly contemporary. For the consequences of the tragic failure of French constitutionalism on later French constitutional history, see, in general, Francois Furet, *Revolutionary France 1770–1880*, trans. Antonia Nevill (Oxford: Blackwell, 1992). On the sharp antagonism of leading French intellectuals in the twentieth century to the American experience, see Tony Judt, *Past Imperfect: French Intellectuals, 1944–1956* (Berkeley: University of California Press, 1992).

There is no correlative feature in French constitutional thought to the American melding of arguments of rights with interpretive analysis of its previous historical constitution, the British Constitution. It is not at all unreasonable that there should have been such a historical component to French constitutionalism. It is, of course, quite true that the French had had no practical experience in democratic politics of a sort that America had enjoyed under the British Constitution, and could not therefore reflect on their own experience in thinking about democratic constitutional forms. But Montesquieu had prominently defended the historical role of the *parlementaires* in enforcing constitutional constraints against the French monarchs, had implicitly criticized the absolute monarchy established by Louis XIV in light of his historical argument, and had urged the revival of this historical institution in contemporary circumstances as an active constraint on monarchical despotism.[91] He had also brilliantly developed a comparative political science, quite influential on the Americans, that urged realism in thinking about constitutional forms in terms of contemporary circumstances, not in terms of anachronistic historical forms (such as the classical republics) that were irrelevant today. The Estates General in 1789 could easily have been self-interpreted in light of Montesquieu's views as an inchoate form of the constitutional structures Montesquieu admired so much in Great Britain, and his arguments of comparative political science could have lent a sober realism to reflections on contemporary French circumstances. Indeed, Mounier roughly took this line (against Sièyes) in the Constituent Assembly of 1789.[92]

In fact, both the substance and the methodology of Montesquieu's constitutionalism were quickly rejected, and French constitutional thought set itself in a direction supposed to be radically discontinuous with French history. Even a suspensive veto for the monarch was resisted (though eventually accepted),[93] and French constitutional

[91] For a good general treatment, see Judith N. Shklar, *Montesquieu* (New York: Oxford University Press, 1987).

[92] See R. R. Palmer, *The Age of the Democratic Revolution*, vol. 1 (Princeton: Princeton University Press, 1959), 489–500.

[93] For a good discussion of the debates surrounding the 1791 constitution, see Keith M. Baker, "Constitution," in Francois Furet and Mona Ozouf, eds., *A Critical Dictionary of the French Revolution*, trans. Arthur Goldhammer (Cambridge, Mass.: Belknap Press of Harvard University Press, 1989), at 479–93.

thought, once a republic was established, resisted any form of strong independent executive that would remind them of the now discredited monarchy. The Girondist project of an executive council independently elected by the people was thus violently rejected by Saint-Just as "the most dangerous threat of all to the unity of the Republic and popular sovereignty,"[94] and when the 1795 constitution adopted an executive, it was a five-person executive council (the Directory) elected by the legislative branches.[95] Those who disown history are proverbially doomed to repeat it, and it is surely an important confirmation of this truth that probably the most enduring political legacy of the French Revolution is the bureaucratic centralism fostered by the French monarchy and perfected under Bonaparte's dictatorship.[96] Indeed, Bonaparte's quite popular dictatorship may be regarded as the return of the repressed, the vengeance of a French constitutional history of absolute monarchy on a generation obsessed by its total repudiation. From this perspective, Bonaparte, unlike the republicans, better understood the force of history when he gave the French what they had come to expect of government, namely, the competent absolute monarchy that the Bourbons had proved unable to give them.

Correspondingly, French constitutional thought learned little from the brilliant political science of comparative constitutionalism of one of its most penetrating constitutional thinkers, Montesquieu.[97] Montesquieu had urged the importance of commerce in contemporary circumstances as a pacifying agent of mutually advantageous relations among peoples, and he had suggested that the classical republics, focused on militaristic imperialism, were anachronistic in the eighteenth century; in their place, he urged the development of competing centers of power that would appropriately moderate the excesses of political power in the service of a humane respect for personal security.[98] French revolutionary constitutionalists ignored the wisdom of

[94] J. L. Talmon, *The Origins of Totalitarian Democracy* (Harmondsworth, Middlesex: Penguin, 1952), at 103.

[95] See William Doyle, *Oxford History of the French Revolution* (Oxford: Clarendon Press, 1989), at 319.

[96] Cf. Alexis de Tocqueville, *The Old Regime and the French Revolution*, trans. Stuart Gilbert (Garden City, N.Y.: Doubleday Anchor, 1955).

[97] See Bernard Manin, "Montesquieu," in Furet, *Critical Dictionary*, at 728–741.

[98] For a good treatment of these points, see Thomas L. Pangle, *Montesquieu's Philosophy of Liberalism* (Chicago: University of Chicago Press, 1973).

Montesquieu's constitutionalism, supposing, unlike the Americans, that his rejection of republicanism in contemporary circumstances disqualified him from making any contribution to constitutional thought (as if republican constitutionalism did not need to worry—a tragically false supposition, in view of the Terror—about the paralyzing, debilitating, and stifling abuses of power that so shaped Montesquieu's political theory and science). French constitutionalists were moved, instead, as we shall see, by Rousseau's quite pure-hearted advocacy of republicanism, and some of them were fatefully attracted by the model of classical republicanism defended by Rousseau.[99] Whereas the Americans used Montesquieu and Hume in distinguishing their own project from classical republicanism, the French embraced this latter model, including its legitimation of militaristic imperialism (in particular, the European wars of liberation fought by the republican armies of France). Constant's later analysis of the liberty of the ancients and moderns was a criticism of this anachronistic way of thinking and its disastrous consequences for a French constitutionalism ostensibly committed to human rights.[100] The Americans had seen the point earlier and made it integral to their constitutional enterprise.

The kinds of extensive empirical and historical inquiries that concerned American constitutionalists were not a French concern, a point that John Adams had made against Turgot in 1787–1788.[101] Adams objected to the French constitutionalism that later developed in the same terms, taking particularly bitter objection to the perfectionist strain in French constitutional thought, its Rousseauean belief that human nature under republicanism would be transformed in ways that would obviate fears of a mass psychology hostile to respect for human rights.[102] American republican experience was quite to the contrary, and Adams thus linked the nonempirical grounding of the

---

[99] See Bernard Manin, "Rousseau," in Furet, *Critical Dictionary*, at 829–843.

[100] See Benjamin Constant, "The Liberty of the Ancients Compared with That of the Moderns," in Biancamaria Fontana, ed., *Constant: Political Writings* (Cambridge: Cambridge University Press, 1988), 308–28.

[101] See John Adams, *A Defence of the Constitutions of Government of the United States of America*, in Charles Francis Adams, ed., *Works of John Adams* (Boston: Little, Brown, 1851, vol. 4, at 278–588; vol. 5, at 3–496; vol. 6, at 3–220).

[102] See, e.g., John Adams, *Discourses on Davila*, in Adams, ed., *The Works of John Adams*, vol. 6 at 279. See, in general, Zoltan Haraszti, *John Adams and the Prophets of Progress* (Cambridge, Mass.: Harvard University Press, 1952).

French institutions to a lack of concern for the pathologies of political power, which was, as we have seen, an important American concern.

Finally, the U.S. Constitution of 1787–1788 innovated a status for constitutional argument distinct from ordinary politics and supreme over it; the French did not. French constitutional thought certainly did not share the Harringtonian dream of an immortal commonwealth for posterity that so moved leading American constitutionalists like Madison; their thought was much closer to Jefferson's defense (in one of his few disagreements with Madison)[103] of a constitution newly made by each generation; surely, the five republics of French constitutional history (with intervening dictatorships and restorations of monarchy) suggest Jefferson's approach.[104] But that, in itself, cannot explain the French failure to develop an independent status for constitutional argument; constitutions, newly made each generation, can certainly— as Jefferson argued they must—immunize constitutional from ordinary political argument.

Americans did not have to struggle with one issue that was of much concern to French constitutionalists, namely, background consensus. Americans, in contrast to the French, had developed a strong national consensus on republican values and thus did not think of constitutionalism as a way of creating such values; their constitutional debates were not over how to forge republican consensus but over which constitutional forms were most adequate to preserve and elaborate that consensus over time. But the need to forge a republican consensus is not inconsistent with the development of a distinctive role for constitutional argument. Americans might very well have taken this goal more seriously, and much better served their posterity than they did. American constitutional thought in 1787–1788 may have become too complacent about the independent power of this republican consensus; Americans' toleration, for example, of the republican abomination of slavery may have rested on the quite wrongheaded idea that the republican consensus in the country could be depended on to end slavery.[105] In the light

<hr>

[103] See Richards, *Foundations*, 102, 103, 105, 132, 134, 136, 142, 156, 180, 288, 289.

[104] See, in general, Alfred Cobban, *A History of Modern France*, 3 vols. (Harmondsworth, Middlesex: Penguin, vol. 1, 1963, vol. 2, 1965, vol. 3, 1965); Furet, *Revolutionary France*.

[105] See Herbert J. Storing, "Slavery and the Moral Foundations of the American Republic," in Robert H. Horwitz, ed., *The Moral Foundations of the American Republic*, 3d

of history, that was a tragic misunderstanding of the proper role of republican constitutionalism in maintaining a commitment to basic republican principles, a misunderstanding that led eventually to a civil war that cost more American lives than any other military conflict in American history.[106] The American constitutionalists of 1787–1788 might well have profited from a greater dosage of the republican idealism of the French revolutionary constitutionalists, who did not, because they could not, separate the questions of republican consensus and constitutionalism.

The French, like the Americans, were committed to the idea of republican constitutionalism, which surely must embody some kind of operative distinction between constitutional and ordinary political argument. However, the constitutional forms they did develop were notoriously distorted by ordinary political argument in a way that self-destructively aborted the practicability during this period in France of establishing a tradition of republican constitutional argument with a force supreme over ordinary political argument. In effect, French constitutionalism was stillborn, because it fatefully confused constitutionalism with ordinary politics. That suggests a self-defeating contradiction at the very heart of the French revolutionary and constitutional project. In fact, this contradiction was implicit in the way the French interpreted the normative conception of popular sovereignty they shared with the Americans.

POPULAR SOVEREIGNTY IN FRENCH CONSTITUTIONALISM

French revolutionary and constitutional thought rested on the idea of inalienable human rights and, if necessary, the right of revolution in defense of those rights. Indeed, the French constitution of 1791, in contrast to the American Constitution of 1787–1788, was prefaced by the Declaration of Rights of Man and Citizen[107] (though certain rights are

---

ed.(Charlottesville: University Press of Virginia, 1986), 313–332. But cf. Paul Finkelman, "Slavery and the Constitutional Convention: Making a Covenant with Death," in Richard Beeman et al., eds., *Beyond Confederation: Origins of the Constitution and American National Identity* (Chapel Hill: University of North Carolina Press, 1987), 188–224.

[106] See James M. McPherson, *Battle Cry of Freedom: The Civil War Era* (New York: Ballantine Books, 1988), at 854.

[107] See Marcel Gauchet, "Rights of Man," in Furet, *Critical Dictionary*, 818–828.

guaranteed by the U.S. Constitution, the most important rights are protected by the 1791 amendments that we now call the Bill of Rights). American state constitutions, including the important Virginia constitution of 1776,[108] were, however, often prefaced by bills of rights, and the French may, in this matter, have taken instruction from the American state constitutions, with which they were familiar.[109] For both the French and the Americans, the protection of the inalienable rights of the person was clearly fundamental to both their revolutionary and their constitutional thought. Differences on this issue appear to be largely matters of expository style.[110] To understand the real differences between American and French revolutionary constitutionalism, we must repair to the deeper examination of the normative perspective they share.

The idea of republican constitutionalism—which both America and France shared—rested on an abstract political theory of legitimate government, namely, that legitimate political power must respect the status of all persons as equal bearers of inalienable rights and common interests.[111] That political theory, often called popular sovereignty, supposes that political power, in order to be legitimate, must be justified and be seen to be justified in terms of the ultimate moral sovereignty of persons understood to be free and equal bearers of rights. The Americans and the French shared this political theory and the associated view that many traditional forms of political authority (in particular, absolute monarchy) were illegitimate on such grounds. Both shared the Enlightenment idea that much traditional political power had corruptly deprived people of their capacity to know, let alone claim, the equal rights of their human nature; both therefore invested the idea of constitutionalism with the moral urgency of so reordering political relations that people were emancipated from such unjust ser-

---

[108] Francis Newton Thorpe, *The Federal and State Constitutions*, vol. 7 (Washington, D.C.: Government Printing Office, 1909), at 3812–3819.

[109] See Gauchet, "Rights of Man," at 819.

[110] See Palmer, *The Age of the Democratic Revolution*, vol. 1, at 487–8; Thomas Paine, *Rights of Man*, ed. Henry Collins (Harmondsworth, Middlesex: Penguin, 1969), at 132–34. For additions made by the constitution of 1793 (much in the spirit of Jacobin direct democracy), see James Miller, *Rousseau: Dreamer of Democracy* (New Haven: Yale University Press, 1984), 154.

[111] For fuller discussion of this conception, see Richards, *Toleration and the Constitution*; John Rawls, *A Theory of Justice* (Cambridge, Mass.: Harvard University Press, 1971).

vility and subjugation and achieved a sense of themselves as free and equal bearers of rights.

That common emancipatory impulse was, for both the Americans and the French, a moral vision. Illegitimate political power had, on this view, flourished because it had systematically degraded the moral powers of persons to be morally independent originators of reasonable thought and deliberation about both personal and ethical life, let alone about their just claims on the political order.[112] In effect, structures of political power had embedded people in unquestioned and unquestionable hierarchies of deference and submission in which the order of personal, ethical, and political life was imposed and specified by the place of persons in the hierarchy. The deepest damage of such illegitimate political power was its corruption of ethics: people were disabled from experiencing their personal powers as morally accountable creative agents living complete lives in a community of free and equal persons. Both American and French revolutionary and constitutional thinkers interpreted their project as establishing a political community of popular sovereignty in which people would be emancipated from such illegitimate political power and thus be capable of moral independence and sovereignty. On this point, John Adams expressed views quite similar to those he had read in Jean-Jacques Rousseau.[113]

Popular sovereignty is, however, an essentially contestable normative concept, subject to a range of different and often conflicting interpretations.[114] Much that is crucial to the distinctive constitutional trajectories of America and France must be understood from the perspective of the different interpretations each nation accorded the foundational normative concept they both conspicuously shared.

Americans, consistent with their religious traditions, crucially adopted a Protestant interpretation of popular sovereignty. Their political theory of popular sovereignty was clearly that of Lockean contractualism: political power is legitimate only if it can be reasonably justi-

---

[112] See Richards, *Foundations*, at 24–32.

[113] See John Adams, "A Dissertation on the Canon and Feudal Law," in Adams, *Works of John Adams*, vol. 3, at 448–74. Adams had read Rousseau's *The Social Contract* as early as 1765, and its vocabulary (if little else of its constitutionalism) influenced him. See Palmer, *The Age of the Democratic Revolution*, vol. 1, at 223–224.

[114] See W.B. Gallie, "Essentially Contested Concepts," in Gallie, *Philosophy and the Historical Understanding*, ch. 8.

fied to all as consistent with their inalienable human rights (in particular, the right to conscience to which Locke and the Americans give such prominent weight).[115] But respect for the right to conscience carries with it, as we have seen, a probing analysis of the corruptibility of political power by sectarian convictions, and Lockean constitutionalism, which generalized the argument for religious toleration to political power as such, interpreted the normative demands of popular sovereignty accordingly. That interpretation had two crucial features: first, a theory of human nature in politics as fundamentally flawed (the theories of faction and of fame), and, second, a theory that all political institutions are tainted by such flaws and must be treated skeptically. American constitutionalism, as we have seen, was for this reason a kind of metareflection on the corruptibility of all forms of political power (including republican political power) and the appropriate constraints on political structures that might, in light of both American political experience and the best political science available, be more likely to constrain the corruptibilities of political power in ways that would over-all tend to treat persons as equal bearers of rights and of common interests. The American idea of constitutionalism thus interpreted popular sovereignty as imposing a sufficiently complex and demanding system of constraints on political power that will, in the interstitial space left by the competing and mutually checking centers of corruptible political power, accord people a fair opportunity and capacity to know and to claim their inalienable rights of reasonable self-government and will hold political power accountable to them.

Both French revolutionary and constitutional thought were, of course, much preoccupied with the criticism and rectification of what they took to be the wholly corrupt complicity of the Catholic Church in the legitimation of the absolute monarchy.[116] But the religious and political history, which the French revolutionary constitutionalists struggled totally to repudiate, set the stage (in the same way that I earlier characterized as the return of the repressed) for the distinctive interpretation they accorded popular sovereignty, an interpretation I would call Catholic. That designation characterizes two features of French revolutionary and constitutional thought: first, its conception of

---

[115] See Richards, *Foundations*, 78–97.

[116] See Mona Ozouf, "De-Christianization," in Furet, *Critical Dictionary*, at 20–32; Francois Furet, "Civil Constitution of the Clergy," ibid., 449–457.

the basic good of human nature, which illegitimate politics had warped, and, second, its assumption that republican institutions, properly designed to be consistent with human nature thus understood, could themselves be depended on to accomplish the work of regenerating human nature and thus to create a community of free and equal persons. In effect, properly designed republican institutions could be depended on to create or restore a human nature now free of all corruptibility.

The political theory of Jean-Jacques Rousseau gave powerful imaginative expression to the interpretation of popular sovereignty that absorbed French republican thought.[117] No writer in France more piercingly articulated for French revolutionary and constitutional thinkers the indignities that the ancien régime inflicted on human nature or more powerfully appealed to their moral imaginations for his morally independent expression of the rights of human nature, his stance as a republican (unlike Voltaire)[118] who, in support for the rights of the common man, had refused to toady to a corrupt political order.[119] Rousseau spoke to the French about the depth and extent of their corruption, not only in politics but also in the family[120] and intimate life[121] and in the authenticity and integrity of personal emotion, thought, and deliberation,[122] and he suggested the kinds of transformations of education and family life, as well as of politics, that would be required to reassert the rights of human nature. No writer was at once so incisively personal and so uncompromisingly politically republican in shaping the French sense of the immensity of the task at hand.

French revolutionary and constitutional thought—fired by a moral vision of popular sovereignty—faced a far more intractable political

---

[117] See Bernard Manin, "Rousseau," in Furet, *Critical Dictionary*, at 829–43; Keith M. Baker, "Sovereignty," in ibid., pp. 844–59.

[118] See Mona Ozouf, "Voltaire," in Furet, *Critical Dictionary*, 869–78.

[119] For a sympathetic treatment of Rousseau from this perspective, see Judith N. Shklar, *Men and Citizens: A Study of Rousseau's Social Theory* (Cambridge: Cambridge University Press, 1985).

[120] Jean-Jacques Rousseau, *Emile*, trans. Barbara Foxley (London: J. M. Dent & Sons, 1961).

[121] See Jean-Jacques Rousseau, *La Nouvelle Heloise*, trans. Judith H. McDowell (University Park: Pennsylvania State University Press, 1968).

[122] See Jean-Jacques Rousseau, *The Confessions*, ed. Lester G. Crocker (New York: Pocket Books, 1956).

history than that faced by its American counterpart; in particular, it confronted the residues of antirepublican prejudices left by an absolute monarchy and an aristocracy whose loss of effective political power had led to an all the more insulting insistence on its prerogatives as superior to those of common people. Americans had long lived a life of democratic equality that their revolution reaffirmed and elaborated; the French had lived in a political order of arbitrary privilege that their revolution had both to end and regenerate. American constitutionalism elaborated an already existing consensus on republican government; the consensus in France was, in comparison, much more insecure and unstable. Rousseau appealed to French republicans precisely because he, more than any other thinker, anatomized the corruption of morality that the illegitimate political order had inflicted on the human heart and mind and articulated an alternative vision of popular sovereignty that promised, as if magically, the requisite moral regeneration. Both the diagnosis of human goodness (corrupted by illegitimate politics) and the remedy of regenerative political action gave the French the theory they believed they needed.

Rousseau had, of course, given his political theory contractualist expression in terms of the abstract political ideal he called the General Will, against which the legitimacy of political power was to be tested.[123] That political ideal is probably best understood, as Kant was later to interpret it,[124] as an abstract test of legitimate government, namely, that political power was legitimate only when it could be reasonably justified to all those subject to political power as consistent with both their rights and the use of power for the public good. Such an abstract test would be a kind of criterion against which any political order or action could be tested for legitimacy. On this view, when Rousseau insists that the General Will cannot be represented,[125] he is making a point that,

---

[123] See Jean-Jacques Rousseau, *The Social Contract*, in *The Social Contract and Discourses*, trans. G. D. H. Cole (New York: Dutton, 1950), 3–141. For pertinent commentary, see Roger D. Masters, *The Political Philosophy of Rousseau* (Princeton: Princeton University Press, 1968).

[124] See Immanuel Kant, "On the Common Saying: 'This May be True in Theory, but It Does Not Apply in Practice'," in Hans Reiss, ed., *Kant's Political Writings* (Cambridge: Cambridge University Press, 1970), 61–92. Kant calls the conception "an idea of reason," 79.

[125] See Rousseau, *The Social Contract*, at 94. For a fuller discussion of Rousseau's views on representation, see Richard Fralin, *Rousseau and Representation* (New York: Columbia University Press, 1978).

from his perspective, applies to any polity: the legitimacy of the polity's actions (its justice, for example) must be independently assessed, and no polity can itself be the last word on this question.

Such an abstract theory of political legitimacy is, of course, consistent with a range of constitutional alternatives (Rousseau himself suggested a range).[126] Indeed, a not unreasonable interpretation of it would render it consistent with the very different constitutionalism of the Americans, to whom the Constitution had been justified in very much such terms (namely, that the Constitution was reasonably justifiable to all by virtue of its rendering political power consistent with their rights and the common good). But Rousseau interprets this normative ideal in light of a conception both of human nature and of political institutions that leads to a quite different constitutionalism. In particular, in his main work of abstract political theory, Rousseau gave particular prominence to the kind of direct democracy associated with the small city-states of the classical republics.

Rousseau's focus on these models was, like so much of his work, motivated by his concern for instituting the kind of political education that would be the most bracing antidote to the corruption of a basically good human nature and thus would enable people, through the discipline of thought and imagination required to think of people as equals, to transform themselves and their society into a moral community of free and equal persons. Human nature had, Rousseau argued, been corrupted by illegitimate politics and by the kinds of false and empty wants (for example, conspicuous consumption) that this politics had spawned; in effect, human nature had become shallow, reactive, and incapable of the reasonable self-government of morally independent agents. The task of a constitutional founder, whom Rousseau—following Machiavelli—identified with an inspired man of power,[127] must be the political structure most likely to regenerate human nature. Rousseau, like Madison, saw faction (understood as persons' isolation in parochial and narrow concerns and obsessions) as the root of political pathology; unlike Madison, he assumed (human nature being good) that this pathology could be removed and that political struc-

---

[126] See, e.g., Jean-Jacques Rousseau, *Considerations on the Government of Poland*, in F. M. Watkins, ed., *Rousseau: Political Writings* (Edinburgh: Thomas Nelson, 1953), 159–274; also, *Constitutional Project for Corsica*, in ibid., 277–330.

[127] See Rousseau, *The Social Contract*, at 37–42.

tures must be constitutionally designed accordingly. In effect, the constitutional structures that were most reasonable (i.e., consistent with the General Will) were those that rendered political power most transparent to a people of republican virtue, a people now capable of moral abstraction and impartiality in the service of human rights and the public good. For this reason, simple democratic political forms were always to be preferred over complex ones because simple forms required people to think together, rather than in isolated factions; small direct democracies were optimal because they rendered politics more transparent to the republican virtue of the people, who were both empowered and competent to exercise such virtue; the classical republics (in particular, Sparta and Rome, not Athens) were the best model for such direct democracies because they made the greatest moral demands on people (without the corruptions of either commerce or art) and created a civil religion of the state that reinforced moral commitment and devotion (including, importantly, the military service fundamental to the militaristic imperialism of Machiavelli's vision of classical republicanism).[128]

Madison had, of course, offered arguments (quite well known to French constitutionalists) maintaining that the classical republics had egregiously violated human rights (he had, however, conceded in a letter to Jefferson that the violations of human rights might be less likely in a quite small, undeveloped, and homogeneous society, the society that Rousseau was imagining).[129] Rousseau certainly had as strong a sense of the personal dimension of human rights as Madison or, indeed, any other writer of the age, that is, how such rights establish the foundation of a morally independent and authentic personal self-government, including the kind of critical self-consciousness and privacy that Rousseau exemplified and celebrated in his own life.[130] But he did not think of constitutionalism, as Madison had, in terms of a generalization of the argument for religious toleration—the tendency of political power to corrupt and subvert moral conscience itself (the con-

---

[128] See Mark Hulliung, *Citizen Machiavelli* (Princeton: Princeton University Press, 1983).

[129] See Madison's letter to Jefferson of October 24, 1787, where Madison grants that a "savage" and quite homogeneous small society might not involve the oppression of the minority by the majority. See Rutland, *The Papers of James Madison,* vol. 10, at 212.

[130] See, e.g., Rousseau, *The Confessions.*

sciences of both politicians and the people). Rather, Rousseau assumed that political power—when structured in an appropriately simple and accountable way—could render politics expressive of the moral competences of self government by a free and equal people; such politics would, by definition, respect both their rights and the public good. Rousseau assumed that political power under a properly designed republic would remove faction, that is, that it would make republican political power not subject to the corruptions to which other forms of political power were subject. If it did not, his constitutionalism would, in his own terms, not be legitimate: it would not preserve and foster respect for human rights.

Rousseau's preferred constitutional alternative was, of course, not feasible in the enormous, well-populated, and commercially and culturally advanced France of the late eighteenth century, and the sheer anachronism of his preferred model might lead one to think that his constitutionalism would be regarded, as it was by Americans,[131] as idle. In fact, Rousseau's interpretation of popular sovereignty imaginatively framed French constitutional thought to a remarkable extent. The model for republican constitutionalism was not, as it was for the Americans, complex structures motivated by distrust of both human nature in politics and of institutions, but the simplicity and unity of political power that gave expression to the regenerated and dependable goodness of man's political nature.

Sièyes's seminally important *Qu'est-ce que le Tiers Etat?*[132] thus posed the basic issues for French constitutionalism in Rousseau's terms; he rejected the idea of separate representation of classes in the Estates General precisely because only a unicameral representative body would be a political structure appropriate to the kind of national unity it must have in order to embody the General Will. Sièyes certainly did not agree with Rousseau about the virtues of direct democracy and argued against the idea (advocated by Rousseau)[133] that representative

---

[131] See, e.g., Madison's dismissal of "[t]heoretic politicians," in Cooke, *The Federalist*, 61. For a useful general study, see Paul Merrill Spurlin, *Rousseau in America 1760–1809* (University: University of Alabama Press, 1969).

[132] Emmanuel Sièyes, *Qu'est-ce que le Tiers Etat?* (Paris: Press Universitaires de France, 1982).

[133] See Rousseau, *Considerations on the Government of Poland*, in Watkins, *Rousseau*, at 193.

government, if acceptable at all, must be subject to binding mandates from the people.[134] But Sièyes basically interpreted the project of French constitutionalism within the framework of Rousseau's assumptions: the design of a simple political structure that gives transparent expression to the General Will.

Sièyes' argument for a representative system was thus quite different from Madison's. Madison regarded faction as an ineradicable feature of human political nature in a republican polity committed to respect for human rights, and he assumed that guarantees of human rights would foster diverse sources of economic, religious, and moral pluralism (and thus forms of faction). The point was not to eliminate but constructively to use the human propensity to form the factions in ways that limit the opportunity for their oppressions and enlarge their utility in serving the ends of justice and the common good. Madison's argument for federalism was thus that the representative principle, extended to a sufficiently large territory and a heterogeneous population (guaranteed its rights) and expressing different constituencies in constitutionally independent centers of power (e.g., a bicameral legislature, an independent executive), would tend to produce a kind of deliberative public argument that would find common ground among these diverse constituencies and thus be more likely to respect the equal rights and common interests of all.[135] The application of the representative principle to a supreme unicameral legislature (especially one concerned not to maintain heterogeneity but to promote homogeneity) would not, for Madison, produce the desirable centers of competing power fundamental to American constitutionalism; instead, it would be likely to produce simply another form of factionalized majority rule and thus not address the republican dilemma, the tendency of majority rule to give unthrottled expression to a factionalized denigration of the rights and interests of minorities. Sièyes's argument is innocent of the republican dilemma and thus of American worries about the corruptibility of political power; he believed, following Rousseau, that an appropriately simple structure of political power would suffice to produce the desirable exercises of political power. Where Madison celebrated heterogeneity and pluralism

---

[134] For a good statement of Sièyes's views, see Keith M. Baker, "Sièyes," in Furet, *Critical Dictionary*, 313–322.

[135] See Richards, *Foundations*, 107–119.

(including guarantees of religious and moral diversity) as crucial to the aims of representative government, Sièyes emphasized homogeneity and unity.

This mode of constitutional thinking has the dangerous tendency of encouraging the republican leadership to suppose that it transparently embodies republican virtue either in itself or because it represents the republican virtue of the people; this temptation may be irresistible if you believe that political institutions have now rendered political power in general, or your political power in particular, incorruptible.

The issue is, of course, fundamental to the very idea of republican constitutionalism, which requires that political bodies be held to some appropriate degree of accountability regarding the principles of the republican political legitimacy of the constitution itself. In effect, republican constitutionalism aspires to domesticate the revolutionary theory of political legitimacy that brought it to power, holding republican politics to the standards of respect for human rights and the public interest. But the tendency of French constitutional thought to assume that its simple and centralizing political structures had rendered political power benign led it not to take seriously the requirement that it develop constitutional processes that continually subject power to critical assessment in light of whether it is, in fact, politically legitimate. This failure might not have been fatal if, in the highly volatile circumstances of French republican politics, the absence of such processes had not left a perceived vacuum of political legitimacy that was rapidly filled with an interpretation of popular sovereignty that undermined the very idea of republican constitutionalism.

Rousseau's preference for direct democracy was at this point interpreted to vindicate a conception of popular sovereignty that justified the role of the Parisian mobs (suitably advised by the political clubs) as the ultimate expression of popular sovereignty and thus as supreme over constitutional processes (in particular, the legislature). Robespierre and Saint-Just—at least when they agreed with the mob—expressed this view.[136] Such direct political action was regenerative, in

---

[136] See, for pertinent discussion, Carol Blum, *Rousseau and the Republic of Virtue: The Language of Politics in the French Revolution* (Ithaca: Cornell University Press, 1986), at 166–7, 173–4, 198, 249, 273. See also Norman Hampson, *Will and Circumstance: Montesquieu, Rousseau and the French Revolution* (Norman: University of Oklahoma Press, 1983).

Rousseau's sense, because it allowed the insurrectionary mob to express its republican virtue. In fact, the mobs were manipulated by one group of the republican leadership against another in a way that was blatantly antidemocratic (for example, excluding the Girondin opposition to the Jacobins from the National Convention)[137] and subverted any reasonable constitutional processes related to the limits on state power required by respect for human rights and the public good.

The political forces unleashed by this development framed the constitutional debates in 1793 over the proposed Girondin constitution of Condorcet and the enacted but never effective Montagnard constitution of the Jacobins. These constitutional debates did not resolve the issue; the direct political response of the National Convention was the Terror, the attempt to substitute for the insurrectionary violence of the mob the more terrible power of the state against any form of suspected disloyalty.[138] Its political theory was yet another interpretation of the twin assumptions of Rousseauean constitutionalism, a human nature warped by the effects of political illegitimacy and a political power that could regenerate it. Robespierre was clear on these points:

> the strength of popular government in revolution is at once *virtue* and its emanation *terror*: terror without virtue is malignant; virtue without terror is impotent.[139]

The Terror can hardly be regarded as a realistic response to external and internal threats to the republic when its greatest excesses took place when these threats were no longer realistic.[140] The Terror, rather, was driven by a reductio ad absurdum of Rousseau's constitutionalism of regenerative political power, driven by the self-righteous belief of men intoxicated by power that the discipline of the Terror was itself incorruptible and could render others incorruptible. The Rousseauean idea of the incorruptibility of republican political power had become, for Robespierre, identified with his own incorruptibility, and that conviction had, in turn, legitimated his conviction that he spoke for and

---

[137] See Ozouf, "Girondins," in Furet, *Critical Dictionary*, at 351–61.

[138] See Francois Furet, "Terror," in Furet, *Critical Dictionary*, at 137–150.

[139] Cited in Carol Blum, *Rousseau and the Republic of Virtue*, at 259.

[140] For a good discussion of this point, see Simon Schama, *Citizens: A Chronicle of the French Revolution* (New York: Alfred A. Knopf, 1989), at 726–792.

could identify the incorruptible virtue of the people. One of the articles added by the 1793 constitution to the earlier Declaration of the Rights of Man and Citizen drew the conclusion that justified the Terror: any dissenter from republic virtue, presumably as Robespierre transparently identified him, was guilty of "usurping the sovereign [and] should be immediately put to death by free men."[141]

The Terror was, of course, extreme and soon repudiated. But the theme of moral pedagogy, of which the Terror is the most dramatic example, pervaded French revolutionary and constitutional thought precisely because the aims of that thought were so absorbed by the search for the uses of political power that would render it transparent to republican virtue. That gave French revolutionary argument the violent self-righteousness of rhetoric (mirrored in the grisly violence of David's republican art)[142] that anticipated and set the stage for its later violence of action.[143] The very way it understood the aims of its constitutionalism led French republican thought disastrously and uncritically to assume that republican political power (whether of the state or of the people) was self-justified and to fail to hold itself accountable to reasonable independent standards of legitimate republican government.

This incoherence subverted the central enterprise of French revolutionary constitutionalism, its drive for the political reeducation of the French people into an enduring consensus of republican principle. The republican leadership, convinced of its own republican virtue, used its political power in increasingly sectarian ways that, over time, imposed even on republicans tests of loyalty that made it impossible for there to be any acceptable politics of the loyal opposition. The seeds of this problem were implicit in the decision of the French republic about how it would treat religion. A comparison of the American and the French views on this subject is instructive, for it suggests that the difficulties in French constitutionalism were implicit in the earliest constitutional consensus of the republican leadership well before they began their descent into division, recrimination, and the hell that was the Terror.

---

[141] See Miller, *Rousseau: Dreamer of Demcracy*, at 154.

[142] See, e.g., Jean Starobinski, *1789: The Emblems of Reason*, trans. Barbara Bray (Charlottesville: University Press of Virginia, 1982), at 99–124.

[143] This is a prominent theme of Simon Schama's excellent study of these events. See Schama, *Citizens*.

It was a decisively important fact in the distinctive formation of American constitutionalism that Americans, following Locke, regarded religious beliefs, properly understood, as vehicles of moral and political emancipation.[144] Locke and his American adherents thus faced frontally the central puzzle for religious Christians and democrats: that a religion like Christianity (a religion, for Locke, of democratic equality and civility) had long been associated in the West with the legitimation of antidemocratic institutions such as hereditary monarchy. Lockean Americans thus confronted the tension in traditional Christianity between a conception of radical freedom from existing roles and the coercive claims (for example, heresy prosecutions) of the Christian political community over the minds and hearts of people.[145] This critical interrogatory was particularly poignant for Locke and the Lockean revolutionary and constitutionalist Americans a century later since they believed that a properly understood Protestant Christianity supplied the ethics of personal self-government that made possible the theory and practice of democratic self-government. How, for long millennia, could Christianity have thus betrayed its essential emancipatory purposes, degrading a just human freedom into acceptance of morally arbitrary hierarchies of religious and political privilege and power?

The American constitutional tradition chose to answer the interrogatory in a way that repudiated the alternative Erastian conception of civil religion familiar to the American founders in the classical republican tradition elaborated by Machiavelli[146] and Rousseau.[147] The challenge to all republican theorists after the ancient world was to understand whether and how republican political practice could exist in a nonpagan world—in particular, in the world of commitment to the Judaeo-Christian religious synthesis. After all, the great historical examples of republican rule—Athens, Sparta, Rome, Carthage, and the like—were all pre-Christian or pagan societies, and the reawakening of interest in republican theory and practice in the Renaissance naturally

---

[144] See, in general, Heimert, *Religion and the American Mind.*

[145] For an illuminating recent study of this tension from the perspective of issues of gender, see Elaine Pagels, *Adam, Eve, and the Serpent* (New York: Random House, 1988).

[146] See Machiavelli, *The Discourses,* ed. Bernard Crick, trans. Leslie J. Walker (Harmondsworth: Penguin, 1970), at 139–152.

[147] See Rousseau, *The Social Contract and Discourses* trans. G. D. H. Cole (New York: Dutton, 1950), at 129–41.

posed the question whether and how republicanism could be squared with Christian commitments.

The classical republican answer by Machiavelli, Rousseau, and Marx[148] was the Erastian conception of civil religion, an established church regulated by state power to appropriately emancipatory ends. On this analysis, the great defect in the relationship of church and state since Constantine was the independence of the church from state control and its consequent capacity to corrupt republican aims and values in the service of theocratically defined ends. This view was naturally, though not inevitably, linked to the kind of Voltairean anticlericalism familiar to Europeans from republican Venice and Florence and the associated classical republican tradition revived by Machiavelli.[149] On this view, Judaeo-Christian values, whatever their truth value, were intrinsically politically dangerous and must be cabined and tamed to the ends of secular authority by the assertion of supreme secular authority over religious life on the model of Roman or Spartan civil religion. Even the political science of Montesquieu and Hume— although not endorsing classically republican civil religion—supported Erastian established churches.[150]

Americans like Jefferson and Madison gravitated to a quite different constitutional conception that culminated in the religion clauses of the First Amendment[151] because they took a different view of how Judaeo Christian belief and republican values interconnected, namely, the familiar American union of equally intense personal religiosity *and* republicanism. On this view, stated by Locke, the essential moral message of Christian belief—namely, the democratic liberty and equality of all persons—supported republican values of equal liberty under law but had been corrupted from its proper supportive role by Constantine's wholly heretical and blasphemous establishment of Christianity

[148] See Karl Marx, *On the Jewish Question,* in *Karl Marx: Early Writings,* trans. T. B. Bottomore (London: C. A. Watts, 1963), at 1–40.

[149] See William J. Bouwsma, *Venice and the Defense of Republican Liberty* (Berkeley: University of California Press, 1968), 1–51, 417–638. For a good general study of Machiavelli's subversive attitude toward Christian thought and practice, see Hulliung, *Citizen Machiavelli.*

[150] For commentary on Montesquieu's Erastian conception of religion, see Pangle, *Montesquieu's Philosophy of Liberalism,* 249–59. On Hume, see David Miller, *Philosophy and Ideology in Hume's Political Thought* (Oxford: Clarendon Press, 1981), 117–8.

[151] See, in general, Richards, *Toleration and the Constitution,* chs. 4–5.

as the church of the Roman Empire. The problem was not that Constantine had opted for the wrong form of established church—one subordinating secular to religious authority—but that, as Americans like Jefferson and Madison came increasingly to see,[152] he had wedded religious to secular authority *at all*. A more radical separation of religious and political authority was required in order to preserve the integrity of each, in particular, to preserve the moral independence of conscience against which the legitimate claims of state power could then be assessed.

In contrast, French revolutionary and constitutional thought identified traditional religion as an enemy to republican morality and asserted, following Rousseau, a role for the state as the religious pedagogue of republican morality. The policy of de-Christianization,[153] including the Civil Constitution of the Clergy in 1790,[154] thus set the course of the French republic in support of alternative political institutions of civil religion. The French disagreed among themselves about the appropriate forms of civil religion; Robespierre, for example, took violent objection to the festival of reason but sponsored his own festival of Rousseauean republican religion.[155] Whereas Americans were skeptical about any political role in these matters, the French—consistent with the assumptions of their constitutionalism—undertook to define the *proper* political role, that is, the proper institution of civil religion that would be morally regenerative.

We should not, of course, underestimate the immensity of the task that the French revolutionary constitutionalists faced in comparison with their American counterparts, in particular, the problem of a lack of a secure republican consensus in France.[156] But the normative conception of popular sovereignty that framed their thinking led them to

---

[152] Americans elaborate this principle beyond Locke, whose arguments focus on free exercise and are not antiestablishment. For discussion of the ways Americans adapted and elaborated Locke's arguments, see Richards, *Toleration and the Constitution*, 88–116.

[153] See Ozouf, "De-Christianization," in Furet, *Critical Dictionary*, at 20–32.

[154] See Furet, "Civil Constitution of the Clergy," in Furet, *Critical Dictionary*, at 449–457.

[155] See Ozouf, "Revolutionary Religion," in Furet, *Critical Dictionary*, at 560–570.

[156] For a range of other contrasts, see Patrice Higonnet, *Sister Republics: The Origins of French and American Republicanism* (Cambridge, Mass.: Harvard University Press, 1988).

think ahistorically and uncritically about this task, adopting models of political power unconsciously in thrall to the absolutist institutions they thought they were repudiating. The institutions that republicans thought were morally regenerative (for example, de-Christianization) in fact imposed an unreasonable moral orthodoxy on many pious citizens, violated their right to conscience, rendered the republican consensus in France narrower and more unstable, and provoked both the opposition of the king and violent counterrevolution in several parts of the country.[157] In contrast, efforts at political reeducation like the public festivals[158] were idle rituals, since they were not accompanied by the development of constitutional forms that would themselves engage the hearts and minds of the French people and thus form an enduring republican consensus. The politically sectarian abuses of power by the members of the republican leadership led them eventually to take the most disastrously self-destructive steps in frustrating the creation of a republican consensus that was among their central ambitions; in particular, they repeatedly failed to respect their own constitutional representative institutions whenever it was convenient to do so (including the use of the Parisian mob to secure political ends they were unable to secure through electoral politics). The politics of participation of the Parisian mobs thus flourished as actual voting by the people understandably declined.[159]

That fact—mobs over voters—illuminates the tragic trajectory of French republicanism into Napoleonic imperialistic dictatorship based on bureaucratic centralization. Voting not only enables voters to register their personal preferences for public goods and services and corresponding tax burdens; it also allows the electorate to formulate, discuss, and express its deliberative views about how public policy should address issues of both justice and the common good. The resolution of political controversy in this way is fundamental to the conception of democratic civility among citizens of a free society—their capacity to resolve differences deliberatively via an informed and critically independent public opinion that (because of guarantees of free speech) is

---

[157] For a vivid narrative of these events, including the effects of de-Christianization in eliminating any sympathy Louis XVI may have felt for the revolution, see, in general, Simon Schama, *Citizens*.

[158] For colorful description of these festivals, see, in general, Schama, *Citizens*.

[159] See Patrice Gueniffey, "Elections," in Furet, *Critical Dictionary*, at 37.

not itself hostage to the state's authority and control. The substitution of the Parisian mobs (controlled by politicians) for voting undermined the conception of reasonable public justification fundamental to constitutional government as such, making impossible the development of reasonable political discourse among holders of diverse views, all of which are respected. In effect, the republican leadership manipulated the mobs to achieve its own ends and thus eroded any possibility of a critical public opinion that could impose reasonable constitutional constraints on the exercise of political power. The consequence was a dynamic that narrowed the conception of what counted as reasonable and tolerable political disagreement (in effect, assimilating any opposition to treason), thus further eroding the breadth of support available to the leadership and reducing it to a level below that which republicanism must have if it is to be viable. Republicanism had appealed to the French in the terms of the Declaration of Rights of Man and Citizen, just as it had moved Americans in the form of a constitutionalism centered on Madison's piercing observation of the contradiction between mobs and the constitutional processes that protect human rights. Republicanism increasingly repelled the French, as it would have Americans, when it took the form of the inverted world of Robespierre's republicanism, in which the mob was the voice of human rights.

Even after the suppression of the mobs after Thermidor, the self-destructive pattern of republican leadership persisted. The 1795 constitution was in part designed to secure a more deliberative republican politics through a constitutional design of independent centers of power, a bicameral legislature and an executive elected by the legislature (the Directory).[160] There was, however, still no serious concern to innovate some impartial processes to ensure that political bodies (e.g., the Directory) adhered to the constitution; Sièyes's recommendation of a constitutional jury for this purpose, for example, was not accepted.[161] Even if Sièyes's recommendation had been heeded, it would have made little difference. If the republicans of 1795 had painfully learned to think skeptically about the political virtue of the people, they had not learned to be skeptical about their own virtue. The new constitutional forms were just that, forms, drained of any weight by a republican

---

[160] See Doyle, *Oxford History of the French Revolution*, at 319.
[161] See Keith M. Baker, "Sièyes," in Furet, *Critical Dictionary*, at 322.

leadership that, secure in its belief about its own republican virtue over that of the people, flouted the results of elections whenever it suited its political convenience. The Directory's repeated disrespect for electoral processes sowed the seeds for the public acceptability of the Napoleonic dictatorship.[162]

It was a disastrous political education in republican values for leaders thus to substitute political convenience for constitutional forms; in effect, the normative theory of popular sovereignty (with its controlling weight on the republican virtue of either the leadership or the people) legitimated clearly unconstitutional uses of political power that alienated many from the idea of republican government. The deepest damage of these developments was, of course, done to the concept of respect for inalienable human rights, the same concepts that French revolutionary constitutionalists had once explained to the French people as the very point of the entire republican project. The forms of French constitutionalism during this formative period did not and were publicly seen not to protect rights, for they did not exercise significant independent constraint on, or protect the rights of the people against, the leadership's pursuit of its own convenience. Indeed, one such development, based on a grotesque appeal to Rousseauean popular sovereignty, unleashed the mobs of Paris, with their murderous violations of anything that respect for human rights could mean or reasonably be taken to mean. Edmund Burke, who had supported the claims of the revolutionary constitutionalism of the Americans as reasonable interpretations of the basic rights of British constitutionalism,[163] violently repudiated French revolutionary constitutionalism because it had proven itself to be at war with a reasonable understanding of the basic normative aims of liberal constitutionalism.[164]

It is surely good evidence for the constitutional wisdom of the American skepticism about the self-deceiving corruptibilities of human nature that these events could have been sponsored by politicians in the name of Rousseau's elevated and humane vision of a polit-

[162] See Doyle, *Oxford History of the French Revolution*, 318–340.

[163] See Edmund Burke, "Speech on Moving His Resolutions for Conciliation with the Colonies," March 22, 1775, in *The Works of Edmund Burke*, 6th ed. (Boston: Little, Brown, 1880), vol. 2, at 101–186.

[164] See, in general, Ross J. S. Hoffman and Paul Levack, eds., *Burke's Politics* (New York: Alfred A. Knopf, 1959), at 277–400.

ical community alive with respect for human rights. The French night-mare of democratic reason was an American nightmare, invoked by Madison in some of his darkest and most prescient pages. It was the tragedy of the democratic constitutionalism of the late eighteenth cen-tury—shared by two intelligent and enlightened peoples—that one of them, moved by a vision of its own goodness, had to live out that night-mare to its final bitter and disillusioned end.

The failure of the French Revolution to lead to a constitutionalism adequate to its normative demands discredited revolutionary constitu-tionalism in France and long delayed the formation of a national con-sensus on republican institutions.[165] Indeed, for European thinkers, the events in France discredited the very idea of a constitutionalism based on revolutionary normative ideals of respect for human rights, as if Amer-ica had never and Britain barely existed;[166] the impact of such a defective model on the tragic trajectory of Italian post-Risorgimento constitution-alism is the subject of the next chapter. Revolutions, which in both Britain and America had been motored by liberal constitutional ideals, were associated in subsequent European thought with such apparently antiliberal ideologies as Marxism;[167] consistent with this self-fulfilling view, modern revolutions do not usually culminate in liberal constitu-tionalism.[168] After the debacle of the French experience, the culture of Europe (including Italy and Germany) could barely grasp even the idea of an attractive revolutionary constitutionalism, let alone implement it.

RIGHTS SKEPTICISM AND THE POSITIVISTIC CHALLENGE TO GERMAN CONSTITUTIONALISM

The great interest of the comparative study of American and French revolutionary constitutionalism is that it demonstrates how a norma-

[165] See Furet, *Revolutionary France 1770–1880*.

[166] For a fuller development of this argument, see, in general, Hannah Arendt, *On Revolution* (Harmondsworth: Penguin, 1973). On the complex impact of the French Rev-olution on British thought, including the delay of liberal constitutional reforms, see Sea-mus Deane, *The French Revolution and Enlightenment in England 1789–1832* (Cambridge, Mass.: Harvard University Press, 1988).

[167] See Arendt, *On Revolution*.

[168] See, in general, John Dunn, *Modern Revolutions: An Introduction to the Analysis of a Political Phenomenon*, 2d ed. (Cambridge: Cambridge University Press, 1989).

tive conviction of inalienable human rights, shared by two forms of constitutionalism at their respective revolutionary foundings, may, in light of other assumptions, lead to radically different institutional forms, some of which frustrate respect for human rights and thus delegitimate such forms of constitutionalism. Indeed, some institutional forms are so radically defective in this regard that the very role of the language and thought of human rights, as a constraint on political power, takes no deep historical roots in the cultural heart of a people; rather, constitutional history reveals a checkered and sometimes bitterly disappointing version of what revolutionary constitutionalism should reflect—the struggles of a free people better to realize respect for universal human rights.[169] We focus here, from this perspective, on Germany; in the next chapter, on Italy.

The great interest of the comparative historical-interpretive study of American and German constitutionalism lies in their quite different approaches to the normative conviction of the protection of human rights that is ostensibly central to the very notion of liberal constitutionalism. The current German constitution, the Basic Law,[170] was importantly addressed, under significant American influence in the wake of World War II,[171] to the need for basic rights-based constitutional institutions that would reconstruct and reframe the legal and political culture that had made possible the moral nightmare of Hitler's totalitarianism; against this background, the interpretation of the Basic Law by the Federal Constitutional Court has, consistent with its textual guarantees of basic rights (including a textual guarantee of the revolu-

---

[169] For a probing critique of French constitutionalism along these lines, see Tony Judt, "Rights in France: Reflections on the Etiolation of a Political Language," *Tocqueville Review* 14, no. 1 (1993), 66–108; on the complicity of French intellectuals in these developments, see Tony Judt, *Past Imperfect;* on French complicity with the racial genocide of Jews, see Tony Judt, "Betrayal in France," *New York Review of Books* 40, no. 14 (August 12, 1993), at 31–34. See also Liah Greenfeld, *Nationalism: Five Roads to Modernity* (Cambridge, Mass.: Harvard University Press, 1992), at 89–188.

[170] See *Basic Law of the Federal Republic of Germany* (Bonn: Press and Information Office of the Federal Government, 1987).

[171] See Carl J. Friedrich, "Rebuilding the German Constitution," 43 *American Political Science Review* 461–82, 705–20 (1949); Carl J. Friedrich, "The Constitution of the German Federal Republic," in E. H. Litchfield, ed., *Governing Postwar Germany* (Ithaca: Cornell University Press, 1953), at 117–51. For general background, see John Ford Golay, *The Founding of the Federal Republic of Germany* (Chicago: University of Chicago Press, 1958); Richard Hiscocks, *Democracy in Western Germany* (London: Oxford University Press, 1957).

tionary right to resist illegitimate authority),[172] prominently deployed rights-based interpretive arguments.[173] The Basic Law is thus very clearly an interpretation of the genre of revolutionary liberal constitutionalism, but its constitutionalism is not the expression of revolution on the model of American or French constitutionalism or even of civil war on the model of the American Reconstruction Amendments. Nonetheless, its constitutionalism is, in the context of the larger history of German constitutional experience,[174] an invocation of revolutionary constitutionalism in profound criticism of the legal and political culture that made Hitler thinkable and even acceptable. The interest of the comparative study of American and German constitutionalism arises in the examination of this criticism of German constitutional traditions.

We have already examined a related form of criticism in the revolutionary constitutionalism of the American Reconstruction Amendments. The focus of that criticism, as we have seen, was on proslavery constitutionalism, in particular, Calhoun's skepticism about rights as a political value, which required that the Constitution be interpreted without reference to the normative demand of the protection of human rights forthrightly stated, for example, in the American Declaration of Independence. As an expression of this criticism, the Reconstruction Amendments unambiguously affirmed a nationally enforceable conception of equal protection of basic human rights.

The German form of this criticism must be understood against the background of the relatively late construction of German constitutional identity. This construction was based on a deeply romantic conception of authentic ethnic-cultural nationality that negatively defined itself by its cultural resistance to the French doctrine of universal human rights and to that doctrine's most profound German exponent, Immanuel

---

[172] See *Basic Law*, Article 20 (4).

[173] For a useful review of the relevant opinions, see Donald P. Kommers, *The Constitutional Jurisprudence of the Federal Republic of Germany* (Durham: Duke University Press, 1989). For my understanding of this jurisprudence I am much indebted to a seminar on comparative German American civil liberties given at the N.Y.U. School of Law in the spring term of 1992 with my colleague Professor Thomas M. Franck and with a visiting professor at the School of Law, Dr. Georg Nolte of the Max Planck-Institut fur Auslandisches Offentliches Recht unde Volkerrecht, Heidelberg, Germany.

[174] See E. M. Hucko, *The Democratic Tradition: Four German Constitutions* (Leamington Spa, U.K.: Berg, 1987), H. W. Koch, *A Constitutional History of Germany* (London: Longman 1984).

Kant[175] (in Italy, Mussolini was correspondingly to defend fascism as the antithesis of the principles of the French revolution of 1789, principles of free speech, liberty of conscience, and equality before the law).[176] The analogy to American proslavery constitutionalism is striking: Calhoun defined Southern constitutional identity in terms of cultural resistance to Jefferson's rights-based Declaration of Independence.[177] In nineteenth-century Europe, culture was the rallying call of national identity; linguistic unity was seen as the basis of a larger cultural and ultimate national unity (thus, Pan-Germanism). German national unity was increasingly identified with the forging of a cultural orthodoxy centered on the purity of the German language, its ancient "Aryan" myths,[178] its high culture. This search for cultural unity arose in part in reaction to the French imperialistic and assimilationist interpretation of universal human rights. That history invited the search for an alternative, linguistically and culturally centered concept of national unity.

But, cultural unity—when hostile to universal human rights—is, as it was under Southern slavery, an unstable, highly unprincipled, and sometimes ethically regressive basis for national unity. It may unreasonably enforce highly sectarian values by deadly polemical reaction to its imagined spiritual enemies, and it is all too comfortable identifying those enemies with a group already historically degraded as culturally inferior. Blacks served as this group in America, reflected in Justice Taney's definition of American national identity in *Dred Scott* in terms of white supremacy; in Europe, this role was performed by Jews, a highly vulnerable, historically stigmatized cultural minority—the paradigm case

---

[175] See, for a persuasive interpretation of German nationalism along these lines, Liah Greenfeld, *Nationalism: Five Roads to Modernity*, at 277–395. For a specific focus on the contrasting definitions of citizenship in Germany and France, see Rogers Brubaker, *Citizenship and Nationhood in France and Germany* (Cambridge, Mass.: Harvard University Press, 1992). On Kant's rights-based political philosophy, see Patrick Riley, *Kant's Political Philosophy* (Totowa, N.J.: Rowman & Littlefield, 1983); on Rousseau's influence on Kant, see Ernst Cassirer, *The Question of Jean-Jacques Rousseau*, trans. Peter Gay (New Haven: Yale University Press, 1989).

[176] See Denis Mack Smith, *Mussolini* (New York: Vintage, 1983), 140.

[177] See Richards, *Conscience and the Constitution*, at 32.

[178] For a superb treatment, see Leon Poliakov, *The Aryan Myth: A History of Racist and Nationalist Ideas in Europe*, trans. Edmund Howard (London: Sussex University Press, 1971).

of cultural heresy. In the German case, where there was little solid, humane historical background of moral pluralism on which to build, romantic aesthetic values increasingly dominated over ethical ones. In Italy, in contrast, Mussolini had the history of longstanding Roman pluralistic tolerance of Jews to appeal to in rebuking Hitler's very German anti-Semitism and acquiesced in German anti-Semitism in Italy only under pressure from Hitler, by then his indispensable ally (a complicity that led to notable resistance by the people of Italy).[179] Richard Wagner, a major influence on the development of German anti-Semitism, preposterously regarded his artistic genius as sufficient to entitle him to articulate, in the role of prophetic moral leader like Lincoln, an ethical vision for the German people in the Aryan myth embodied in *Parsifal*. This confusion of the categories of aesthetic and ethical leadership reflects the underlying crisis in ethical and political culture.[180]

The force of this crisis in German constitutional culture was prominently exemplified in the period of Weimar constitutionalism by the constitutional theory of Carl Schmitt. Schmitt's complicity with the Nazis[181] places him, with Heidegger,[182] among the leading intellectuals of their period who exemplify the culture that made Hitler both thinkable and acceptable; what is interesting about Schmitt in particular is his pivotal role as a leading constitutional theorist who was highly critical of Weimar constitutionalism.

Schmitt's critique was based on a rights-skeptical theory of the ineradicable nature of political power, which he saw as based on a polarity of friends and enemies[183] in which political sovereignty was

---

[179] On Mussolini's rejection of anti-Semitism, see ibid., p. 70. On the striking history of the Italians in not persecuting and sometimes protecting Jews both in Italy and in the territories occupied by Italy, see Susan Zuccotti, *The Italians and the Holocaust: Persecution, Rescue, Survival* (New York: Basic Books, 1987); Meir Michaelis, *Mussolini and the Jews: German-Italian Relations and the Jewish Question in Italy, 1922–1945* (Oxford. Clarendon Press, 1978); and Jonathan Steinberg, *All or Nothing: The Axis and the Holocaust, 1941–1943* (London: Routledge, 1990).

[180] See Poliakov, *The Aryan Myth*. See also Leon Poliakov, *The History of Anti-Semitism*, vol. 3, trans. Miriam Kochan (New York: Vanguard Press, 1975), ch. 11.

[181] See Joseph W. Bendersky, *Carl Schmitt: Theorist for the Reich* (Princeton: Princeton University Press, 1983).

[182] See Victor Farias, *Heideigger and Nazism* (Philadelphia: Temple University Press, 1989).

[183] See Carl Schmitt, *The Concept of the Political*, trans. George Schwab (New Brunswick: Rutgers University Press, 1976), at 26.

ultimately defined by "the orientation toward the possible extreme case of an actual battle against a real enemy."[184] For Schmitt, consistent with the German nationalistic tradition he reflects, these polarities were founded on retaining the purity of the nation's already constitutive ethnic homogeneity, requiring, as the condition of national integrity, "first homogeneity and second—if the need arises—elimination or eradication of heterogeneity."[185] His criticism of Weimar constitutionalism was aimed not at its political democracy, but at its liberalism, its demand for a kind of rights-based equal treatment that was inconsistent with the friend-enemy polarities of politics as such.[186] From this perspective, the rights-based demand for liberal dialogue and mutual respect (centering on respect for rights of conscience, free speech, and association) was a kind of antipolitics that was fundamentally inconsistent with the exigencies of political action.[187] Liberalism was, for Schmitt, unacceptable as a political theory for the same reason that he had earlier argued German political romanticism was unacceptable: its passivism when political action was required.[188]

Schmitt could characterize his views as democratic, albeit illiberal, on the basis of a positivistic interpretation of the ultimate basis for political legitimacy, namely, the will of a people to act politically. The interpretation is positivistic because, in contrast to both the American and the French rights-based conceptions of popular sovereignty, the will of the people was amorally defined, for Schmitt, by however a people bonded themselves as a homogeneous unit against an enemy in possible war irrespective of "ideals or norms of justice" and without regard to moral questions.[189] The view was supposedly democratic because it defined legitimate politics as the authentic expression of the people's will, whatever it turned out to be.

Of course, thus mystically understood, democracy would not necessarily be defined even by respect for minimal conditions of majority

[184] Ibid., at 39.

[185] See Carl Schmitt, *The Crisis of Parliamentary Democracy*, trans. Ellen Kennedy (Cambridge, Mass.: MIT Press, 1985), at 9.

[186] See Schmitt, *The Crisis of Parliamentary Democracy*, at 8–13.

[187] See Schmitt, *The Concept of the Political*, at pp. 69–93.

[188] See Carl Schmitt, *Political Romanticism*, trans. Guy Oakes (Cambridge, Mass.: MIT Press, 1986).

[189] See Schmitt, *The Concept of the Political*, at 49.

rule expressed through regular and fair elections.[190] Schmitt thus famously argued for the broadest possible construction of executive powers under article 48 of the Weimar constitution not as an expression of majority rule or democratic processes (which such an interpretation would often frustrate) but in order to facilitate politically decisive action that would preserve national integrity against what Schmitt took to be the anti-German forces of disorder (including the democratic expression of those forces through electoral politics).[191] The crucial point about healthy politics, for Schmitt, was not its reasonableness but its willful decisiveness: "[l]ooked at normatively, the decision emanates from nothingness."[192] Consistent with this view, after Hitler's accession to power, Schmitt publicly defended the legality of Hitler's purges as appropriately decisive action to preserve national integrity.[193]

Schmitt's theory of politics, understood as a descriptive theory of political psychology, is not inconsistent with liberal constitutionalism. Indeed, a form of such a theory (Madison's theory of faction) plays a prominent role among the six ingredients of American revolutionary constitutionalism. For Madison, however, the fact of faction in politics was just that: an ineradicable fact of political psychology. The task of liberal constitutionalism is not to deny facts (in the way French constitutionalism apparently did) but to take them seriously in the construction of constitutional institutions that will better achieve the normative ends of liberal constitutionalism, respect for human rights, and the public interest.

But Schmitt interpreted such facts not descriptively but normatively. He gave these facts a normative interpretation that rests not on the facts but on normative assumptions of what appears superficially to be a radical, indeed avowedly nihilistic, rights skepticism: "an absolute decision created out of nothingness."[194] On the basis of this skepticism,

[190] For a fuller exploration of the nature of democratic processes, see Robert A. Dahl, *Democracy and Its Critics* (New Haven: Yale University Press, 1989).

[191] See Carl Schmitt, *Political Theology*, trans. George Schwab (Cambridge, Mass.: Harvard University Press, 1985), at 11–12; for background, see George Schwab's introduction at xix–xxiii.

[192] See Schmitt, *Political Theology*, at 31–32.

[193] See Bendersky, *Carl Schmitt: Theorist for the Reich*, at 212–18.

[194] See Schmitt, *Political Theology*, at 66.

the recommended course is to resist any appeal to universalistic constraints on national aspirations and to follow the leader who best expresses national authenticity. The underlying normative assumptions, while certainly nihilistic about rights, are not, however, ultimately normatively nihilistic. If they were ultimately nihilistic, any choice might be as good as any other. But, Schmitt offered us one choice as clearly the one demanded, namely, respect for the person who is most politically decisive in uniting a people against its putative enemies. That is a normative choice—the worship of power—that has had its self-conscious defenders in political philosophy since Callicles defended the view in Plato's *Gorgias*.[195] Schmitt, however, offered no normative argument; indeed he willfully denied the need for one, because he failed to understand that he had taken and indeed defended a normative choice.

Schmitt's incoherence during this period was publicly echoed to similar effect by the philosopher Martin Heidegger: the self-conscious appeal to moral nihilism is offered as a ground for following the mandates of the most politically powerful and nationally unifying man of the hour, Adolf Hitler.[196] The argument made in both cases cannot be defended, because it is fundamentally incoherent and therefore indefensible. But, both the argument and its appeal can be understood against the historical background of German nationalism to which I earlier referred. German national cultural identity was forged, as we have seen, in negative opposition to ideas of universal equal human rights, an opposition that had been philosophically deepened for Heidegger in particular by what he took to be Nietzsche's nihilistic attack on these ideas.[197] Both Schmitt and Heidegger profoundly identified

[195] See Plato, *Gorgias*, trans. Walter Hamilton (Harmondsworth: Penguin, 1973).

[196] For a persuasive argument that Schmitt and Heidegger share a common position on these normative issues, see Richard Wolin, *The Politics of Being: The Political Thought of Martin Heidegger* (New York: Columbia University Press, 1990), at 29–30, 31–32, 38, 39–40, 106; see also Pierre Bourdieu, *The Political Ontology of Martin Heidegger*, trans. Peter Collier (Cambridge: Polity Press, 1991). On Heidegger's complicity with Nazism, see, in general, Farias, *Heidegger and Nazism*; cf. Jean-Francois Lyotard, *Heidegger and "the jews,"* trans. Andreas Michel and Mark Roberts (Minneapolis: University of Minnesota Press, 1990). For a sympathetic and probing account of Heidegger's contributions to other areas of philosophy, see Hubert L. Dreyfus, *Being-in-the-World: A Commentary on Heidegger's Being and Time, Division I* (Cambridge, Mass.: MIT Press, 1991).

[197] On Neitzsche's profound influence on Heidegger, see Wolin, *The Politics of Being*, at 98, 141–42.

with this negatively defined German cultural tradition as the communitarian source of all affirmative value in living. Their appeal to moral nihilism was thus self-understood as the therapeutic rejection of discredited ideas of universal human rights; in contrast, obedience to the mandates of the nationally unifying man of the hour was interpreted as the way of preserving what they took to be the only ultimate value in living—the cultural tradition of the German people. Heidegger thus quite clearly wed a person's solitary pursuit of personal authenticity with a passivist subordination to the communitarian demands of the hour, an interpretation of the essential historical-cultural values of German culture as expressed by the supposedly great political interpretive artist of the hour, Adolf Hitler.[198]

As I earlier remarked, cultural unity—when hostile to universal human rights—can be an ethically regressive basis for national unity, founding national unity on forms of religious, ethnic, or racial subjugation. The European form of this nationalist subjugation, anti-Semitism, arose in the context of the tense relationship between emerging European principles of universal human rights, sponsored by the French Revolution, and nineteenth-century Europe's struggles for a sense of national identity and self-determination. When the French Revolution took the form of Napoleonic world revolution, these forces became fatally contradictory. The emancipation of the Jews occurred in this tense environment, and the Jews became, over time, its most terrible victim. The Jews, whose emancipation was sponsored by an appeal to universal human rights,[199] were identified with a culture hostile to the emergence of national self-determination.[200] Their very attempts at assimilation into that culture were, according to this view, marks of their degraded inability to participate in a true national culture.

In Germany, political anti-Semitism became, under Hitler's leadership, the very core of the success of Nazi politics in a nation humiliated by the triumphant democracies in World War I.[201] Nazism was self-

---

[198] See Wolin, *The Politics of Being,* at 60–61.

[199] See Arthur Hertzberg, *The French Enlightenment and the Jews* (New York: Columbia University Press, 1990).

[200] See Uriel Tal, *Christians and Jews in Germany,* trans. Noah Jonathan Jacobs (Ithaca: Cornell University Press, 1975).

[201] See Peter Pulzer, *The Rise of Political Anti-Semitism in Germany and Austria,* rev. ed. (Cambridge, Mass.: Harvard University Press, 1988); Jacob Katz, *From Prejudice to Destruction* (Cambridge, Mass.: Harvard University Press, 1980).

consciously at war with the idea and practice of human rights, including the institutions of constitutional government motivated by the construction of a politics of public reason that respects human rights.[202] Schmitt's constitutional theory was congenial to Nazism's aims because his normative theory of politics, based on both rights skepticism and the polarity of friends and enemies, would permit war against any enemy, no matter how unjust, to be the basis of authentic national identity, again without addressing issues of morality. Hitler's irrationalist and immoral war against the Jews would thus be legitimate precisely because it attacked human rights (identified, as we have seen, with the Jews) and provided the kind of enemy that unified the German people as a people.

From the perspective of comparative revolutionary constitutionalism, the interest of Schmitt's form of rights skepticism is in its central justifying role in so radically and self-consciously an anticonstitutional ideology as Nazism. By comparison, Calhoun's proslavery constitutionalism, albeit rights skeptical, was still recognizably a form of constitutionalism: the theory of concurrent majorities articulates certain constraints on political power in the interest of a larger utilitarian public good.[203] Schmitt, however, legitimates the removal of any and all such constraints to the extent that such removal enables a political leader to mobilize authentic national unity in the required way. If Calhoun offered us a defective form of what retained at least some elements of liberal constitutional procedures, Schmitt offered us not constitutionalism, but anticonstitutionalism in one of its most blatant forms, totalitarianism.[204]

Schmitt's anticonstitutionalism, like Heidegger's, rested on the legitimation of whatever dominant political leaders manipulatively regard as necessary to secure national will and identity. All the sophistication of Schmitt's and Heidegger's argument serves this most ultimate and irrationalist of political parochialisms, in which ultimate value in living is self-consciously defined by the irrationalist romantic appeal Adolf Hitler held for the German people. Intellectuals like Schmitt and Heidegger and many others in Europe (including

---

[202] See Hannah Arendt, *The Origins of Totalitarianism* (New York: Harcourt Brace Jovanovich, 1973).

[203] For discussion, see Richards, *Conscience and the Constitution*, at 32–36.

[204] See Arendt, *The Origins of Totalitarianism*.

France)[205] failed to offer what liberal constitutionalism clearly requires of its public culture and the role of intellectuals in that culture: rigorous and morally independent support for and cultivation of critical and reasonable normative standards of decency in politics against which politicians may be tested and, if found wanting, be resisted on the grounds of revolutionary constitutionalism. The genuine moral nihilism in Schmitt and Heidegger is the moral and intellectual irresponsibility of their bovine worship of political power, their stultification of the moral and intellectual powers of independent critical thought that is fundamental to the exercise of our inalienable human rights of dissent and resistance against tyranny.

The liberal constitutionalism of the Basic Law must be understood against this background and the longer cultural history it reflects. If it succeeds, it will be because it fundamentally reconstructs and reframes German national identity in terms of respect for universal human rights and empowers the competence of the German people to understand and demand in their own voice that politicians respect such rights; if it fails, it will be because it dilutes respect for rights to the traditional measure of uncritically parochial German ethnic solidarity. The test for liberal constitutional institutions in Europe, at both the national and the European level, will be the degree to which they foster in the lives of their people a national and a European identity expressed through respect for human rights, not in antagonism to them. If American constitutional experience is at all relevant, an institutionally enforceable conception of European human rights may be central to such a cultural reconstruction.[206]

SUMMARY AND CONCLUDING REMARKS

The genre of liberal constitutionalism can be interpreted in terms of the six ingredients of revolutionary constitutionalism, and useful compar-

---

[205] See Judt, *Past Imperfect*.

[206] For European developments along these lines, see Mark W. Janis and Richard S. Kay, *European Human Rights Law* (Hartford, Conn.: University of Connecticut Law School Foundation, 1990). For an argument that Britain should foster these developments by internally entrenching a bill of rights, see Ronald Dworkin, *A Bill of Rights for Britain* (London: Chatto & Windus, 1990).

isons may be made in these terms among interpretations of this genre. Two comparisons were offered to illustrate this point. The first examined the quite different interpretations given in America and in France of the normative ideal of human rights to which those nations' revolutions appealed, and the different experiences with constitutionalism and cultural support for human rights to which those different interpretations led. The second compared the different role of rights skepticism in American and German constitutional experience and the challenge a cultural history of such skepticism poses for the success of constitutionalism in Europe today.

The motive of my inquiry has been to explore the renewed interpretive and critical relevance, in the late twentieth century, of the kind of interest in constitutionalism that characterized America and France and many other peoples in the late eighteenth and early nineteenth centuries; thus, a German neo-Kantian liberal, Francis Lieber, who fled political persecution in his native country and immigrated to the United States during the antebellum period brought to the study of American constitutional institutions perhaps the best interpretive studies of the universalistic values of revolutionary constitutionalism and the ways in which American constitutionalism might better reflect these values (including Lieber's advocacy of the Reconstruction Amendments).[207] Constitutionalism, especially in the late eighteenth century, was regarded as a reflection of the interest of all civilized peoples in the application of reason to politics in order to promote values of universal human rights that are the property of no religion or race or ethnicity or gender or sexual preference but the universal moral claims of humankind.[208] Humankind may be in a better position today fruitfully to continue this dialogue than it has been at any time since the high point of the political Enlightenment in the late eighteenth century. We need a conception of comparative law more fitting to this extraordinary opportunity to enrich and deepen the political imagination of all peoples and to support their demand for their human rights, including their political right to forms of constitutional government that respect all their rights. Comparative revolutionary constitutionalism, as I have explained and defended it here, affords normative and empir-

---

[207] See Richards, *Conscience and the Constitution*, at 43, 46–49, 141–43, 210–11, 223, 238, 255.

[208] See, in general, Richards, *Foundations*.

ical resources fundamental to this great and humane project. We must now use and cultivate these resources, which make possible, as I shall argue, an illuminating interpretive and critical framework that allows us to understand the promise and betrayal of Italian revolutionary constitutionalism as the background of the Southern Italian emigration. Indeed, on this basis, multicultural identity, suitably understood and elaborated, may itself be a cultural resource that may advance reasonable discourse about better understanding and implementing the values of liberal nationalism, both in America and abroad.

3

The Promise and Betrayal of Italian Revolutionary Constitutionalism: The Southern Italian Emigration

IN THIS CHAPTER I present relevant interpretive background for the emigration of millions of Southern Italians in the late nineteenth and early twentieth centuries, a period during which a politically reunited Italy had ostensibly achieved the goals of the revolutionary constitutionalism of the Risorgimento. I proceed in three stages: first, the promise of the Risorgimento as a form of revolutionary constitutionalism; second, the compromises of principle that led to the reunification of Italy under a constitutional monarchy; and third, the sense of betrayal of the promises of reunification from the perspective of the experience of Southern Italians.

THE RISORGIMENTO AS REVOLUTIONARY CONSTITUTIONALISM

The nineteenth-century Italian movement of revolutionary constitutionalism, which we call the Risorgimento, had two aims: first, to end the occupation of Italy by foreign powers and their surrogates (for example, the Bourbon royal house that ruled the South),[1] and, second, to establish in its place, consistent with the aims of revolutionary constitutionalism, a legitimate form of republican constitutionalism that would harness political power to respect the human rights and advance the aims of justice and the public good for the people of

---

[1] See, on this royal house, Harold Acton, *The Bourbons of Naples 1734–1825* (London: Methuen, 1956); Harold Acton, *The Last Bourbons of Naples (1825–1861)* (New York: St. Martin's Press, 1961).

Italy.[2] In its first aim, the Risorgimento expressed long-standing ambitions, expressed throughout post-Roman Italian history, to end the balkanizing occupation of Italy by foreign powers, including, among others, Spain, France, and Austria-Hungary.[3] Both Dante and Machiavelli had called for the reunification of Italy, Dante by making the Ghibelline case in terms of the monarchy of the emperor,[4] Machiavelli by ending *The Prince* with his "exhortation to liberate Italy from the barbarians."[5] In *The Discourses*, Machiavelli clearly regards republican government on a properly interpreted Roman classical republican model (with a citizen militia) as the best way of realizing this aim.[6] The second aim, while prefigured by Machiavelli, is much more recent, crucially appealing to the theory and practice of modern revolutionary constitutionalism, in particular, that of France.

Of these two aims, the second, Italian revolutionary constitutionalism, was much more interpretively contestable and contested. European interpretations of nationalism in the nineteenth century were, as we have already seen in the cases of France and Germany (chapter 2), much in debate and included both liberal and illiberal interpretations. Even an ostensibly liberal normative interpretation like revolutionary constitutionalism served, as in Napoleonic France, illiberal ends. To the extent the Risorgimento was modeled on French revolutionary consti-

[2] See, for good general studies of this period of Italian history, Denis Mack Smith, *Modern Italy: A Political History* (Ann Arbor: University of Michigan Press, 1997), 3–92; *Victor Emanuel, Cavour, and the Risorgimento* (London: Oxford University Press, 1971); *Cavour and Garibaldi 1860: A Study in Political Conflict* (Cambridge: Cambridge University Press, 1954); *Cavour* (New York: Alfred A. Knopf, 1985). For useful background readings, see Denis Mack Smith, ed., *The Making of Italy 1796–1870* (New York: Walker and Company, 1968).

[3] For concise reviews of this complex history, see Reinhold Schumann, *Italy in the Last Fifteen Hundred Years: A Concise History* (Lanham, Md.: University Press of America, 1986); George Holmes, ed., *The Oxford History of Italy* (New York: Oxford University Press, 1997).

[4] See, on this point, Charles B. Schmitt and Quentin Skinner, eds., *The Cambridge History of Renaissance Philosophy* (Cambridge: Cambridge University Press, 1988), at 410–11; Rachel Jacoff, ed., *The Cambridge Companion to Dante* (Cambridge: Cambridge University Press, 1993), 67–99.

[5] See Niccolò Machiavelli, *The Prince and Discourses*, ed. Max Lerner (New York: Modern Library, 1950).

[6] See, for illuminating commentary on these points, Schmitt and Skinner, *Cambridge History of Renaissance Philosophy*, at 430–41.

tutionalism, its ostensible liberalism was ideologically unstable and, as we shall see, destructively distorted to illiberal ends. The last step in this process was Mussolini's reinterpretation of the Risorgimento drained of its "foreign," liberal elements and harnessed to the patriotic ends of fascism.[7] The antebellum interpretive debates over American revolutionary constitutionalism are analogous, as Calhoun and others increasingly interpreted its aims in rights-skeptical terms (chapter 2). We need to be clear about the degree to which revolutionary constitutionalism, whether in Italy or America, was thus subject to various interpretations, some of them (as in the case of Mussolini or Calhoun) self-consciously illiberal. Since the liberal interpretation is clearly to be normatively preferred, we need also to understand how it was distorted and even subverted into politically powerful interpretations at war with both the theory and the practice of respect for human rights.

I develop my interpretation of Italian revolutionary constitutionalism from the perspective of a group of Italians, the people of the South, who suffered acutely from this process of distortion and subversion; I explain this process in part in terms of uncritical racist assumptions that rationalized it. It is consistent with the interpretive validity of this account that other Italians (including some Southerners who, having moved to the North, helped develop the policies of the government) did not share the Southern sense of the growing political illegitimacy of the nation; indeed, if I am right, the coherence of the account requires that there was a profound interpretive disagreement about these issues among Italians, the kind of chasm of disagreement (also reflecting racism) that increasingly existed in antebellum America between the North and the South about the meaning and validity of the American union. To this extent, my account focuses on an interpretation of the Risorgimento that was certainly not mainstream in Italy and was, if anything, increasingly marginal. While aspects of its argument clarify some aspects of Italian history, its aim is to understand the background of the emigration from the South to the United States and the degree to which the disappointment of the people of the South in Italian revolutionary constitutionalism ideologically framed their attitude toward the promises of American liberal nationalism. To understand this background, we need to be clear about the development of Italian revolu-

---

[7] See Smith, *Mussolini*, at 132–3.

tionary constitutionalism, including its distortion and subversion to illiberal ends.

The paradoxical background of this development in Italy was, as Denis Mack Smith makes clear, not

> reformist movement from within, but rather the revolutionary con-
> quests of Napoleon after 1796. It was Napoleon's invasions which
> destroyed the existing state system; just as the ideas of the French
> Revolution, which arrived with the invaders, completely upset old
> categories of thought and behavior . . . Napoleon could also rely on
> considerable support from many Italians who looked on his invasion
> as a deliverance . . . It was from families who gained power or wealth
> under Napoleon that the leaders of the nineteenth-century risorgi-
> mento emerged.[8]

Notably, the three leading figures in the Risorgimento, Mazzini, Garibaldi, and Cavour, were born subjects of France.[9]

> In other ways, too, the Napoleonic occupation of Italy had important
> effects on the growth of nationalism. Not only did the French bring
> something positive to Italy, but the high taxes which they imposed,
> and which Napoleon's wars made necessary, in time generated a
> strong opposition which took its place in the development of national
> consciousness. Whereas the reformers of the eighteenth century had
> worked happily in a context of enlightened despotism, this generation
> and the next were open to much more radical aspirations for political
> liberty; and a causal chain was to lead from ideas of popular sover-
> eignty to those of Italian patriotism.[10]

I have already discussed some of the problematic features of French revolutionary constitutionalism, that clarify its tragic trajectory into Napoleonic imperialistic dictatorship (chapter 2). If that trajectory was tragic for republican constitutionalism in France, it was even more so for the nations of Europe, including Italy, that formed their consti-

---

[8] See Smith, *The Making of Italy, 1796–1870*, at 5–6.

[9] Denis Mack Smith, *Italy: A Modern History* (Ann Arbor: University of Michigan Press, 1969), at 18.

[10] See Smith, *The Making of Italy, 1796–1870*, at 6.

tutional ambitions for nationhood in reponse, either affirmatively or negatively, to the model of Napoleon's decadently Caesarist and imperialistic interpretation of revolutionary constitutionalism (which justified Napoleon's wars, including the invasion of Italy, as wars of national liberation). The problem for the Risorgimento (as an interpretation of revolutionary constitutionalism) was not only the intrinsic substantive defects of such a model but the fact that, as a model that had rationalized yet another foreign conquest of Italy, it corruptively suggested the legitimacy of an Italian constitutionalism that, both internally and externally, required a comparable form of enlightened elitist imperialism (whether, as we shall see, an unjust domination by the North of Italy of the South or Italian imperialistic adventures in Africa, both rationalized in racist terms).

Of course, the problems faced by the Risorgimento were more daunting than those faced by revolutionary France. France, like both revolutionary Britain (in the English Civil War) and America (in the American Revolution), addressed the task of revolutionary constitutionalism on the basis of long historical cultural experience as a people or nation; the task in revolutionary France was not to forge a sense of nationality (which already existed) but to forge an enduring reasonable consensus on republican government (in contrast to absolute monarchy). As I suggested in my comparison of American and French constitutionalism (chapter 2), we should not underestimate the difficulty of such a task in a nation, like France, that has a long history of centralized political and religious absolutism and that is unaccustomed to the kind of reasonable reflection on the corruptibility of political power so important to serious constitutional theory and practice. The challenge facing the Risorgimento was even more daunting. Italy, in contrast to France, had to forge a sense of nationhood out of the balkanized historical experience of Italy since the fall of Rome, as well as a reasonable consensus on republican values; in D'Azeglio's words on the attainment of political unity, "We have made Italy; now we have to make the Italians."[11] The Risorgimento was, of course, unified by the sense of a common external enemy (the illegitimate foreign occupations), against which Italians were justly in rebellion on grounds of revolutionary constitutionalism. But, once the enemy was

---

[11] Quoted in Benedetto Croce, *A History of Italy 1871–1915*, trans. Cecila M. Ady (New York: Russell & Russell, 1929), at 97.

expelled, Italy would face a historical and cultural vacuum of national identity that France did not.

It was this fact, I believe, that gave a special ideological instability to the Risorgimento: consistent with the aim of expelling the foreign occupations, the vacuum could be filled in quite different ways. The political moralist of the Risorgimento, Joseph Mazzini, thus argued that "[t]he republic is the only legitimate and logical form of government"[12] because it alone accorded appropriate respect for inalienable human rights:

> Personal liberty; liberty of locomotion; liberty of religious belief; liberty of opinion on all subjects; liberty of expressing opinion through the press or by any other peaceful method; liberty of association so as to be able to cultivate your own minds by contact with the minds of others; liberty of trade in all the productions of your brains and hands: these are all things which no one may take from you.[13]

However, Cavour, the political architect of the reunification of Italy and a life-time opponent of Mazzini's republican theory and practice, most admired the utilitarian philosophy of Jeremy Bentham[14] and defended constitutional monarchy as "the only type of government which can reconcile liberty with order."[15]

This fundamental instability in the normative theory of the Risorgimento mirrored a corresponding instability in its practice. Mazzini's revolutionary constitutionalism required that the people, sensible of their status as bearers of human rights, exercise their Lockean human right to revolt against an illegitimate government that abridged their basic human rights; Mazzini, however abortively, thus supported and fomented revolutionary activity, including participation in the short-lived Roman republic of 1849.[16] Giuseppe Garibaldi's often inspired leadership of guerrillas assumed the legitimacy and importance of popular

[12] See Joseph Mazzini, *The Duties of Man and Other Essays* (London: J. M. Dent & Co., 1860), 78.

[13] See ibid., at 79. On Mazzini's important role in the Risorgimento, see Denis Mack Smith, *Mazzini* (New Haven: Yale University Press, 1994); Roland Sarti, *Mazzini: A Life for the Religion of Politics* (Westport, Conn.: Praeger, 1997).

[14] See Smith, *Cavour*, at 8.

[15] Cited at p. 23, Smith, *Italy: A Modern History*.

[16] See Smith, *Mazzini*, at 64–76.

resistance to injustice, but, to the disgust of Mazzini, Garibaldi (though a self-proclaimed republican and socialist) "meekly surrendered to the king the dictatorial powers over the half of Italy which he had conquered in 1860. His confusion of mind helped the process by which most of the republicans and revolutionaries rallied to the throne."[17] Cavour regarded the strategic manipulation of foreign policy and the use of ordinary troops of the kingdom of Piedmont-Sardinia (including the strategic invasion of the Papal States in 1860) as the keys to the reunification of Italy under the constitutional monarchy of the House of Savoy. Cavour effectively coopted Garibaldi's revolutionary successes through plebiscites in Naples and Sicily that were strategically "needed in order to stop the diffusion of revolutionary sentiments" (Cavour).[18]

When, in the twentieth century, the great Italian antifascist political thinkers Benedetto Croce and Antonio Gramsci debated how and why an evil like fascism should first have arisen and triumphed in Italy, understandably they interpretively contested the meaning of the Risorgimento as a form of revolutionary constitutionalism. Croce, as an ethical liberal[19] and a defender of the liberal nationalism of the constitutional monarchy, offered interpretive histories of his native Naples[20] as well as of Italy[21] and even of Europe generally[22] in which the Risorg-

[17] See Smith, *Italy: A Modern History*, at 15.

[18] See Smith, *Cavour*, at 232. For an important study of the conflict of Garibaldi and Cavour, see Smith, *Cavour and Garibaldi 1860*.

[19] See, for example, Benedetto Croce, *Politics and Morals*, trans. Salvatore J. Castiglione (New York: Philosophical Library, 1945), at 111–25. For Croce's main philosophical works, see Benedetto Croce, *Aesthetic As Science of Expression and General Linguistic*, trans. Douglas Ainslie (New Brunswick: Transaction, 1995); *Logic as the Science of the Pure Concept*, trans. Douglas Ainslie (London: St. Martin's, 1917) and *Philosophy of the Practical: Economic and Ethic*, trans. Douglas Ainslie (London: St. Martin's, 1913). For commentary, see Ernesto G. Caserta, *Croce and Marxism: From the Years of Revisionism to the Last Postwar Period* (Napoli: Morano Editore, 1987); Herbert Wildon Carr, *The Philosophy of Benedetto Croce: The Problem of Art and History* (London: Macmillan, 1917); Gian N. G. Orsini, *Benedetto Croce: Philosopher of Art and Literary Critic* (Carbondale: Southern Illinois University Press, 1961); Angelo A. De Gennaro, *The Philosophy of Benedetto Croce: An Introduction* (New York: Greenwood Press, 1968); Cecil Sprigge, *Benedetto Croce: Man and Thinker* (Cambridge: Bowes & Bowes, 1952); and Angelo Crespi, *Contemporary Thought of Italy* (New York: Alfred A. Knopf, 1926).

[20] See Benedetto Croce, *History of the Kingdom of Naples* trans. Frances Frenaye (Chicago: University of Chicago Press, 1970).

[21] See Croce, *A History of Italy 1871–1915*.

[22] See Benedetto Croce, *History of Europe in the Nineteenth Century*, trans. Henry Furst (London: George, Allen & Unwin, 1953).

imento arises "not from economic interests, religious fanaticism, or pride of race, but from an intellectual concept of human dignity, not narrowly patriotic but imbued by fraternal feelings toward other peoples, both friends and enemies, and the wish to see Italy take its place at their side in the common effort to create a modern civilization."[23] In contrast to fascist chauvinism, Croce insisted on the intrinsic cosmopolitanism of Italian culture generally and on its culturally pluralistic nature, including French influences on the Risorgimento in particular.[24] Consistent with his ethical liberalism, he argued that the interpretive study of history must focus on the critical lessons to be learned from history as the story of the struggle for liberty, including both its triumphs and its defeats.[25] Such interpretive study, for Croce, could enable a people, like the Italians under and after fascism, critically to understand and recover the best elements of their defensible liberal traditions.[26] Such study may direct attention to small ethical minorities who articulated, defended, and maintained these liberal traditions, including, as the Neapolitan Croce makes quite clear, the important role in the Risorgimento of liberals of the South.[27] For Croce, fascism was an irrationalist nationalism (influenced by German sources) wholly inconsistent with and deviational from the only defensible liberal tradition Italy had produced,[28] and its racism expressed an irrationalist naturalism[29] that was, like Marxism,[30] fundamentally at odds

---

[23] See Croce, *History of the Kingdom of Naples*, at 236–7.

[24] See ibid., at 151–2, 164–5, 199–201; Croce, *A History of Italy*, at 26–7; Croce, *History of Europe in the Nineteenth Century*, at 13–14, 341–2.

[25] See, for Croce's methodology on this point, Benedetto Croce, *History as the Story of Liberty*, trans. Sylvia Sprigge (New York: W. W. Norton, 1941); see also Benedetto Croce, *History Its Theory and Practice*, trans. Douglas Ainslie (New York: Harcourt, Brace, and Co., 1923). For illuminating commentaries, see David D. Roberts, *Benedetto Croce and the Uses of Historicism* (Berkeley: University of California Press, 1987); Edmund E. Jacobitti, *Revolutionary Humanism and Historicism in Modern Italy* (New Haven: Yale University Press, 1981). For a development of a similar view of history, inspired in part by Croce, see R. G. Collingwood, *The Idea of History*, rev. ed., ed. Jan Van Der Dussen (Oxford: Oxford University Press, 1994).

[26] See, on this point, Croce, *History as the Story of Liberty*, at 43–5, 47–8, 244.

[27] See Croce, *History of the Kingdom of Naples*, at 195–6, 236–7, 247–8.

[28] See, on these points, Croce, *A History of Italy*, at 239–42, 248–51, 266–7, 279, 280–1.

[29] See Croce, *History of Europe in the Nineteenth Century*, at 257–9; see also 322–3, 340–1.

[30] See ibid., 140–2, 322–3, 340–1.

with a liberal respect for rights of moral personality, including "political liberty or liberty of conscience."[31] Fascism must thus interpretively be sharply walled off from the Risorgimento, "the masterpiece of the European liberal spirit."[32]

Gramsci, a Marxist and a founding figure of the Italian Communist Party, questioned Croce's interpretive history of the Risorgimento as "passive revolution" "without an organic treatment of the French Revolution and the Napoleonic Wars"[33] on the ground that it subverted Croce's ostensible antifascism. This elitist picture "contributed to a reinforcement of fascism—furnishing it indirectly with an intellectual justification, after having contributed to purging it of various secondary characteristics, of a superficially romantic type but nevertheless irritating to his classical serenity modeled on Goethe."[34] In effect, on Croce's interpretation of the Risorgimento, fascism "corresponds to the movement of moderate and conservative liberalism in the last century."[35] For Gramsci, the Risorgimento was more fundamentally flawed as an interpretation of revolutionary constitutionalism than Croce supposed, precisely because it had largely the culturally elitist character that Croce ascribed to it. Gramsci concurs that Italian thought in all its complex forms, both secular and religious, artistic and scientific, as well as political, had from Rome to the Renaissance and beyond had the cosmopolitan character that Croce emphasized,[36] but he arugues that culture in all these forms was limited to and cultivated by cultural elites; whatever its humane cosmopolitanism, it did not appeal to, enjoy, and energize the level of popular support required as the basis for the democratic theory and practice of revolutionary constitutionalism. Italy had certainly pioneered the glories of the Renaissance, but, from the perspective of defensibly democratic political values, paradoxically "in Italy a great scientific, artistic and literary flowering coincided with the period of political, military, and State decadence."[37] What Italy needed and never had was the democratizing and liberalizing ferment of the Protestant Reformation (as the

---

[31] See ibid., 141.

[32] See ibid., 253; see also 209–28.

[33] See Gramsci, *Prison Notebooks*, at 118.

[34] See ibid., at 119.

[35] See ibid.

[36] See, for example, Gramsci, *Prison Notebooks*, at 63, 117–8, 173–5, 274–5.

[37] See ibid., at 275.

background to the English Civil War and the American Revolution) or the Enlightenment (as the background for the Jacobins in the French Revolution).[38] Italy, like Spain, had, however, sponsored the Counter-Reformation, combining, as it did, baroque artistic glories with the repression of dissent.[39] Without an experience of the theory and practice of democratic freedom (including, importantly, "freedom of thought and of the expression of thought"),[40] there could be no enduring liberal consensus in civil society to sustain the institutions of democratic constitutionalism. From Gramsci's perspective, whatever liberal consensus there was in the Risorgimento was too small and too elitist to give rise to an acceptable form of democratically accountable and responsive liberal constitutionalism. The elitist hegemony of the moderates (including, initially, Croce), who dominated the Italian constitutional monarchy,[41] was easily corrupted into forms of Caesarism and militarism that anticipated and certainly supinely failed to resist the rise of fascism and the dictatorship of Mussolini.[42] What Italy needed, Gramsci argued, was a movement of theory and practice (which he associated with a properly understood form of democratic Marxism,[43] as "The Modern Prince")[44] that would combine the best elements of the Renaissance and the Reformation[45] and

---

[38] See ibid., at 394–5.

[39] See Fernand Braudel, *Out of Italy: 1450–1650*, trans. Sian Reynolds (Tours: Flammarion, 1991), 193–211. On the importance of the impact of the Counter-Reformation on Spanish and thus Mexican culture in a reasonable understanding of the cultural differences between Mexican and American constitutionalism, see Octavio Paz, *The Labyrinth of Solitude*, 357–76.

[40] See Gramsci, *Prison Notebooks*, at 350.

[41] On the hegemony of the moderates, see Gramsci, *Prison Notebooks*, at 55–90.

[42] On the increasing demagogy of the moderate elite, see ibid., 89–90; on Caesarism, see ibid., at 219–223. On the tendencies to dictatorship, including rule by decree, in Italy prior to Mussolini, see Smith, *Italy: A Modern History*, 138–40, 144–6, 175–97. On the growing importance of antiliberal nationalistic imperialism in Italian politics prior to Mussolini, see ibid., at 268–71, 272–3. On the complicity of the monarchy and liberals, including (for a period) Croce, in the rise of fascism, see ibid., 340–2, 354–5, 383.

[43] See Gramsci, *Prison Notebooks*, at 350–1, 352, 360, 364–5.

[44] See ibid., at 125; for a comparison of Machiavelli and Marx, see ibid., at 133–6.

[45] For illuminating discussion of this point, see Joseph V. Femia, *Gramsci's Political Thought: Hegemony, Consciousness, and the Revolutionary Process* (Oxford: Clarendon Press, 1987), at 122–3; on the crucial importance of Croce in the development of Gramsci's thought, see ibid., at 81–101, 112, 123–4.

make possible a reasonable public understanding of revolutionary constitutionalism and the institutions that would sustain that understanding.[46] Italy needed, as Bobbio was also later to observe,[47] what it had not yet had, namely, a democratic Risorgimento that sustained the theory and practice of revolutionary constitutionalism.

AMERICAN, FRENCH, AND ITALIAN REVOLUTIONARY AND CONSTITUTIONAL THOUGHT COMPARED

To understand the background of Croce's and Gramsci's contesting interpretations of the Risorgimento, we need to evaluate the constitutionalism to which the Risorgimento led from the perspective of the six elements of comparative revolutionary constitutionalism. Italian constitutionalism was, as we have seen, adapted from French revolutionary constitutionalism under circumstances that, if anything, uncritically exemplified its most problematic features as an interpretation of revolutionary constitutionalism. We may see this difficulty in each of the ways Italian constitutionalism adapted the French model to Italian circumstances.

Revolutionary Principles

While rights-based revolutionary principles had been stated and defended by Mazzini and put into practice in the popular military successes of Garibaldi, these principles enjoyed the support of the leaders of the Risorgimento only as a rationale for the expulsion of the foreign occupations of Italy, not as a basis for the constitutional construction of Italian unification. Cavour had shrewdly coopted the more revolutionary achievements of Garibaldi to his purposes, but those purposes rejected Mazzini's republican constitutionalism entirely.[48] Instead, Cavour secured reunification of Italy on the basis of the constitutional monarchy of the House of Savoy as expressed in the *statuto* of 1848,

---

[46] On this point, see Gramsci, *Prison Notebooks*, at 394–5.

[47] See, on this and related points (including the merits and demerits of the Italian resistance at the end of World War II as such a theory and practice), Norberto Bobbio, *Ideological Profile of Twentieth-Century Italy*, trans. Lydia G. Cochrane (Princeton: Princeton University Press, 1995), 109, 117, 148, 157.

[48] See, for good general studies, Smith, *Cavour*; Smith, *Cavour and Garibaldi*.

granted by Carlo Alberto to his Kingdom of Sardinia[49] and republished by Mussolini as the fundamental constitution of the realm as late as June 1939.[50] The terms of Article 65 of the *statuto* laid down that "the king nominates and dismisses his ministers"[51] and was under no obligation to follow their advice; the constitution contained only generalities about ministerial power. By its failure to state explicity who had the chief responsibility for initiating legislation, the *statuto* left open the path to the development of British-style constitutional conventions. The king, for example, developed the power of issuing proclamations that had the force of law, and he appointed all members of the Senate. The king summoned and dissolved parliament and in the early years even presided at cabinet meetings. Article 5 provided that:

> The king alone has the executive power. He is the supreme head of the state, commands all the armed forces by sea and land, declares war, makes treaties of peace, of alliance, of commerce, but giving notice of them to the two Houses as far as security and national interests permit. Treaties which demand any financial burden, or which would alter the territorial boundaries of the state, shall not have any effect until after the two Houses have consented to them.[52]

Constitutional Principles of the British Constitution

Nothing in the logic of revolutionary constitutionalism requires that only a republican constitution can reasonably effectuate its aims; even the Americans, who rejected the constitutional monarchy of the British Constitution, did so not because it was a constitutional monarchy but because it had departed from what the Americans regarded as its legitimate principles, principles that constrained what the Americans took to be the extravagant taxing and other powers asserted in the name of British parliamentary supremacy over its American colonies. As we have seen, Americans took pride in being participants in the British common-law tradition of dissent that had fired the English Civil War and triumphed in the Glorious Revolution of 1688. Americans like

---

[49] See Smith, *Italy: A Modern History*, at 27.
[50] See ibid., at 439.
[51] See ibid., at 27.
[52] See ibid., at 28.

Adams, Jefferson, Wilson, Hamilton, and Dickinson[53] thus argued that the British Constitution of parliamentary supremacy had betrayed its own basic principles of legitimacy, and they sought to establish an alternative form of government that would use the lessons of British constitutional corruption to construct a government more in tune with the true principles of the British Constitution. In that sense, American revolutionary thought was based as much on a view of the true nature of British-style constitutionalism as it was on a belief in the inalienable rights of the person; it would be the test of the legitimacy of the American Revolution, thus understood, that it would yield a more adequate conception of constitutionalism than the British understanding of these matters in 1776.

American revolutionary constitutionalism thus importantly assumed and indeed elaborated the British tradition of revolutionary constitutionalism, even taking up republican proposals made during the period that followed the English Civil War (including those of Harrington) but not implemented in Britain, which returned to constitutional monarchy as limited by the Glorious Revolution of 1688 and subsequent developments. Americans contested whether those developments had yielded an appropriately constrained, legitimate rights-based constitutionalism, certainly rejecting any form of hereditary monarchy in its constitutional arrangements. But, some form of British-style constitutional monarchy, appropriately constrained, could, in principle, not be excluded as a form of legitimate revolutionary constitutionalism. That Britain had, for example, abolished slavery long before the United States might be taken, as it was by Lincoln, as a challenge to the comparative legitimacy of the American constitutional experiment in contrast to British constitutional monarchy (on the basis that Britain better protected human rights over all).[54] Cavour's preference for constitutional monarchy as "the only type of government which can reconcile liberty and order"[55] might be justified along these lines.

But, it is one thing to justify constitutional monarchy against the background of British historical experience with rights-based traditions embedded in the common law and quite another to justify the Italian choice of constitutional monarchy against the background of the

---

[53] See Richards, *Foundations*, at 65.

[54] See, on this point, Richards, *Conscience and the Constitution*, at 53.

[55] See Smith, *Italy: A Modern History*, at 23.

Italian experience of both Napoleonic popular imperialistic dictatorship and the lack, as Gramsci noted, of any comparable popular traditions of rights-based dissent. In particular, the powers in foreign affairs in general and the war powers in particular that were constitutionally accorded the monarch importantly legitimated the militarism of the House of Savoy[56] (on the model of Napoleonic imperialism), which increasingly defined Italian nationalism in terms of exorbitantly expensive imperialistic adventures abroad[57] that required, in consequence, universal conscription[58] and the highest levels of taxation in Europe.[59] The political franchise was narrowly distributed,[60] reinforcing "the traditional apoliticism and passivity of the great popular masses."[61] The politics of compromise among elites (known as transformism)[62] led to a weak party system that failed to encourage or express reasonable public dialogue among well-defined alternative positions. Expansion of the franchise, corresponding to widening literacy, did not break this pattern; "[t]he history of Italy, like that of Germany, was to prove that a broadening of the electorate could be harnessed to the cause of the strong state and in itself signified no necessary advance in liberalism."[63] Indeed, such reforms enfranchised the cities more than the countryside, the North more than the South, and thus exacerbated an unjust differentiation that culminated in the legitimation crisis that was the background, as we shall see, of the massive Southern Italian emigration to the United States.

It is not at all unreasonable that there should have been a historical component in Italian constitutionalism analogous to the American melding of arguments of rights with interpretive analysis of the previous historical constitution, the British Constitution. While the Italians had not had the practical experience in democratic politics that America had enjoyed under the British Constitution, Italy's lack of a long tra-

---

[56] See ibid., at 28–29. See, for an illuminating general treatment of this matter, Denis Mack Smith, *Italy and Its Monarchy* (New Haven: Yale University Press, 1989).

[57] See Smith, *Italy: A Modern History*, at 81, 119

[58] See ibid., at 120.

[59] See ibid., at 105.

[60] See ibid., at 31; see also 34–5; on the later expansions of the franchise, see ibid., at 133–4, 257–8.

[61] See Gramsci, *Prison Notebooks*, at 203.

[62] See Smith, *Italy: A Modern History*, 110–12.

[63] See ibid., at 134.

dition of absolute monarchy like that in France made available to it what the French had not had, experience in diverse political forms on which it could reflect in thinking about constitutional forms. These included both the diverse republican forms (for example, in Renaissance Florence and Venice) which were carefully studied by Americans, and the pathbreaking and influential political science of Machiavelli which arose from this republican experience, as well as the important later developments of Machiavelli's thought—in the work of Harrington, Montesquieu, and Hume—that, as we have seen, had such a powerful impact on American constitutional thought.

The enormous historical diversity of political and cultural experience within Italy since the fall of Rome might also have been interpretively harnessed to a better understanding of the responsibilities of a rights-based constitutional construction of a unified Italy. The remarkably original and prophetic interpretive human science of the Neapolitan Giambattista Vico had used the very diversity of Italian cultural experience, both diachronically and synchronically, to suggest how the charitable interpretation of cultures must resist imposing on them any simplistic model of the physical sciences or uniform progress but must rather contextualize their symbolic forms to their circumstances.[64] Vico was certainly no democrat,[65] but he brought to his sensitive studies of culture a moral ideal of people "equal in human nature"[66] and thus "equal in civil rights"[67] and a vision of the role of jurisprudence in studying and elaborating this ideal (perfected, for Vico, in Roman law). Vico's methodology of humane respect for equality and for diverse cultural forms suggests powerful resources on which Italian constitutional thought might also profitably have drawn.

---

[64] See Giambattista Vico, *The New Science of Giambattista Vico*, ed. Thomas Goddard Bergin and Max Harold Fisch (Ithaca: Cornell University Press, 1948); trans. Max Harold Fisch and Thomas Goddard Bergin, *The Autobiography of Giambattista Vico*, (Ithaca: Cornell University Press, 1944). For illuminating commentary, see Isaiah Berlin, *Vico and Herder: Two Studies in the History of Ideas* (London: Hogarth Press, 1976), 1–142; Leon Pompa, *Vico: A Study of the "New Science,"* 2d ed. (Cambridge: Cambridge University Press, 1990); Peter Burke, *Vico* (Oxford: Oxford University Press, 1985); Mark Lilla, *G. B. Vico: The Making of an Anti-Modern* (Cambridge, Mass.: Harvard University Press, 1993).

[65] See Isaiah Berlin, *Vico and Herder*, at 62.

[66] See Vico, *The New Science*, at 20.

[67] See ibid., at 411.

In fact, such historical resources were largely ignored, as Italian constitutional reflection, taking French thought as its model, set itself in a direction supposed to be radically discontinuous with Italian history. In effect, the historical model for Italian constitutionalism was not its own rich, diverse interpretive complexity but the bureaucratic centralism fostered by the French monarchy and perfected under Bonaparte's dictatorship, an approach to these matters that corresponds to Vico's worries about the rationalist excesses of "the barbarism of reflection."[68]

Analysis of Political Pathologies

When Italy thus uncritically adopted the bureaucratic centralism of French constitutional thought, it took on as well the French failure, reflected in the constitutional thought of Rousseau, either to reflect on or to take seriously the pathologies of political power as the reasonable background for understanding and implementing the aims of revolutionary constitutionalism. In my earlier discussion of Rousseau's influential conception of popular sovereignty (chapter 2), I attributed the cultural power in France of Rousseau's interpretation to a preoccupation of French revolutionary constitutionalism with the wholly corrupt complicity of the Catholic Church in the legitimation of the absolute monarchy. The uncritical Italian acceptance of this already internally flawed French perspective importantly was shaped by what was, if anything, an even more serious worry about the traditionally illiberal role that the Catholic Church had often played and continued to play in Italian political and cultural life.[69] Italy was the traditional home of the Papacy, an intransigent opponent of the national movement to Italian reunification, which had ended the Church's political powers over the Papal States.[70] By 1860, not only did patriotic Italians find themselves under "a kind of collective excommunication,"[71] but in December 1864 the papal encyclical *Quanta cura* condemned all the major principles of liberalism, including respect for the basic human rights to conscience and free speech,[72]

---

[68] See ibid., 424.

[69] On the repressive impact of Catholic religious intolerance, in the wake of the Reformation, on Italian culture, see Braudel, *Out of Italy*, at 194–5.

[70] See George Holmes, ed., *The Oxford History of Italy* (New York: Oxford University Press, 1997), at 192, 208, 235–6.

[71] See Smith, *Italy: A Modern History*, at 89.

[72] See ibid., 90–91.

and the Church even prohibited Catholics from voting (many faithful ignored the ban).[73] Notably, the Catholic Church later accepted fascism and rejected liberalism and communism.[74] Against this wall of opposition, Italian constitutional thought, perhaps understandably, found appealing the French interpretation of popular sovereignty and its associated Machiavellian aim of taming an antirepublican Church by imposing a civil religion (as opposed to the American separation of state and religion as morally independent spheres). These aims legitimated the powers of the bureaucratic centralism of the national government in forging a sense of national citizenship; both Italian universal conscription[75] and compulsory education[76] make sense, as forms of republican political reeducation, against this background.

We should not, of course, underestimate the immensity of the task that the Italian constitutionalists, like the French, faced in contrast to the American Founders, namely, the need to develop a secure consensus on liberal values. But, the authoritarian conception of popular sovereignty that framed Italian thinking, drawing on the French, subverted its ostensible liberalism. The Italian emphasis on universal conscription certainly could draw upon Machiavelli's classical republican emphasis on an armed militia of citizen-soldiers as the basis for stable legitimate government,[77] but its aims were less republican (let alone rights-based) than unjustly imperialistic in the Napoleonic mode. The increasingly imperialistic character of Italian nationalism, which culminated in fascism, had its roots in a perversely illiberal political education that "grotesquely looked upon war as a test of progress and civilization."[78] The ideological war between the state and the Catholic Church failed to engage, in the sense of a legitimate national community, the often humane and liberal sentiments of pious Italian Catholics in the tradition of Manzoni; the way was thus open for a manipulative, cynical politician like Mussolini to make a settlement with the Church that enlisted the popular support of many religious Italians for his authoritarian fascism.[79]

---

[73] See ibid., 97–98.

[74] See, on this point, ibid., at 441, 443.

[75] See ibid., 120.

[76] See ibid., 260–1; Croce, *A History of Italy*, at 57.

[77] See, on this point, Gramsci, *Prison Notebooks*, 132.

[78] See Smith, *Italy: A Modern History*, at 81.

[79] See Smith, *Mussolini*, 159–69.

The Italian lack of constitutional skepticism about the corruptibil-ity of political power led to the development of a particularly corrupt tradition of the exercise of political power from which Italy continues to suffer.[80] This tradition included failing to prevent corruption,[81] indulging the authoritarian intolerance of the elites who felt threatened by what they took to be class war,[82] and fostering a politics based not on principles developed by debate among different political convictions but on clientage to a common patron.[83] In effect, "since 1860 the central-ization of government had proceeded apace, without a parallel devel-opment in representative institutions to ensure the essential freedoms and enough public criticism."[84] The consequence of such fundamental defects in constitutional thought and institutions placed at odds liberal principles and the more democratic expansion of the franchise, as many Italian liberals warned.[85] Universal suffrage, when it came, "was thus to assist in destroying the liberal party: the old liberal ruling classes were soon so afraid of the new popular parties, whether socialist or Catholic, that to combat them they signed their own death warrant by supporting Mussolini."[86] Croce himself supported fascism for a period[87] though, as we have seen, he was later to repudiate it as foreign to Italian cos-mopolitan culture.[88] A constitutionalism, so unconcerned with the republican dilemma of majority factions hostile to human rights, was thus devoured by a mass politics at reactionary war with liberalism.[89]

Use of Comparative Political Science

Just as French constitutional thought learned little from the brilliant political science of comparative constitutionalism of its most penetrat-ing constitutional thinker, Montesquieu, Italian thought failed as well to take seriously Montesquieu or, indeed, as we earlier noted, the inven-

---

[80] See, for relevant recent history, Smith, *Modern Italy: A Political History*, 417–97.

[81] See Smith, *Italy: A Modern History*, 198.

[82] See ibid., at 199.

[83] See ibid., at 202.

[84] See Smith, *Italy: A Modern History*, 198.

[85] See, on this point, ibid., at 208–9, 258–9, 288, 391.

[86] See ibid., at 259.

[87] See ibid., 383, 411.

[88] See ibid., 399–400.

[89] See Smith, *Mussolini*, at 140.

tion of modern political science in Machiavelli or of interpretive human science in Vico. It is astonishing that a people with such a rich interpretive tradition of dealing with political culture (including the later pioneering contributions of Mosca and Pareto)[90] should have so little used it in reflecting on the challenge of Italian revolutionary constitutionalism. Such a use of comparative political science might reasonably have opened the Italian constitutional mind to take more seriously than it did Cattaneo's proposal for a federal constitution, in which he prophetically warned that the bureaucratic centralism of the Italian state would undermine personal freedom, and foreign wars would then lead to the militarization of society.[91] The diversity of Italian regional cultures would, from this perspective, be a republican strength, not a weakness, since regions would be accorded the constitutional powers, where appropriate, democratically to develop and pursue a conception of justice and the public good rooted in their own circumstances and values.

Political Experience

The failure to use comparative political science is one with the failure to build upon Italian political experience, including not only the republican experiments in Northern Italy but the tradition (since 1130) of absolute monarchical rule by outside powers or their surrogates in the South.[92] The resulting cultural division between the North and the South was one between traditions of communal engagement, on the one hand, and alienated disengagement, on the other, with consequences that any form of reasonable constitutional thought must take seriously.[93] The centralized powers of a government, based on wholly inadequate political representation of the people and interests of the South, enforced an effectively imperialistic rule on the South, perpetuating rather than challenging the traditional status of the South as a colony ruled by outside pow-

[90] See, on their respective roles in Italian political argument, Smith, *Italy: A Modern History*, 208, 258, 288.

[91] See ibid., at 56. See also Smith, *Victor Emanuel, Cavour, and the Risorgimento*, 251–2. On Cattaneo, see Thom, "More than a Lombard patriot," *Times Literary Supplement*, July 3, 1998, at 25.

[92] See Holmes, *Oxford History of Italy*, 48–56.

[93] See, for a classic treatment of the consequences of this division for political life, Robert D. Putnam, *Making Democracy Work: Civil Traditions in Modern Italy* (Princeton: Princeton University Press, 1993).

ers. This callous disregard of experience forged a constitutionalism that, in the view of many in the South, was a mockery of liberal values.[94]

Constitutional Argument as a Work of Political Reason

The bankruptcy of Italian constitutionalism, like that of its French model, was crystallized in its failure to support the legitimacy of constitutional argument as supreme over ordinary political argument. Such a distinction can have force only if constitutional institutions (like federalism, separation of powers, and judicial review) can reasonably be regarded as securing constraints on the exercise of political power that render it consistent with the respect for basic human rights and the pursuit of justice and the public good. But, Italian constitutionalism observed no such checks and balances; the powers of the monarchy (Croce notwithstanding),[95] for example, exercised no such liberalizing restraint. Rather, the executive—the king and his ministers—possessed a preponderance of power under the 1848 *statuto*; the judiciary was hardly distinct from the executive; there were few if any political forums outside parliament, no wide circle of newspaper readers, no well-developed party organizations linking rural areas with the capital; the Senate rarely evinced independence, and, in the Lower House, a skillful premier could build a majority by patronage.[96] The construction of Italian constitutionalism had been based not on the exercise of public reason and discussion but on plebiscites with manhood suffrage[97] annexing the South to Piedmont; Cavour, with Garibaldi's complicity, shrewdly used such plebiscites to forestall the more popular revolutionary forces that threatened landowners.[98] The consequence was that Italian constitutionalism did not afford the reasonable constraints on political power that would have legitimated a distinction between constitutional and ordinary political argument; the resulting politics, not subject to any such reasonable constraints, fatefully con-

---

[94] See Smith, *Italy: A Modern History*, at 134–5.

[95] For Croce's rationale of the monarchy along these lines, see Croce, *A History of Italy 1871–1915*, at 40.

[96] See, on these points, ibid., at 199; on other defects in Italian constitutionalism, see ibid., at 198–210.

[97] See ibid., 198.

[98] See Holmes, *Oxford History of Italy*, 204–5; Smith, *Italy: A Modern History*, 40–43.

fused constitutionalism with ordinary politics. The trajectory of Italian constitutionalism to fascism, which triumphed first in Italy, was thus possible within the terms of an authoritarian constitutionalism that amorally imposed no effective limits on ordinary politics.

The deepest damage of these developments was, of course, to respect for the inalienable human rights to which revolutionary constitutionalism appealed as the very point of the project. A constitutionalism that affords no effective institutional protection for such rights degenerates easily into the theatrical mass politics of Mussolini's fascism which arose from a reactionary war on the threat posed by both liberalism and socialism to dominant interests.[99] Aesthetic values, as in Germany, increasingly dominated ethical values, exemplified by the poet Gabriele D'Annunzio's extraordinary innovation of a populist, theatrical politics (culminating in his reign for a year as military dictator of Fiume), which helped prepare the way for Mussolini's mass politics.[100] Mussolini's fascism, rooted in Sorel's romantic celebration of the role of transformative violence in forging a community based on myth,[101] built upon forces long implicit in Italian constitutionalism: the same often unemployed or underemployed educated classes that fired the Risorgimento and were later a significant force in the triumph of Mussolini;[102] the acceptance, when convenient for the political leadership, of dictatorship[103] and rule by decree;[104] and imperialistic militarism under the leadership of the House of Savoy.[105] Mussolini himself rationalized fascism as a new kind of revolution at war with the

[99] See Smith, *Italy: A Modern History*, 340–2, 354–5, 385; see also, for a good general discussion of Mussolini, Smith, *Mussolini*.

[100] See, in general, John Woodhouse, *Gabriele D'Annunzio: Defiant Archangel* (Oxford: Oxford University Press, 1998); for illuminating further commentary, see Alexander Stille, "The Candidate of Beauty," *London Review of Books*, July 2, 1998, at 3–6; Adrian Lyttelton, "The First *Duce*," *Times Literary Supplement*, July 24, 1998, at 6–7. For Croce's criticism of D'Annunzio's political irrationalism and its detrimental effects on Italian politics, see Croce, *A History of Italy 1871–1915*, at 239–42, 248–51, 265–7, 279, 280–1.

[101] See, for an illuminating discussion of these and related points in the origins of Italian fascism, Zeev Sternhell, *The Birth of Fascist Ideology: From Cultural Rebellion to Political Revolution* (Princeton: Princeton University Press, 1994).

[102] See Smith, *Italy: A Modern History*, 37.

[103] See ibid., 138–40, 175–88.

[104] See ibid., 188–97.

[105] See ibid., 28–9, 81, 119.

revolutionary constitutionalism of the French Revolution and, in particular, with its conception of respect for equal human rights of conscience and speech.[106] Mussolini could thus contest the very meaning of revolutionary constitutionalism because Italian constitutionalism had drained the concept of any intrinsic moral meaning. Mussolini, the amoral political artist, could effectively fill this vacuum with an unstable, highly theatrical politics, manipulated by his grandiloquent and cowardly egotism and essentially journalistic skills, in which imperialistic militarism played an increasingly important and ultimately fatal role.[107] The way was thus prepared ideologically (Hitler genuinely admired Mussolini)[108] for the development of a German fascism, as we have seen (chapter 2), even more aggressively at war with human rights. Under the impact of his growing servile dependence on Germany, Mussolini, initially hostile to what he took to be the madness of Hitler's very German anti-Semitism, enacted a similar policy in Italy and attempted, against the considerable resistance of the Italian people, to implement it (85 percent of Italian Jews survived).[109]

THE LEGITIMATION CRISIS OF ITALIAN CONSTITUTIONALISM: THE EMIGRATION FROM SOUTHERN ITALY

The defects in Italian constitutionalism were the cultural background for the legitimation crisis that was an important factor in the massive emigration from Southern Italy to the United States in the late nineteenth and early twentieth centuries. Importantly, that emigration, sharply limited in the United States by the National Origins Quota system of 1924,[110] took place largely before Mussolini's rise to power in Italy in 1922.[111] Its cultural context was thus the Risorgimento and the resulting Italian constitutional development I have discussed at some length. Our task now is to understand the impact of both on

---

[106] See Smith, *Mussolini*, 140.

[107] See, for a good examination of all these points, Smith, *Mussolini*.

[108] See ibid., at 172–3.

[109] See Zuccotti, *The Italians and the Holocaust: Persecution, Rescue, and Survival*, xxv, 272. See, in general, on Mussolini's change in policy and Italian resistance, ibid.; Michaelis, *Mussolini and the Jews*; Steinberg, *All or Nothing*.

[110] See Smith, *Civic Ideals*, at 443.

[111] See Smith, *Mussolini*, at 52–68.

Southern Italy, in particular, on the Southern Italians who found emigration to the United States, despite all its cultural dislocations, the reasonable course. My argument has both economic and ideological components. The economic crisis in the South was perceptibly the consequence of national policies hostile to the interests of the people of the South. My interpretive aim is reasonably to put the response of the people of the South to this economic crisis in a context of ideological disappointment framed by the ostensible aims of Italian revolutionary constitutionalism.

Italians have historically been among the most mobile Europeans in patterns of migration both within and outside Europe.[112] In the years between 1876 and 1976 alone, an estimated 26 million people emigrated from Italy.[113] The massive bulk of the emigration to the United States was distinctively from Southern Italy during the period 1890–1920, when Southern Italians experienced, more brutally than any other Italians, the consequences of the defects in Italian constitutionalism. My concern here is with the grounds for emigration of these Italians (obviously, different explanations may be needed for other groups and periods). We need to understand both what happened and how Southern Italians not unreasonably interpreted these events in terms of the promise and betrayal of Italian revolutionary constitutionalism, creating a legitimation crisis that justified the revolutionary act of emigration, a course of action that seemed to many of them both more legitimate and more hospitable to their ambitions.

To understand their interpretive attitude, we must start with an important fact in the history of Italian revolutionary constitutionalism, namely, that the part of that history that most clearly reflects a popular movement of such constitutionalism was the brilliantly successful revolt fomented and led in the South by Garibaldi, which culminated in his dictatorship of half of Italy in 1860.[114] Garibaldi had won the trust and cooperation of many southerners by his integrity, good nature, and honest concern with their welfare,[115] but his gifts were military, not

---

[112] See, for a good general study, Thomas Sowell, *Migrations and Cultures: A World View* (New York: BasicBooks, 1996), especially, ch. 4 at 140–74.

[113] See ibid., at 140.

[114] See Smith, *Italy: A Modern History*, 14–16; see, for a good general study, Smith, *Cavour and Garibaldi 1860*.

[115] See Smith, *Cavour*, 238.

political, let alone constitutional. Pressure from Sicilian landowners forced Garibaldi to abandon the sweeping promises of land reform that had been instrumental in his winning the support of the peasants; once the Bourbon army was no longer a threat, Garibaldi's forces opened fire on peasant rebels in Sicily, sending the message to landowners in Sicily and Naples that his redshirts were defenders of order, not of social revolution; the alliance with the landowners guaranteed the collapse of the Bourbon State but drained Garibaldi's expedition of its radical aims.[116] Garibaldi's loyal surrender of his troops to the king of Piedmont was followed by plebiscites annexing Sicily and Naples to the kingdom of Piedmont which passed overwhelmingly on the basis of the enthusiasm generated by Garibaldi but certainly did not reflect any specific constitutional agreement to bureaucratic centralism (indeed, some assurances had been given that local government would be secured).[117] Garibaldi's subsequent retirement from politics was not what the people of the South expected.[118]

Garibaldi's victories and the subsequent unification of Italy were crucially made possible by the revolt of the peasants in Southern Italy in 1860; the peasants were instrumental not only in undermining the Bourbons at a decisive moment but also in compelling landowners to turn to Piedmont as the defender of social order. Otherwise, the common people were irrelevant to Italian nationalism, which explains why the new constitutional order made so little effort to win them over; in fact, they faced a more oppressive government than the one they had helped replace.

Before 1860 the South was a country of low taxes and negligible national debt, with the capital asset of large domanial lands and led by a paternal government that tried to keep food cheap. After 1861 it lost its autonomy, taxes leaped up, and by 1865 the loss of industrial protection (the low tariffs of Piedmont were extended nationwide) had forced the closure of many factories.[119] The new national government was thus associated with conscription, high taxation, and a free hand for landowners in local governments (peasants could not vote); even expenditure on elementary education was resented because peasants

---

[116] See Holmes, *Oxford History of Italy*, 204–5.

[117] See, on these points, Smith, *Cavour and Garibaldi 1860*, 387–8, 392–410.

[118] See ibid., 408–410.

[119] See Smith, *Italy: A Modern History*, 231–2.

relied on the labor of their children in the fields.[120] To balance the enormous expenditures on public works and railroad building, the Italian state not only raised taxes but sold royal and Church lands in a hurry for whatever prices it could get.[121] The appropriation of Church lands and wealth by the state worsened the position of most of the peasants; for them, the change of ownership meant harder tenancy terms and greater difficulty in access to credit.[122] It is not surprising that many in the South entertained growing doubts about the united Italy or that the peasants in many areas actively supported the anti-Piedmontese "Brigandage" of the early 1860s.[123] The response of the Turin government was harsh and repressive. Over a period of eighteen months, the police reported having summarily executed 1,038 people, most of whom were suspect because they were found to be carrying personal weapons, a common practice in Naples. Another three thousand were imprisoned without due process of law. The government sent some sixty battalions of crack combat soldiers to teach a lesson to the Southerners. In about a year, they killed some three thousand Neapolitan rebels. Their severity escalated hostilities, and by 1865 the national government had a virtual army of occupation, 120,000 soldiers, in the South to repress the populace.[124] In 1864 Garibaldi informed the king that the semimilitary government of Turin was hated more in Naples than that of the Bourbons, and ten years later a newspaper campaign was opened there with the slogan "We are Neapolitans before we are Italians."[125]

In the 1880s the government raised tariffs, including prohibitive duties imposed on imported French goods. This act provoked retaliation from Italy's trading partners, and 40 percent of Italian exports were dammed up as a result. This hit the South particularly, taking capital away from southern agriculture and putting it into northern industry.[126] A general agricultural depression (arising from a reduction

---

[120] See Holmes, *Oxford History of Italy*, 236.

[121] See Hughes, *The United States and Italy*, 47–8.

[122] See Holmes, *Oxford History of Italy*, at 236–7.

[123] See Hughes, *The United States and Italy*, 48.

[124] See Gambino, *Blood of My Blood*, at 50–1; see also ibid., 264–5; on repression of Sicilian revolts then and later, see ibid., 51–2, 63–4.

[125] See Smith, *Italy: A Modern History*, 232.

[126] See Smith, *Italy: A Modern History*, 157–62.

in shipping charges, which allowed the produce of North America and Argentina to flood the European market) caused another setback in the South;[127] the price of wheat fell as the minister of the treasury chose at that moment to increase the tax on grain and to raise the price of salt. This hit both landowners and peasants in the predominantly rural South, for the region paid as much in taxes as the much wealthier region of Lombardy and three times as much as Venetia. Meanwhile, the decline in agricultural prices made it increasingly difficult for southerners to pay the debts they had incurred by their recent enormous increase in vineyard acreage, and each year many smallholders forfeited their holdings. The South had to pay with its depreciated products for manufactured goods that protection now made dearer, and thus still more capital was drained from the South in a deliberate policy of capital accumulation in the North, where it was thought the money could be better employed.[128] Increasingly violent peasant unrest in Sicily in 1893 led to a government crisis, resulting in the sending of additional government troops to repress the insurrection.[129]

For these reasons, the universal scholarly consensus is that the South was palpably very much worse off after unification.[130] There has been less scholarly interest in the question of how the people of the South interpreted this fact in light of the promises made to them at the time of Italy's unification about the benefits of an Italian nationalism that was, after all, foreign to their history and experience. Those promises plausibly raised normative expectations in the people of the South that they could reasonably hold this new government to the terms of the revolutionary constitutionalism in terms of which it had justified the expulsion of the foreign occupations of Italy, including southerners' participation in the overthrow of the House of Bourbon in the Kingdom of the Two Sicilies.[131] If we take the leading Southern defender of the Risorgimento and unification, the Neapolitan philoso-

---

[127] See Holmes, *Oxford History of Italy*, 238.

[128] See Smith, *Italy: A Modern History*, 232.

[129] See ibid., 174–5; Gambino, *Blood of My Blood*, 63–4.

[130] See Lopreato, *Italian Americans*, 25; Smith, *Italy: A Modern History*, 230–42; Holmes, *Oxford History of Italy*, 236–8; Hughes, *The United States and Italy*, 47–8; Croce, *A History of Italy*, 58–60; P. A. Allum, *Politics and Society in Post-War Naples* (Cambridge: Cambridge at the University Press, 1973), at 20–3, 37–8, 64–6.

[131] See, for an illuminating treatment of the background of these expectations, including rising Neapolitan interest in Jacobin ideas, Croce, *History of the Kingdom of Naples*.

pher Benedetto Croce, as a not unreasonable benchmark for how those expectations of the political legitimacy of the unified Italy were interpreted in the South,[132] we may begin to understand the dimensions of the legitimation crisis, which was, as I shall argue, an important component in the massive emigration from Southern Italy to the United States that is my concern in this book.

Croce had defended the Risorgimento as "the masterpiece of the European liberal spirit,"[133] which arose not "from economic interests, religious fanaticism, or pride of race, but from an intellectual concept of human dignity, not narrowly patriotic but imbued by fraternal feelings toward other peoples, both friends and enemies, and the wish to see Italy take its place at their side in the common effort to create a modern civilization."[134] In his remarkable interpretive study of European liberalism, Croce's student Guido de Ruggiero elaborated this political morality in terms of a progressive conception of respect for certain equal liberties that begins with "the first great affirmation of modern liberalism: religious freedom"[135] as an aspect of the more abstract inalienable right to conscience, "the principle of free examination,"[136] "that inviolable stronghold of consciousness in which all human liberties have their birth and their growth."[137] This right was later generalized reasonably to include as well other aspects of moral freedom, "[g]oods, relations between man and man, family life, even of his own body," namely, "freedom to express and communicate his own thought, personal security against all oppression, free movement, economic liberty, juridical equality, and property,"[138] and, more recently, "the right to a fair share of the moral and economic wealth of the community"[139] and the right to association among workers.[140]

---

[132] For Croce's relevant works defending the Risorgimento and the resulting Italian constitutionalism of a unified Italy, see Croce, *History of the Kingdom of Naples, A History of Italy 1871–1915, History of Europe in the Nineteenth Century.*

[133] See Croce, *History of Europe in the Nineteenth Century,* 253.

[134] See Croce, *History of the Kingdom of Naples,* 236–7.

[135] See Guido de Ruggiero, *The History of European Liberalism,* trans. R. G. Collingwood trans. (Boston: Beacon Press, 1964), at 17.

[136] See ibid., at 20.

[137] See ibid., 23.

[138] See ibid., 26.

[139] See ibid., 72; see also ibid., 26–32.

[140] See ibid., 142.

Croce, like De Ruggiero and others, regarded liberalism as consistent with concerns for economic and social distributive justice.[141]

A liberal conception of Italian nationalism of this sort held out to the people of the South the promise that their unification with the rest of Italy under a common government would afford them something they had lacked under their Bourbon rulers and their predecessors, namely, a government that would be legitimate in terms of the liberal conception, extending to all persons equal respect for their human dignity (expressed in respect for basic human rights) and the use of political power to pursue justice and the public good on fair terms. For this reason, the people of the South may reasonably have expected much more of the new unified government than they had of previous governments or even of government generally. The long historical experience of the people of the South under occupying powers, in contrast to the communal and even republican experience that characterized the North, has been offered as an explanation for the greater recent success of democracy in the North than in the South.[142] But, from the longer perspective of Italian history since the Risorgimento, it is not at all clear that the problem lay in the South as opposed to the North; the fundamental defects in Italian constitutionalism were products, as we have seen, of a Northern hegemony that uncritically absorbed and imposed a model of Napoleonic centralism on Italian complexity; fascism, which arose in the intellectual life and politics of the North, expressed a similar, if more malign, uncritical authoritarianism.[143] From this perspective, the vaunted individualism of the Italians may,[144] as Luigi Barzini argued, express not reflective moral individualism but uncritical communal attachments.[145] In contrast, the

---

[141] See Croce, *History of Europe in the Nineteenth Century*, at 35, 313–4, 319–20. See, for a similar position, Carlo Rosselli, *Liberal Socialism*, trans. William McCuaig (Princeton: Princeton University Press, 1994). See, for subsequent development of a similar position, Norberto Bobbio, *The Future of Democracy: A Defence of the Rules of the Game*, trans. Roger Griffin (Minneapolis: University of Minnesota Press, 1987); Norberto Bobbio, *The Age of Rights*, trans. Allan Cameron (Cambridge: Polity, 1996); *Liberalism and Democracy*, trans. Martin Ryle and Kate Soper (London: Verso, 1990); *Ideological Profile of Twentieth-Century Italy*. Bobbio explicits connects such a position with the political contractarianism of John Rawls; see Bobbio, *The Future of Democracy*, at 131–37.

[142] See, in general, Putnam, *Making Democracy Work: Civic Traditions in Modern Italy*.

[143] See, for a good general study, Smith, *Mussolini*.

[144] See, on this point, Jacob Burckhardt, *The Civilization of the Renaissance in Italy*, trans. S. G. C. Middlemore (London: Penguin, 1990), at 99, 101, 114, 214, 289, 319.

[145] See Luigi Barzini, *The Italians* (New York: Atheneum 1965), 217–8.

people of the South brought to a reunified Italy a skepticism about political power in general that made many of them, Croce included, among the most morally independent liberal critics of Italian politics, including fascism.[146]

Skepticism does not, of itself, lead to a liberal attitude toward politics; it may, as in the profound skepticism about values of a Carl Schmitt (chapter 2), lead to a bovinely amoral worship of fascist power. But, there was, as we have seen, a substantive moral content to the promises of the Risorgimento that reasonably focused the traditional political skepticism of the people of the South on the demands that liberalism imposes on politics. In particular, the promise of respect for human dignity, as a value in politics, may have suggested relief for the sources of Southern unhappiness called *la misèria*. This unhappiness certainly had an economic component, but it also had a moral component, a sense of humiliating injury inflicted by the servility demanded of peasants by the petty officials (with their contempt for manual labor) who lorded over them, an affront to the self-respect due persons.[147] *La misèria*, understood as "the result of humiliation," is a matter about which a person, in the light of rising moral expectations, will "become far more sensitive."[148] The Risorgimento was a veritable high tide of such rising moral expectations in the people of the South.

If the legitimacy of the new unified Italy was now to be assessed in terms of the degree to which the new government (in contrast to the old) secured respect for the basic rights of human dignity and harnessed political power to justice and the common good, it was fundamentally defective. To start with, there was no change in the social relations in the South of the sort that one might reasonably have expected; rather, the old rulers were replaced with new, much more distant ones, and the landowners

[146] For Croce's early support of fascism and later repudiation, see Smith, *Italy: A Modern History*, at 383, 399–400, 411. See also, on this and related points, Giuseppe Casale, *Benedetto Croce between Naples and Europe* (New York: Peter Lang, 1994); David Ward, *Antifascisms: Cultural Politics in Italy, 1943–46: Benedetto Croce and the Liberals, Carlo Levi and the "Actionists"* (Madison, N.J.: Fairleigh Dickinson University Press, 1996).

[147] See, for illuminating treatment of this important point, Edward C. Banfield, *The Moral Basis of a Backward Society* (New York: Free Press, 1958), 62–66, 160; for a moving treatment based on personal observation, see, in general, Carlo Levi, *Christ Stopped at Eboli* trans. Frances Frenaye (New York: Farrar, Straus and Giroux, 1963).

[148] See Banfield, *The Moral Basis of a Backward Society*, at 160.

alone had the right to vote, reinforcing the traditional master-slave ethos of proprietors over the peasants.[149] The new rulers were, as we have seen, even less responsive than the old ones. The level of benefits to the South worsened (creating the economic crisis) and the corresponding burdens (including higher taxation and conscription) increased.

Such callous injustice perceptibly violated the most minimal requirements of political legitimacy that the people of the South had the right to demand of the new constitutional order, namely, that they should be treated on terms of equal respect with the people of the North. That, after all, was the very basis of the liberal nationalist interpretation of the Risorgimento—that it, in contrast to previous governments, would guarantee the human dignity on equal terms of all the people of Italy. As we have seen, there were reasonable grounds for the people of the South to come to believe that the new government, so narrowly focused on the interests of the North at the expense of the South, flagrantly violated this basic requirement of liberal political legitimacy.

Such unjust treatment was bad enough. What made it much worse, from the perspective of the legitimately rising moral expectations of the people of the South, was the independently unjust basis for such treatment, reflected in the government's practice of attributing responsibility for it to a "Southern problem."[150] It is one thing to treat persons, acknowledged to be persons, unjustly; it is quite another to treat them unjustly and then to rationalize such treatment on the basis of dehumanizing stereotypes of racial difference that unjustly deny their very humanity. As we shall see at greater length in the next chapter, the political evil we call racism arises from a culture that, first, abridges the basic human rights (including the rights of conscience, speech, intimate life, and work) of a class of persons and then rationalizes this abridgment by invoking dehumanizing stereotypes that rest, with vicious circularity, on the cultural entrenchment of the abridgment of basic human rights. In effect, what is at bottom a culturally entrenched injustice is speciously naturalized in terms of alleged facts of nature that explain the subhumanity of a class of persons (who are not, for this rea-

---

[149] See, on this ethos, P. A. Allum, *Politics and Society in Post-War Naples*, 44–45.

[150] See Smith, *Italy: A Modern History*, 230–42; for an important recent treatment of the ways in which this problem was unjustly constructed, see Robert Lumley and Jonathan Morris, eds., *The New History of the Italian South: The Mezzogiorno Revisited* (Exeter: University of Exeter Press, 1997).

son, bearers of human rights). The reunification of Italy, on terms of liberal nationalism, required that all persons be guaranteed equal concern and respect, but that demand was unjustly subverted by indulging irrationalist stereotypes of difference that rested on and reflected a long cultural history that had deprived the people of the South of respect for their basic rights of conscience, speech, intimate life, and work on the fair terms required by liberal principles. Such unjust political irrationalism was rationalized in Italy (as it also was in the United States, Britain, and Germany)[151] in terms of the racist science of the late nineteenth century, popularized, as Gramsci acutely observes, "by the sociologists of positivism."[152] Such racism arises, consistent with what I shall later elaborate as the paradox of intolerance, when the reasonable demands of liberal principles would or should give rise to doubts about the ways in which a problem has been and is being addressed by established political authorities; it is precisely when the culture most reasonably needs to entertain and discuss such reasonable doubts that, paradoxically, it suppresses them by the irrationalist politics of racism. The constitutional treatment of the South in an Italy unified on ostensible grounds of liberal principles would and should have raised doubts about its fundamental justice, let alone decency. Rather than entertain and discuss such doubts, however, the politics of racism suppressed them by invoking the specious certainties of a racist science that naturalized injustice (thus rationalizing, in such racist terms, the excesses in the use of repressive force against civil war in the South).[153]

That cultural racism should have manifested itself under ostensibly liberal nationalism in Italy should be no more surprising than that a similar situation should have arisen under such nationalism in America or Britain during the same period. Defective liberal nationalism familiarly rationalizes cultural injustice in terms of alleged facts of nature. The powerful, culture-shaping political force of racist assumptions in Italy, as elsewhere (see chapter 4), was shown by the way even self-consciously progressive thought was framed, including statements by governing officials (some from the South), in terms of a "Southern problem." It is, of course, a familiar feature of such forms of

---

[151] See, for fuller discussion of these and related points, Richards, *Conscience and the Constitution; Women, Gays, and the Constitution.*

[152] See Gramsci, *Prison Notebooks*, 71.

[153] See, on this point, Smith, *Cavour*, at 238–9.

intractable cultural prejudice (including religious intolerance, racism, sexism, and homophobia) that their unjust cultural assumptions uncritically frame the thought even of some of their victims (thus, the notorious anti-Semitism of Otto Weininger).[154]

The classic example of the construction of Italian racism is Alfredo Niceforo's *L'Italia barbara contemporanea* (Contemporary Barbarian Italy) of 1898. For Niceforo, "Sardinia, Sicily, and the *Mezzogiorno* are three peoples who are still primitive, not completely evolved, less civilized and refined than the populations of the North and Centre of Italy."[155] His portrait of these people reduces them to alleged facts of positivist sociology (rates of crime, education, birth rate, mortality, suicide rate, and economy), grounded in even harder craniometric data of race that "explain" the greater individualism of the South and the sense of organization of the North.[156] On this basis, Niceforo calls for a federal solution that allows the South's government to be authoritarian and the North's to be liberal. Niceforo's argument blatantly confuses culture and nature and, although supposedly for a federal solution, is not at all genuinely federalist, since it supports the then current reality of Italian politics, the authoritarian hegemonic impositions of rule in the South in blatant violation of liberal principles.

This powerfully racist attitude toward the people of the South, rationalized in terms of positivist social pseudoscience,[157] failed to take seriously either southerners' culture or history; it was, in the usual pattern of unjust cultural entrenchment of such prejudices, supported by dehumanizing stereotypes (discussed further in the next chapter), including stereotypes of gender and sexuality (the South as feminine in contrast to the North as masculine).[158] The Neapolitan Croce, the tow-

---

[154] For elaboration of this point, see Richards, *Women, Gays, and the Constitution*, at 332–36.

[155] Excerpt reprinted in John Dickie, "Stereotypes of the Italian South 1860–1900," in Lumley and Morris, *The New History of the Italian South*, 114–47, at 115.

[156] See ibid.

[157] See, on this point, Stephen Jay Gould, *The Mismeasure of Man* (New York: W. W. Norton, 1981).

[158] See, for a good general discussion of this and related points, Gabriella Gribaudi, "The Images of the South: The *Mezzogiorno* as seen by Insiders and Outsiders," in Lumley and Morris, *The New History of the Italian South*, 83–113, especially 95–8; see also John Dickie, "Stereotypes of the Italian South 1860–1900", in ibid., at 114–47. On Mussolini's aim, consistent with this feminizing stereotype, to use fascism to make Italian character less Southern Italian (thus, more masculine and militaristic), see Smith, *Mussolini*, 180–1.

ering Italian intellectual of his period, angrily anatomized the unjust sources of "the Southern problem" in the ways in which facts like agricultural insufficiency were wedded to other facts like race without any interpretive attention to the complexities of Southern Italian culture,[159] let alone

> how these quick-witted, adaptable, and hardworking people withstood the hardships and vicissitudes of the Napoleonic wars and, last but not least, how they have been enterprising enough to emigrate and find work abroad. Italian emigrant works made such an impression upon the fanatical pan-Germanist, Houston Stewart Chamberlain, that, flying in the face of all the theories of head measurement and anthropometry, he called them pure Germans, a typical example of racist absurdity![160]

He analyzed the roots of the problem, as Franz Boas had earlier in the United States (see the next chapter), in an indefensible and undefended reduction of the human to the physical science, thereby removing from study either the power of culture or its interpretive study, let alone concern with the role of moral ideas in culture and its development.[161] The consequence was "lowering in men's minds the moral life and with it this feeling for liberty,"[162] obfuscating issues of personal and collective moral responsibility for the infliction of evil and injustice. For example,

> contributions to the exaltation of violence were brought by the theories of ethnologists and pseudo-historians concerning the struggle of the races, and the artificial political consciousness that men were attempting to build on these of Germanic and Latin races, Slave or Scandinavian or Iberic or Hellenic races—as not only real facts but natural values to be asserted one against the others, and with the subjection or extermination of the others.
>
> Warfare, bloodshed, slaughter, harshness, cruelty, were no longer objects of deprecation and repugnance and opprobrium, but

---

[159] See Croce, *History of the Kingdom of Naples*, at 45–6, 244–7.

[160] See ibid., 245–6.

[161] See Croce, *History of Europe in the Nineteenth Century*, 257–9, 322–3, 340–1.

[162] See ibid., 259.

were regarded as necessities for the ends to be achieved, and as acceptable and desirable.[163]

As Croce's analysis suggests, racism as a potent political force expressed itself during this period in both Europe and the Untied States, not only in the unjust distortion of domestic politics but in the rationalization of unjust imperialistic policies abroad. For example, both America's emergence as a global imperial power in the Spanish-American War and its debates about what to do with the various islands obtained (the Philippines, Guam, and Puerto Rico, accompanied by the final annexation of Hawaii) prominently expressed "evolutionary racial ideologies."[164] Italian imperialism took on this character well before the rise to power of Mussolini, leading to the disastrously abortive Ethiopian War of 1893–95 and the more successful Libyan War of 1911–12.[165] Importantly, the racist motivations for these imperialistic adventures were linked to prejudice against the people of the South, for the drive was to acquire colonies where southerners might emigrate.[166] Mussolini's later, quite explicitly racist attack on Ethiopia aimed at Italian colonization by the people of the South, whom Mussolini regarded as racially inferior.[167]

Such a racist policy of colonization for emigration corresponds to a dynamic in the construction of American racism in the antebellum period, the colonization movement. The American colonization movement, supported by Jefferson among others, argued that the abolition of slavery should be followed by colonization abroad of American blacks, on the ground that African Americans, while entitled to freedom, would not appropriately be integrated into the American political community as equal citizens.[168] Garrison prominently attacked colonization because it legitimated the evil of racial prejudice. The abolitionist accusation was that the American conscience had assuaged its guilt about the evil of slavery by advocating a policy, abolition and colonization, that reinforced the more fundamental evil of racism, upon which both the injustice of slavery and the injustice of discrimination against free

---

[163] See ibid., 341.
[164] See Smith, *Civic Ideals*, 429.
[165] See Smith, *Italy: A Modern History*, at 179–88, 272–81.
[166] See ibid., at 279–81.
[167] See, on these points, Smith, *Mussolini*, 173–4, 190, 180–1, 262.
[168] See Richards, *Conscience and the Constitution*, at 82.

blacks rested. The same accusation can be leveled against Italian public policy; its imperialistic enthusiasm for the colonization of southerners in Africa importantly rationalized its racist failure to integrate the people of the South on equal terms into Italian liberal nationalism. The people of the South, allegedly by nature incapable of liberal freedoms, must therefore be expelled from the polity. Indeed, if the racist analysis of the unjust treatment of the people of the South has reasonable force, it darkly explains not only the rising Italian imperialism during this period but the sense of serious students of the Italian emigration to the United States that emigration was "well-nigh expulsion."[169]

From their perspective, the people of the South must reasonably have found the claims made on behalf of Italian liberal nationalism to be increasingly empty, vapid, and even dangerously rhetorical, demanding, as they did, in support of increasingly inflated imperialistic rhetoric, compulsory conscription and the highest tax rates in Europe, these to support public expenditures one third of which went to the military in sometimes disastrous military adventures.[170] It was certainly the basic right of the people of the South, consistent with a Crocean liberal interpretation of the Risorgimento, to subject the exercise of political power by the Italian state to skeptical scrutiny in light of the requirements for liberal political legitimacy, in particular, its guarantee of basic human rights and its use of political power to advance justice and the public good on fair and equal terms. Such scrutiny confronted them with the sorry record we have now discussed at some length, in which a high factionalized, indeed, racist conception of the proper purposes of the Italian state, including a resurgent imperialism itself motored by racism, was enforced at the expense of the rights and interests of the people of the South. Put simply in the terms they would have used and understood, la misèria—in both its moral and its economic dimensions—not only worsened under a unified Italy but now included a superadded element of unjust moral humiliation, namely, racism.

The people of the South could not reasonably be expected to regard as legitimate a state, allegedly based on liberal principles for all Italians, that had, in fact, increasingly constructed its sense of national identity on a politics based not only on denying to southerners equal respect for

---

[169] See Foerster, *The Italian Emigration of Our Times*, at 49.

[170] See, on these points, *Italy A Modern History*, 105, 119–20, 179–88.

their rights and interests but on subjecting them to a new, nationally imposed insult to the sense of their human dignity that Croce and others had defended as the promise of the new Italy. That promise must have reasonably been interpreted by many in the South as the worst kind of betrayal, as they found themselves now governed not only by the petty tyrannies of local notables but by an arrogant, bureaucratic, Napoleonic centralism in Rome that was based on their racist dehumanization (as not persons and thus not bearers of human rights) and thus on denying to them the right to be seen as the equals of other Italians.

This interpretive attitude explains the legitimation crisis in the allegiance of the people of the South to the Italian state, a crisis, of course, justified by a liberal interpretation of the Risorgimento, which accorded persons the basic human right to reject the legitimacy of a regime that failed to accord them respect for basic human rights and the use of political power for justice and the common good. It is this legitimately revolutionary interpretive attitude that underlies and explains the civil wars in the South, discussed earlier, that emerged after unification and were so violently repressed by the troops of the new nation[171] and the role played during this period in the South, in response to the popular sense of a vacuum in political legitimacy, of organizations like the *camorra* in Naples and the Sicilian *mafia*.[172] It is also, I believe, the appropriate interpretive context for understanding the grounds of both economics and ideology that justified the great emigration from Southern Italy to the United States.

There must have been a heavy burden of both history and culture that had to be overcome in order for the people of the South to justify to themselves their emigration to the United States; the applicable Southern adage would have been very much in point: *Chi lascia la via vecchia e pieglio la via nuova, sa quello che lascia me non sa quello che trova* (He who leaves the old way for the new knows what he leaves but knows not what he will find).[173] The emigrants were, of course,

---

[171] See Smith, *Italy: A Modern History*, 69–75, 82–4.

[172] See, on this point, Jonathan Morris, "Challenging *Meridionalismo*: Constructing a New History for Southern Italy," in Lumley and Morris, *The New History of the Italian South*, 1–19, especially at 12–13; Paolo Macry, "The Southern Metropolis: Redistributive Circuits in Nineteenth-Century Naples," ibid., 59–82, especially at 72–75.

[173] See Covello, *The Social Background of the Italo-American School Child: A Study of the Southern Italian Family Mores and Their Effect on the School Situation in Italy and America*, at 257.

largely composed of populations with the longest continual history of occupying the Italian peninsula, dating from the large migrations from pre-Roman Greece to Magna Graecia.[174] Their culture was thus rooted in Pagan Greece, remnants of which remain in Southern religious concepts and practices.[175] Its culture remains, with that of the rest of Italy, the oldest continually settled basically urban civilization of Europe.[176] Consistent with the conservative tenor of the applicable Southern adage, there must have been something in what they knew that was so unacceptable that the culturally conservative people of the South were willing to undergo the cultural dislocations of emigration, which would for many (though by no means all) be permanent.[177]

What they knew I have now discussed at some length, in particular, an economic crisis interpreted in terms of illegitimate exercises of state power. However, one aspect of the promises of Italian liberal nationalism was met, the extension to the people of the South of a right they had not enjoyed under previous governments, namely, the basic right of movement (including the right to emigrate).[178] Respect for at least that basic human right enabled the people of the South reasonably to address and make a choice (namely, of political allegiance) that they had not previously been able to make. Indeed, making that choice may have been, as Croce's earlier cited defense of them suggests (citing Houston Chamberlain's estimate of them), a way of asserting and proving their humanity against the tradition of racist subjugation that had dehumanized them. Perhaps, the emigration reasonably may have seemed less final because they could return (many came and went between Italy and America many times before making their deci-

[174] See, on this point, Piazza, "Migration and Genetic Differentiation in Italy," in Adams, Lam, Hermalin, and Smouse, *Convergent Issues in Genetics and Demography*, at pp. 81–93. Cf. Luca Cavalli-Sforza, Menozzi, and Piazza, *The History and Geography of Human Genes*, at 277–80.

[175] See, on this point, Covello, *The Social Background of the Italo-American School Child*, at 103–45.

[176] See, for an excellent general study of this matter, Philip Jones, *The Italian City-State: From Commune to Signoria* (Oxford: Clarendon Press, 1997).

[177] About half of the emigrants returned to their homeland; eventually, many settled in the United States. See Nelli, "Italians," in Thernstrom, *Harvard Encyclopedia of American Ethnic Groups*, at 547.

[178] See DeConde, *Half Bitter, Half Sweet*, at 3, 70.

sions to settle in the United States).[179] On this basis, the people of the South could, as one would expect in so understandably skeptical a people, garner some comparative experience and thus more reasonably make their ultimate decisions. The emigrants usually first came as young men, only later bringing over either their wives and children or women they would marry.[180] The comparative experience of life in Italy and the United States gave them a reasonable basis on which to make their decisions on ultimate political allegiance. Nothing could have mattered more to the these young men and women of the South than how the basic unit of Southern cultural life, the family and its honor (*onore della famiglia*),[181] would fare in Italy compared to the United States.

"In Italy, largely, the past is the present."[182] The Italian Risorgimento and its avowed liberal nationalism had promised the people of the South a politics that would improve their past; it had, as we have seen, worsened it. Its injuries were both moral (its racist insults to the sense of honor and self-respect) and economic; the reasons for the emigration were, correspondingly, both moral and economic.[183] The new Italian nationalism had come to confirm southerners' ancient view of government as a thief (*Governo ladro*),[184] and they had accordingly and legitimately developed little or no feeling of national identity as Italians.[185] In their comparison between Italy and the United States, these men and women, looking at the futures available to their families and children, were reasonably struck by the burdens of the Italian past and the more open promises of an American future. One Italian emigrant to the United States movingly described his thinking and feelings about his Americanization along such lines:

> I go about the streets to find the great history, to feel the great emotion
> for all that is noble in America . . . Even in big city like New York I do
> not find much monuments in the great deeds, to the great heroes, and

[179] See Thernstrom, *Harvard Encyclopedia of American Ethnic Groups*, at 547.

[180] See ibid.

[181] See Covello, *The Social Background of the Italo-American School Child*, at 152; see, in general, ibid., 149–91.

[182] See Foerster, *The Italian Emigration of Our Times*, 48.

[183] See ibid., 48–49, 415–22; Lopreato, *Italian Americans*, 33.

[184] Lopreato, *Italian Americans*, 114.

[185] See, on this point, Foerster, *The Italian Emigration of Our Times*, 22, 102, 420, 426–7.

the great artists . . . I do not find the great art to compare with the art of Italy . . . But one day I see very, very big building. My mind is struck. With all I have seen in Italy . . . I have never seen anything like that! It is a giant!

When I went to night school, I had a good impression to me . . . I learn little English, and about the American government, and how the people can make change and progress by legislation without the force of revolution, and I like very much this idea. The teacher told me why not to become an American?

I have good impression to become an American. But I do not become American because I think always of the grandeur of the Italy civilization of the past! . . . [Then he falls in love and] . . . I do not wish at all to go back to Italy. I think to take wife . . . I think about many things, but I think especially about the future. Everything begin to look different. I have not think much about the future before, I have think about the past. Maybe I have son, it is the future for him. American is to be his country. What is the past? It is gone. The future is to be come great time. . . . The grandeur of the Italian cities . . . held Italy in the world's highest place for nearly one thousand years. But the world continue. . . . Now comes the great day for America, the great financial, the great mercantile power, and I think with that the great science, the great art, the great letters. Why to live always in the memory of past grandeur? They were only men. I am a man, and my son will be a man. Why not live to be somebody ourselves, in a nation more great than any nation before, and my son perhaps the greatest of any great man?

And I see that big work to build the future. I see the necessity to learn the English, to become the citizen, to take part in the political life, to work to create the better understanding between the races that they come to love each another, to work for better conditions in industry. For health and safety and prosperity, to work for the progress in science, for the better government, and for the higher morality—and it become more pleasure to work than to take the leisure. Suddenly it looks to me like that is the American, that is what the American is always to do, always to work for the achievement. It come to me, like I am born—I am American![186]

---

[186] Quoted in Lopreato, *Italian Americans*, 173–4.

Italians had emigrated to a nation, the United States, with its own traditions of liberal nationalism, recently reformed and reaffirmed in the wake of the Civil War. How, in contrast to Italy, would Southern Italians fare there?

4

American Liberal Nationalism and the Italian Emigration

WE HAVE NOW investigated what the Southern Italians left and must now more closely examine the nation to which they came, in particular, how its political culture during this period importantly framed their sense of themselves as Italian Americans.

Americans during the nineteenth century took an understandable interest in the developing forms of liberal nationalism in Europe from the perspective of the legitimate aims of revolutionary constitutionalism that had justified their own revolution and the resulting constitutional developments. The Hungarian liberal nationalist Louis Kossuth received a hero's welcome during his 1851–2 visit to the United States,[1] and the United States at various points tried to act as an intermediary to assist Kossuth in his struggles with Austria-Hungary[2] (the British, in contrast, were disinterested in Hungarian nationalism yet supported Italian nationalism).[3] As I earlier noted (chapter 2), the German liberal nationalist Francis Lieber found a home in the United States as one of its prominent political theorists of liberal nationalism, and Irish Americans became increasingly involved in supporting Irish republican nationalism.[4] Americans also actively supported the Risorgimento,[5] notably including the dynamic American transcendentalist and feminist Margaret Fuller; Fuller fell in love with an Italian sup-

---

[1] See Istvan Deak, *The Lawful Revolution: Louis Kossuth and the Hungarians, 1848–1849* (New York: Columbia University Press, 1979), 342–5. On Kossuth's somewhat inconsistent record as a liberal nationalist, see, in general, ibid.; he thus opposed Magyar nationalism, ibid., 122, and even evinced racism, ibid., 127.

[2] See ibid., 206–7, 299–300.

[3] See ibid., 147.

[4] See Patrick J. Blessing, "Irish," in Thernstrom, *Harvard Encyclopedia of American Ethnic Groups*, 536–8; McCaffrey, *The Irish Catholic Diaspora in America*, 138–68.

[5] See DeConde, *Half Bitter, Half Sweet*, 36–58.

porter of Mazzini who fought for the ill-fated Roman republic of 1849 (Fuller tended the wounded in a military hospital and brought together materials for a history of the brief republic); when French troops crushed the republic, Fuller defended the Italians against American claims of unfitness for republicanism in terms of a prejudice akin to American racism:

> ignorant of Italian literature and Italian life, [they] talk about the corrupt and degenerate state of Italy as they do about that of our slaves at home. They come ready trained to that mode of reasoning which affirms, that, because men are degraded by bad institutions, they are not fit for better.[6]

Fuller, her husband, and their young baby tragically drowned when their ship, bringing them to America, foundered off Fire Island.[7] Americans, including Italians who had already emigrated to the United States, gave not only active moral but material support to the political and military struggles of Cavour and Garibaldi for a unified Italy, and some Americans directly aided Garibaldi, even serving as volunteers in his army in the Sicilian campaign of 1860. This American assistance may have been decisive in the victories that led to Garibaldi's dictatorship over half of Italy in 1860.[8] Garibaldi, after early defeats at the hands of the Austrians and others, lived and worked in New York in 1850–51 and later, in 1861, actively supported the Union cause in the American Civil War, even offering to fight in the Union armies;[9] in fact, a number of those who had fought in Garibaldi's forces crossed the Atlantic to volunteer for service in the Union armies.[10] Italians had read translations of Harriet Beecher Stowe's *Uncle Tom's Cabin*, and one of them told Stowe that her humane feelings for the enslaved spoke movingly as well for the "poor slaves still in Italy,"[11] a thought Mazzini had expressed to the leading American abolitionist Theodore Weld on the eve of the American Civil War: "We are fighting the same sacred battle

---

[6] Quoted in ibid., 47.
[7] See ibid., 45–6.
[8] See, on this point, ibid., 54–8.
[9] See ibid., 60–1.
[10] See ibid., 61.
[11] See ibid., 54.

for freedom and the emancipation of the oppressed, you, Sir, against *negro*, we against *white* slavery."[12] After the Union victory in the Civil War, Mazzini appealed to the United States to support the struggles for revolutionary constitutionalism in Europe:

> You have become a Nation-Guide, and you must act as such. You must aid your republican brethren everywhere the sacred battle is fought. . . . This is your mission; this is your glory and safety; this is your future![13]

These relationships between advocates of American and Italian revolutionary constitutionalism suggest important common themes, not least the suggestion, by both Americans and Italians, that the unjust plight of the African Americans held in slavery was importantly analogous to the situation of the Italian people. We must now examine more closely the later development of this common theme in the period after the Civil War, when the massive emigration of Southern Italians to the United States took place. As I earlier noted (chapter 2), the Union victory in the American Civil War was itself justified as a second appeal to American revolutionary constitutionalism against the antebellum decadence of the Constitution of 1787, now appropriately reformed, consistent with that revolutionary constitutionalism, by the Reconstruction Amendments. Both that great conflict and the later interpretive struggles over the meaning of the Reconstruction Amendments importantly were over the political and constitutional evil of American slavery and its attendant racism; and the great Italian emigration occurred during a period now reasonably regarded as one of the most racist in American constitutional history, when that racism applied to recent immigrants, including the Southern Italians. Italian American identity was thus importantly first formed against the background of such injustice, and its development as an identity was shaped by later struggles against this injustice. To clarify all these points, we must first understand the larger background of American principles of antiracism, how they were compromised in early interpretations of the Reconstruction Amendments (during the period of the European immigration under examination here), and how these

---

[12] Quoted in ibid., 60.
[13] Quoted in ibid., 62.

interpretations were later successfully contested. I thus begin my examination with a discussion of the background of the constitutional condemnation of racism as a constitutional evil in terms of a conception of the structural injustice of moral slavery that, in my judgment, best explains our constitutional condemnation not only of racism but of religious intolerance, sexism, and homophobia as well; my discussion focuses on our current understanding of racism as a constitutional evil (with some discussion of religious intolerance, sexism, and homophobia) and then presents a discussion of some of the ways in which such structural injustice was unjustly rationalized. On this basis, I then examine in two stages the impact of these developments on Italian American identity. First, I focus on the period 1890–1920, during the first generation of Southern Italian emigration, when American racism was well entrenched in our law and practice. Second, I examine the subsequent period, during which this racism was increasingly contested, in terms of its impact on the identity of second and third generation Italian Americans. In the next chapter, I address the question of human rights and muticultural identity, comparing the Italian American experience to related forms of multicultural experience in the United States.

RACISM AS A CONSTITUTIONAL EVIL

The struggle for racial justice plays a leading role in our interpretive understanding of the Reconstruction Amendments, both in terms of the hermeneutic background of those Amendments in the antebellum abolitionist movement and in terms of the successful African American struggle, after their ratification, to rectify the crudely racist interpretation they had irresponsibly been given by the judiciary.[14] The success of that later struggle culminated in *Brown v. Board of Education*[15] and the reasonable national consensus that accepts the legitimacy of that opinion as a fixed point in contemporary discussions of judicially enforceable constitutional principles. Contemporary constitutional theories are importantly defined and valued in terms of

[14] I discuss both these matters at length in Richards, *Conscience and the Constitution;* see also Richards, *Women, Gays, and the Constitution.*

[15] *Brown v. Board of Education,* 347 U.S. 483 (1954).

the account they give of the legitimacy of *Brown* and its progeny (including, as we shall see, judicial expansion of its principle to include gender[16] and, most recently, sexual orientation[17]). Some such constitutional theories focus on the political powerlessness of African Americans, supposing judicial intervention to be appropriate to the extent it rectifies such powerlessness, suitably interpreted;[18] others associate the constitutional defect with the basis of the disadvantage (namely, an immutable and salient personal characteristic).[19] Presumably, any plausible elaboration of the principle of *Brown*, as understood by such theories, would require plausible analogies to be made to either the political powerlessness of African Americans or to personal characteristics that, like race, are immutable and conspicuously salient.

A plausible general theory of suspect classification analysis must unify, on grounds of principle, the claims to such an analysis of African Americans, women, and lesbians and gays. Political powerlessness cannot do so. Lack of political power—measured by some statistical norm such as Ackerman's[20] or by Ely's principle of fair representation[21]—does not capture the plane of ethical discourse of suspect classification analysis as it has been developed in authoritative case law. An analysis based on political powerlessness wrongly suggests that the gains in political solidarity of groups subjected to deep racial, sexist, or religious prejudice (in virtue of resistance to such prejudice) disentitle them to constitutional protection,[22] as if the often meager political gains of blacks, women, and gays and lesbians (when measured against their claims of justice) were the measure of constitu-

---

[16] See, for example, *Frontiero v. Richardson*, 411 U.S. 677 (1973); *Craig v. Boren*, 429 U.S. 190 (1976); *United States v. Virginia*, 116 S.Ct. 2264 (1996).

[17] See *Romer v. Evans*, 116 S.Ct. 1620 (1996); but cf. *Bowers v. Hardwick*, 478 U.S. 186 (1986).

[18] See, for example, Bruce Ackerman, "Beyond *Carolene Products*," 98 *Harv. L. Rev.* 713 (1985); John Hart Ely, *Democracy and Distrust: A Theory of Judicial Review* (Cambridge, Mass.: Harvard University Press, 1980).

[19] See, for example, Michael J. Perry, "Modern Equal Protection: A Conceptualization and Appraisal," 79 *Colum. L. Rev.* 1023 (1979).

[20] See Ackerman, "Beyond *Carolene Products*."

[21] See Ely, *Democracy and Distrust*.

[22] Ackerman likewise makes this erroneous suggestion, "Beyond *Carolene Products*," at 718, 740–46.

tional justice.[23] This analysis preposterously denies constitutional protection to women because they are a statistical majority of voters.[24] This approach also proves too much: it extends protection to any political group, though subject to no history of rights-denying prejudice, solely because it has not been as politically successful as it might have been (e.g., dentists).[25] Procedural models of suspect classification analysis suppress the underlying substantive rights-based normative judgments in terms of which equal protection should be and has been interpreted. Such models neither explanatorily fit the case law nor afford a sound normative model with which to criticize the case law.

Suspect classification analysis identifies the political expression of irrational prejudices of a certain sort—namely, those rooted in a history and culture of unjust exclusion of a certain group from participation in the political community as required by their basic rights of conscience, speech, association, and work. The fundamental wrong of racism and sexism has been the intolerant exclusion of blacks and women from the rights of public culture, exiling them to cultural marginality in supposedly morally inferior realms and unjustly stigmatizing identity on such grounds. Similar unjust cultural marginalization and stigmatization also victimize homosexuals, and the rectification of this condition entitles sexual orientation to be recognized as a suspect classification.

Analysis of this sort suggests why immutability and salience do not coherently explain even the historical paradigm of suspect classification of race and therefore cannot normatively define the terms of principle reasonably applicable to other claims to suspect classification

[23] Racial classifications, for example, remain as suspect as they have ever been, irrespective of the political advances of African Americans. See, e.g., *Palmore v. Sidoti*, 466 U.S. 429, 434 (1984) (awarding custody of child on grounds of race of adoptive father held unconstitutional).

[24] The Supreme Court has expressly regarded gender as a suspect classification irrespective of the status of women as a political majority. See, e.g., *Frontiero v. Richardson*, 411 U.S. 677, 686 n.17 (1973); cf. *Craig v. Boren*, 429 U.S. 190, 204 (1976) (holding that gender classification is not substantially related to traffic laws). But cf. Ely, *Democracy and Distrust*, at 164–70 (asserting that women should be denied constitutional protection because they constitute a majority of voters and are noninsular).

[25] The Supreme Court has declined to regard the mere fact of the greater political success of one interest group over another as relevant to a decision on whether to accord closer scrutiny to legislation favorable to one group over another. See, e.g., *United States R.R. Retirement Bd. v. Fritz*, 449 U.S. 166, 174–76 (1980); cf. *Williamson v. Lee Optical*, 348 U.S. 483, 488 (1965).

analysis. The principle of *Brown v. Board of Education*[26] itself cannot reasonably be understood in terms of the abstract ethical ideal that state benefits and burdens should never turn on an immutable and salient characteristic as such. There is no such ethical ideal.[27] It is not a reasonable objection that a distribution of goods may be owed persons on the basic of an immutable and salient characteristic if justice requires or allows such a characteristic to be given such weight. Disabled persons are born with disabilities that often cannot be changed; nonetheless, resources are appropriately accorded them because of their disabilities to accord them some fair approximation to the opportunities of nondisabled persons.

The example is not an isolated one; its principle pervades the justice of rewards and fair distribution generally. For example, we reward certain athletic achievements very highly and do not finely calibrate the components of our rewards on the basis of the extent to which those achievements result from acts of self-disciplined will or from natural endowments. Achievement itself suffices to elicit reward, even though some significant part of it turns on immutable physical endowments that some have and others lack. Or, we allocate scarce places in institutions of higher learning on the basis of an immutable factor such as geographic distribution, an educational policy we properly regard as sensible and not unfair. The point can be reasonably generalized to include that part of the theory of distributive justice that is concerned with maintaining both an economic and social minimum and some structure of differential rewards to elicit better performance for the public good. The idea of a just minimum turns on certain facts about levels of subsistence, not on acts of will; we would not regard such a minimum as any the less justly due if the human sciences were to show us that some significant component of it turned on immutable factors. Differential rewards perform the role of incentives for the kind of performance required by modern industrial market economies; the human sciences may show us that immutable factors such as genetic endowment play some significant role in such a performance. Nonetheless, we would not regard it as unjust to reward the performance so long as the incentives worked out with the consequences specified by the theory of dis-

---

[26] 347 U.S. 483 (1954).

[27] For a similar analysis, see Ronald Dworkin, *Law's Empire* (Cambridge, Mass.: Harvard University Press, 1986), at 381–99.

tributive justice. Our conclusion, from a wide range of diverse examples, must be that immutability and salience do not identity an ethical ideal that could be a reasonable basis for suspect classification analysis.

In particular, race is a suspect classification, not on such grounds (which would include much that we regard as just) but when it expresses a background structural injustice of a certain sort that sustains a rights-denying culture of irrational political prejudice. Persons are regarded as victimized by this prejudice not because they are physically unable to change or mask the trait defining the class but because the prejudice itself assigns intrinsically unreasonable weight to and burdens on identifications that define one's moral personality. Race in America is culturally defined by the "one-drop" rule, under which quite small proportions of black genes suffice for one to be regarded as black, including persons who are for all visibly salient purposes nonblack.[28] Persons who are black by this definition could pass as white; most, including some historically important African American leaders, chose not to do so.[29] Choosing to pass as white would cut them off from intimately personal relationships to family and community that nurture and sustain their self-respect and personal integrity;[30] the price of avoiding racial prejudice would be an unreasonable sacrifice of the basic resources of personal and ethical identity that they do not accept. In effect, one is to avoid injustice by a silencing of one's moral powers to protest injustice, degrading moral integrity into silent complicity with evil. The same terms of cultural degradation apply to all victims of racism whether visibly or nonvisibly black, the demand of supine acceptance of an identity unjustly devalued.

Racial prejudice is an invidious political evil because it is directed against significant aspects of a person's cultural and moral identity and justified on irrationalist grounds of subjugation based on that identity. The point is not that its irrationalist object is some brute fact that cannot be changed but that it is directed at important aspects of moral personality, in particular, "the way people think, feel, and believe, not how they look"—the identifications that make them "members of the black

[28] See, generally, F. James Davis, *Who Is Black?: One Nation's Definition* (University Park: Pennsylvania State University Press, 1991).

[29] Ibid., at 7, 56–57, 77–78, 178–79.

[30] Ibid., at 56–57.

ethnic community."[31] Racial prejudice, thus analyzed, shares common features with certain forms of religious intolerance. In particular, racism and anti-Semitism share a common irrationalist fear—persons who can pass as white or Christian but are nonetheless tainted by an incapacity fully to affirm the majoritarian race or religion.[32] The incapacitating taint is ascribed on the basis of "perceived attitudes and social participation rather than on . . . appearance or lineage."[33] On this basis, any dissent from the dominant racist or anti-Semitic orthodoxy, let alone sympathetic association with the stigmatized minority, is interpreted as evidence of being a member of the defective minority, thus imposing a reign of intellectual terror on any morally independent criticism of racial or religious intolerance and encouraging a stigmatized minority to accept the legitimacy of subordination.[34] The structural resemblance of racism to a form of religious intolerance is an important feature of its American historical background and is fundamental to a sound interpretation of the suspectness of race under American constitutional law.

The interpretive status of race, as the paradigm interpretive case of a suspect classification under the American constitutional law of the Equal Protection Clause, arose against the background of the interdependent institutions of American slavery and racism and the persistence of racism, supported by its judicial legitimation in cases like *Plessy v. Ferguson*[35] and *Pace v. Alabama*[36] long after the formal abolition of slavery. Racist institutions, including race-based slavery and its legacy of American apartheid,[37] evolved from an unjust and constitutionally illegitimate religious intolerance against the culture of African Americans held in slavery. Racist prejudice was thus, in its origins, an

---

[31] Ibid., at 179.

[32] Ibid., at 55–56, 145.

[33] Ibid., at 145.

[34] For exploration of this phenomenon in the form of Jewish anti-Semitism, see, for example, Sander L. Gilman, *Jewish Self-Hatred: Anti-Semitism and the Hidden Language of the Jews* (Baltimore: Johns Hopkins University Press, 1986); Michael Lerner, *The Socialism of Fools: Anti-Semitism on the Left* (Oakland, Calif.: Tikkun Books, 1992).

[35] 163 U.S. 537 (1896) (state segregation by race held constitutional).

[36] *Pace v. Alabama*, 106 U.S. 583 (1863) (stronger penalties for interracial, as opposed to intraracial, sexual relations not racially discriminatory).

[37] For a recent important study of the persistence of this injustice, see Douglas S. Massey and Nancy A. Denton, *American Apartheid: Segregation and the Making of the Underclass* (Cambridge, Mass.: Harvard University Press, 1993).

instance of religious discrimination. This discrimination later developed, in ideological support of the institutions of American slavery, into a systematically unjust cultural intolerance of African Americans as an ethnic group, reflected in their degradation from the status of bearers of human rights, such as the basic rights of conscience, speech, intimate association, and work.[38] Race is constitutionally suspect when and to the extent public law expresses such unjust racial prejudice, reflecting the unjust cultural degradation of a class of persons from their status as bearers of basic human rights.[39] The evil of such prejudice is its systematic degradation of identifications at the heart of free moral personality, including powers to protest injustice in the name and voice of one's human rights.

African American self-understanding of American racism was deepened and energized by the scholarship and activism of W. E. B. Du Bois in exactly these terms. His historical studies challenged the dominant, often racist orthodoxy of the age,[40] and his 1903 book *The Souls of Black Folk*[41] offered a pathbreaking interpretive study of African American culture and the struggle for ethical self-consciousness under circumstances of racial oppression[42]—

a world which yields him [a black person] no true self-consciousness, but only lets him see himself through the revelation of the other

[38] I develop this argument at greater length in Richards, *Conscience and the Constitution: History, Theory, and Law of the Reconstruction Amendments* (Princeton: Princeton University Press, 1993), at 80–89, 150–170; see also, in general, Richards, *Women, Gays, and the Constitution*.

[39] For further development of this argument, see Richards, *Conscience and the Constitution*, at 170–77.

[40] See W. E. B. Du Bois, *The Suppression of the African Slave-Trade*, in *W. E. B. Du Bois*, ed. Nathan Huggins (orig. pub., 1896; New York: Library of America, 1986), 3–356; *Black Reconstruction in America, 1860–1880* (orig. pub., 1935; New York: Atheneum, 1969).

[41] See W. E. B. Du Bois, *The Souls of Black Folk*, in *W. E. B. Du Bois*, ed. Nathan Huggins (orig. pub., 1903; New York: Library of America, 1986), 359–586.

[42] See, in general, David Levering Lewis, *W. E. B. Du Bois: Biography of a Race, 1868–1919* (New York: Henry Holt, 1993); Eric J. Sundquist, *To Wake the Nations: Race in the Making of American Literature* (Cambridge, Mass.: Belknap Press of Harvard University Press, 1993), 457–625; for a more critical, less rights-based reading of Du Bois's theory and practice, see Adolph L. Reed, Jr., *W. E. B. Du Bois and American Political Thought: Fabianism and the Color Line* (New York: Oxford University Press, 1997).

world. It is a peculiar sensation, this double-consciousness, this sense of always looking at one's self through the eyes of others, of measuring one's soul by the tape of a world that looks on in amused contempt and pity. One ever feels his two-ness,—an American, a Negro; two souls, two thoughts, two unreconciled strivings, two warring ideals in one dark body, whose dogged strength alone keeps it from being torn asunder.[43]

The struggle for justice was thus a struggle for self-respecting identity on terms of justice that would transform both:

The history of the American Negro is the history of this strife,—this longing to attain self-conscious manhood, to merge his double self into a better and truer self. In this merging he wishes neither of the older selves to be lost. He would not Africanize America, for America has too much to teach the world and Africa. He would not bleach his Negro soul in a flood of white Americanism, for he knows that Negro blood has a message for the world. He simply wishes to make it possible for a man to be both a Negro and an American, without being cursed and spit upon by his fellows, without having the doors of Opportunity closed roughly in his face.[44]

I describe Du Bois's theory in terms of a normative struggle for redefining identity as a way of making the best sense of his remarkable insights against both the retrospective background of the tradition of abolitionist dissent he both reflects and elaborates and the prospective development of this struggle in the movements for civil liberties that include African Americans, women, and, most recently, gays and lesbians.[45] Du Bois is a towering figure in the history of both the theory and the practice of these movements because he speaks so powerfully from within the experience of the ethical struggle for voice and reasonable discourse as claims of basic human rights against a cultural tradition that both promised and betrayed its guarantees of basic human rights as minimal constitutional conditions of legitimate exercises of

---

[43] See W. E. B. Du Bois, *The Souls of Black Folk*, at 364–65.

[44] Ibid., 365.

[45] See, for further exploration of this retrospective and prospective background, Richards, *Conscience and the Constitution*; Richards, *Women, Gays, and the Constitution*.

state power. The extraordinary importance of African American dissent to American constitutionalism has been not only its demands that these basic rights be extended on fair terms to all persons but its analysis of the ways in which structural injustice (denying a class of persons their very status as bearers of human rights) has been unjustly rationalized in terms of a question-begging entrenchment of that injustice. The most illuminating way to come to terms with the ethical enormity of this structural injustice and the role of claims for identity in protesting it is to start with the inalienable human right that, more than any other, models both the significance and weight of what an inalienable human right is—the right to conscience.

The normative value placed on conscience as an inalienable human right was seminally articulated by Locke and Bayle, who stated the argument for toleration as a constitutive principle of justice in politics.[46] Constraints of principle must be placed on the power of the state to enforce sectarian religious views because the enforcement of such views on society at large entrenches, as the measure of legitimate convictions in matters of conscience, irrationalist intolerance; intolerance is unjustly rationalized by limiting both the standards of debate and speakers to the sectarian measure that supports dominant political and moral authority. The rights-based evil of such intolerance is the inadequate grounds on which it abridges the inalienable right to conscience, the free exercise of the moral powers of rationality and reasonableness in terms of which persons define personal and ethical meaning in living. While this human right, like others, may be abridged on compelling secular grounds of protecting public goods reasonably acknowledged as such by all persons (irrespective of other philosophical or evaluative disagreements), the self-entrenching of a sectarian view cannot suffice.[47]

Locke's and Bayle's argument for toleration was a judgment of and a response to such abuses of political epistemology (the political enforcement at large of a sectarian view). The legitimation of religious persecution by both Catholics and Protestants (drawing authority from Augustine, among others) had rendered a politically entrenched view of religious and moral truth the measure of permissible ethics and religion, including the epistemic standards of inquiry and debate about

---

[46] For full discussion of the terms and scope of their argument and its implications for American constitutionalism, see Richards, *Toleration and the Constitution* at 85–281.

[47] See Richards, *Toleration and the Constitution*, at 244–47.

religious and moral truth. By the late seventeenth century (when Locke and Bayle wrote), there was good reason to believe that politically entrenched views of religious and moral truth (resting on the Bible and associated interpretive practices) assumed essentially contestable interpretations of a complex historical interaction among pagan, Jewish, and Christian cultures in the early Christian era.[48]

The Renaissance rediscovery of pagan culture and learning reopened the question of how the Christian synthesis of pagan philosophical and Jewish ethical and religious culture was to be understood. Among other things, the development of critical historiography and techniques of textual interpretation had undeniable implications for reasonable Bible interpretation.[49] The Protestant Reformation both assumed and encouraged these new modes of inquiry and encouraged as well the appeal to experiment and experience, methodologies associated with the rise of modern science. These new approaches to thought and inquiry made possible the recognition that there was a gap between the politically enforceable conceptions of religious and moral truth and the kinds of reasonable inquiries that the new approaches made available. The argument for toleration arose from the recognition of this disjunction between the reigning political epistemology and the new epistemic methodologies.

The crux of the problem was that unjustly entrenched political conceptions of truth had made themselves the measure both of the standards of reasonable inquiry and of who could count as a reasonable inquirer after truth. But, in light of the new modes of inquiry that became available during the Reformation, this political entrenchment of religious truth was often seen to rest not only on the degradation of reasonable standards of inquiry but on the self-fulfilling degradation of the capacity of persons to conduct such inquiries. In order to rectify these evils, the argument for toleration forbade, as a matter of principle, enforcement by the statement of any such conception of religious truth. The scope of legitimate political concern was acknowledged, as we have seen, to rest on the pursuit of general ends such as life and basic rights and liberties (for example, the right to conscience). The pursuit of such goods was consistent with the full range of ends free people might rationally and reasonably pursue.

---

[48] See Richards, *Toleration and the Constitution*, at 25–27, 84–98, 105, 125.
[49] See ibid., at 125–26.

A prominent feature of the argument for toleration was its claim that religious persecution corrupted conscience itself (both Bayle and Locke, religious Christians, thus argued that religious persecution corrupts ethics and, for this reason, what they took to be Christianity's elevated and simple ethical core of a universal brotherhood of free people). Such corruption, a kind of self-induced blindness to the evils one inflicts, is a consequence of the political enforcement at large of a conception of religious truth that immunizes itself from independent criticism in terms of reasonable standards of thought and deliberation. In effect, the conception of religious truth, though perhaps having once been importantly shaped by more ultimate considerations of reason, ceases to be held or to be understood and defended *on the basis of reason*.

A tradition that thus loses a sense of its reasonable foundations stagnates and depends increasingly for allegiance on question-begging appeals to orthodox conceptions of truth and on the violent repression of any dissent from these accepted conceptions as a kind of disloyal moral treason. The politics of loyalty rapidly degenerates, as it did in the antebellum South's repression of any criticism of slavery, into a politics that takes pride in widely held community values solely because they are community values. Standards of discussion and inquiry become increasingly parochial and insular; they serve only a polemical role in the defense of the existing community values and are indeed increasingly hostile to any more impartial reasonable assessment in light of any independent standards.[50]

Such a politics tends to forms of irrationalism in order to protect its now essentially polemical project. Opposing views relevant to reasonable public argument are suppressed, facts distorted or misstated, values disconnected from ethical reasoning; indeed, deliberation in politics is denigrated in favor of violence against dissent and the aesthetic glorification of violence. Paradoxically, the more the tradition becomes seriously vulnerable to independent reasonable criticism (indeed, increasingly in rational need of such criticism), the more it is likely to generate forms of political irrationalism (including scapegoating of outcast dissenters) in order to secure allegiance. This paradox of intol-

---

[50] See John Hope Franklin, *The Militant South, 1800–1861* (Cambridge, Mass.: Belknap Press of Harvard University Press, 1956); cf. W. J. Cash, *The Mind of the South* (New York: Vintage Books, 1941).

erance (the internal need for criticism generating repression of dissent) works its irrationalist havoc through its war on the inalienable right to conscience, in particular, constructing a group of scapegoats on the basis of the unjust repression of this central human right.

The history of religious persecution amply illustrates these truths; as the American antebellum abolitionist advocates of the argument for toleration clearly saw,[51] no aspect of that history does so more clearly than Christian anti-Semitism. The development of the worst ravages of medieval anti-Semitism (totally baseless and irrational beliefs about ritual crucifixions and cannibalism of Christians by Jews) was associated with growing internal doubts about the reasonableness of certain Catholic religious beliefs and practices (for example, transubstantiation) and the resolution of these doubts by the forms of irrationalist politics associated with anti-Semitism (centered on fantasies of ritual eating of human flesh that expressed the underlying worries about transubstantiation).[52] The politics of this anti-Semitism illustrates the paradox of intolerance, which explains the force of the example for abolitionists. Precisely when the dominant religious tradition gave rise to the most reasonable internal doubts, these doubts were banned from reasonable discussion and debate and transmuted into blatant political irrationalism aimed at one of the more conspicuous, vulnerable, and innocent groups of dissenters. It did not escape the abolitionists, who were critics of American slavery, that irrationalism against Jews was made possible by the long history of Christian Europe's restrictions on Jews (including, e.g. limits on their access to influential occupations, their social intercourse with Christians, and their living quarters), rationalized, as it was, by Augustine, among others, in the quite explicit terms of slavery: "The Jew is the slave of the Christian."[53]

The argument for toleration was importantly developed and elaborated as an internal criticism of cultural traditions so corrupted by construction of cultural identity on terms of injustice that the tradition no longer served reasonable ethical values. Locke and Bayle, for example, forged the argument for toleration as an internal criticism of their own identity as Christians, identifying the unjust abridg-

---

[51] See Richards, *Conscience and the Constitution*, at 59–63, 67–69.

[52] For fuller discussion, see Richards, *Conscience and the Constitution*, at 68–69.

[53] Cited in Gavin I. Langmuir, *History, Religion, and Antisemitism* (Berkeley and Los Angeles: University of California Press, 1990), 294.

ment of the right to conscience as corrupting what they took to be the ethical core of true Christianity and calling for the reconstruction of Christian identity on terms of justice. The American abolitionist elaboration of the argument in order to condemn both American slavery and racism[54] was an internal criticism of their own identities as both Christians and Americans; they called for a reconstruction of Christian and American identity on terms of justice. In particular, abolitionist moral and constitutional thought condemned the corruption of American constitutional guarantees of universal human rights by the structural injustice of slavery and racism.[55] American slavery and racism, like anti-Semitism, rested on the structural justice of the abridgment of the basic human rights of a group of persons on the speciously circular grounds of their alleged incapacity to be bearers of human rights, an incapacity that, in fact, depended on their unjust dehumanization.

The abolitionists, consistent with their argument for toleration, saw slavery and discrimination as religious, social, economic, and political persecution motivated by a politically entrenched conception of black incapacity. That conception enforced its own vision of truth against both the standards of reasonable inquiry and the reasonable capacities of both blacks and whites who might challenge the conception. A conception of political unity, subject to reasonable doubt as to its basis and merits, had, consistent with the paradox of intolerance, unreasonably resolved its doubts in the irrationalist racist certitudes of group solidarity on the basis of unjust group subjugation.

Black Americans were the scapegoats of southern self-doubt in the same way European Jews had been victims of Christian doubt. Frederick Douglass, the leading black abolitionist, stated the abolitionist analysis with a classical clarity:

> Ignorance and depravity, and the inability to rise from degradation to civilization and respectability, are the most usual allegations against the oppressed. The evils most fostered by slavery and oppression are precisely those which slaveholders and oppressors would transfer from their system to the inherent character of their victims. Thus the

[54] See, for further discussion, Richards, *Conscience and the Constitution*, at 73–89.
[55] On abolitionist constitutional theory, see ibid., at 89–107.

very crimes of slavery become slavery's best defence. By making the enslaved a character fit only for slavery, they excuse themselves for refusing to make the slave a freeman.[56]

In his classic account of African American double consciousness, Du Bois had called for a reconstruction of African American identity on terms of justice that would address injustices in the construction of both black ethnic and American identity. Douglas addressed both; he insisted, as Martin Luther King was also later to claim,[57] on holding Americans to their constitutional promises of guarantees of the universal human rights of all persons,[58] but, like other ex-slaves, including Sojourner Truth and Harriet Jacobs,[59] he also addressed the unjust terms of the construction of African American identity. As Du Bois clearly saw, the questions could not be separated: the injustice of American racism (including its rights-denying construction of African American identity as subhuman) was made possible by the unjust construction of American identity as, contradictorily, both rights based and, in light of structural injustices like slavery and racism, rights denying. African American claims for identity on terms of justice thus moved along both parameters, and no aspect of their struggle more profoundly addressed this problem than their demand to speak and be heard in the ethically transformative exercise of their free moral powers of conscience in protest of the terms of their subjugation.

The force of such rights-based claims for identity is well illustrated by the ultimately successful African American struggle, under the leadership of the legal redress committee of the NAACP (in which Charles Houston and Thurgood Marshall played central roles), to secure the judicial repudiation of *Plessy* and *Pace*.[60] Black Americans in

---

[56] "The Claims of the Negro Ethnologically Considered," in Philip S. Foner, ed., *The Life and Writings of Frederick Douglass*, 5 vols. (New York: International Publishers, 1975), 2:295.

[57] For a good general study, see Taylor Branch, *Parting the Waters: Martin Luther King and the Civil Rights Movement, 1954–63* (London: Papermac, 1990).

[58] On the various forms of abolitionist constitutional theory, see Richards, *Conscience and the Constitution*, at 89–107.

[59] See, for further discussion, Richards, *Women, Gays, and the Constitution*, at 115–124.

[60] See Mark V. Tushnet, *The NAACP's Legal Strategy against Segregated Education, 1925–1950* (Chapel Hill: University of North Carolina Press, 1987) and *Making Civil Rights*

the South and elsewhere asserted and were finally accorded some measure of national protection by the Supreme Court (reversing early decisions to the contrary)[61] in the exercise of their First Amendment rights of protest, criticism, and advocacy.[62] On this basis, Martin Luther King brilliantly used and elaborated the rights of conscience and free speech to protest American racism. Very much in the spirit of the strategy of Garrisonian nonviolence in the antebellum period,[63] he appealed, as he did in his classic "Letter from Birmingham City Jail,"[64] for the need for "nonviolent direct action . . . to create such a [moral] crisis and establish such creative tension that a community that has constantly refused to negotiate is forced to confront the issue."[65] Like Garrisonian radical abolitionists in the antebellum period, King demanded his basic human rights of conscience and free speech to engage in reasonable public discourse about basic issues of justice, including criticism of the racist orthodoxy "that degrades human personality" and is therefore "unjust."[66]

No aspect of that criticism was more profound than the attack on the foundations of American racism, as it had been legitimated in *Plessy* and *Pace*. The foundations of that racism lay in eighteenth-century thought. The eighteenth-century comparative science of human nature, developed by Montesquieu and Hume, had seen human nature as more or less constant but subject to modification by the environment, history, institutional development, and the like. Both writers discussed race differences from this perspective. Montesquieu's position was one

---

Law: Thurgood Marshall and the Supreme Court, 1956–1961 (New York: Oxford University Press, 1994); Genna Rae McNeil, *Groundwork: Charles Hamilton Houston and the Struggle for Civil Rights* (Philadelphia: University of Pennsylvania Press, 1983); Jack Greenberg, *Crusaders in the Courts: How a Dedicated Band of Lawyers Fought for the Civil Rights Revolution* (New York: BasicBooks, 1994).

[61] See *Gitlow v. New York*, 268 U.S. 652 (1925) (First Amendment held applicable to states under Fourteenth Amendment).

[62] See, in general, Harry Kalven, Jr., *The Negro and the First Amendment* (Chicago: University of Chicago Press, 1965).

[63] For further discussion, see, in general, Richards, *Conscience and the Constitution*, ch. 3.

[64] See Martin Luther King, "Letter from Birmingham City Jail," in *A Testament of Hope: The Essential Writings of Martin Luther King, Jr.*, ed. James Melvin Washington (orig. pub., 1963; repr. ed., New York: Harper & Row, 1986), 289–302.

[65] Ibid., 291.

[66] Ibid., 293.

of ironic skepticism.[67] Hume, however, departed from the model of a uniform human nature to suggest significant, constitutionally based race differences inferred from comparative cultural achievements.[68] Hume's suggestion of separate races had an antitheological significance; it was thus condemned, notably by James Beattie,[69] as part of a larger repudiation of the Christian ethics of equality based on the biblical idea of one divine creation of humans. Hume's suggestion was later developed, in the nineteenth century, into polygenetic theories of human origins by American ethnologists and others,[70] who thought of their theories as part of the battle of progressive science against reactionary religion.

In the nineteenth century, this artificially drawn contrast hardened into a division between certain approaches to the human sciences and nearly anything else. These approaches, very much under the influence of models of explanation drawn from the physical sciences, assumed that good explanations in the human sciences must be crudely reductive to some physical measure, like brain capacity or cephalic indices. There was little attention to, let alone understanding of, culture as an independent explanatory variable, and thus no concern with the interpretive dimension of human personality in general and of our moral powers in particular. To the extent culture was attended to at all, cultural transmission was thought of in Lamarckian terms[71] (even Du Bois may have accepted such a view),[72] which suggested that the efforts and resulting achievements of one generation were, as it were, wired into the physical natures of the

---

[67] For further discussion, see Richards, *Conscience and the Constitution*, 74.

[68] See David Hume, "Of National Characters," in David Hume, *Essays Moral Political and Literary* (Indianapolis: LibertyClassics, 1987), 208 n. 10.

[69] See James Beattie, *An Essay on the Nature and Immutability of Truth* (New York: Garland Publishing, Inc., 1983), 479–84. See also James Beattie, *Elements of Moral Science* (Delmar, N.Y.: Scholars' Facsimiles & Reprints, 1976), 183–223.

[70] See William Stanton, *The Leopard's Spots: Scientific Attitudes toward Race in America, 1815–59* (Chicago: University of Chicago Press, 1960); George M. Fredrickson, *The Black Image in the White Mind: The Debate on Afro-American Character and Destiny, 1817–1914* (Middletown, Conn.: Wesleyan University Press, 1971); Thomas F. Gossett, *Race: The History of an Idea in America* (New York: Schocken Books, 1965).

[71] See George W. Stocking, Jr., *Race, Culture, and Evolution: Essays in the History of Anthropology* (New York: Free Press, 1968), 47–48, 124, 234–69.

[72] See Adolph L. Reed, Jr., *W. E. B. Du Bois and American Political Thought*, 39, 58.

offspring of that generation. As a result, any cultural advantage that one people might have had was not only peculiarly its own (not necessarily transmissible to other peoples), but a matter of rational pride for all those born into that people. The cultural advances in question were never accidents of time and circumstances but products of the achieving will, with each generation playing its part in further acts of progressive will, building on the achievements of past generations.

These views not only failed to appreciate what culture is, let alone its explanatory weight in the human sciences. They confused culture with acts of will, failing to understand the nature of cultural formation and transmission, the role of contingency and good luck in cultural progress, and the complete impropriety of taking credit for such advances simply by virtue of being born into such a culture. This whole way of thinking naturally created ethical space for explanations in terms of superior and inferior races as a proxy for the comparison between the remarkable scientific advances in Western culture in the nineteenth century and the putative lack of comparable advances nearly everywhere else.[73] If the least progress appeared to have been made in African cultures, African peoples must be inferior; if Egyptian culture clearly had been, for some long period, advanced and had an important impact on progressive cultures like that of ancient Greece, then Egyptians could not be black.[74]

It was assumptions like these that explain why the Supreme Court in *Plessy* could be so ethically blind, in the same way proslavery thinkers had been blind, to the ignoble and unjust contempt that its legitimation of the further cultural degradation of blacks inflicted on black Americans.[75] For the *Plessy* Court, race was not morally arbitrary but a physical fact crucially connected with other physical facts of rational incapacity for which blacks, being from a nonprogressive culture, must be ethically responsible. In contrast, white Americans, taking rational ethical pride in their willed success in sustaining a progressive culture, should take the same pride in their race and might reasonably protect their achievements from those of another race who were culpa-

[73] Ibid., 234–69.

[74] See, for example, Stanton, *The Leopard's Spots*, 50.

[75] On the roots of *Plessy* in the dominant racist social science of the nineteenth century, see Charles A. Lofgren, *The Plessy Case* (New York: Oxford University Press, 1987).

bly nonprogressive by nature. Race, a physical fact supposed to be causally connected to other physical facts, had been transformed into a character trait. The highly moralistic mind of nineteenth-century America had no problem, once having bought the idea of such a transformation, protecting people of good moral character from those who were culpably of unworthy character.

Abolitionist thought had taken the moral insularity of proslavery defenses as an example of the corruption of conscience so common in the history of religious persecution,[76] and modern racism in both America and Europe exemplified one of human nature's more artfully self-deceiving evasions of the moral responsibilities of liberal political culture—illustrated, in *Plessy*, by the way in which the culture's respect for science had been manipulated to serve racist ends. Fundamental public criticism of this view of the human sciences must, by its nature as a form of public reason bearing on constitutional values, reshape constitutional argument.

The pivotal figure in such criticism was a German Jew and immigrant to the United States, Franz Boas, who fundamentally criticized the racial explanations characteristic of both European and American physical anthropology in the late nineteenth century.[77] Boas argued that comparative anthropological study did not sustain the explanatory weight placed on race in the human sciences; there was more significant variability within races than there was among races.[78] Indeed, many of the human features that were supposed to be unchangeably physical (like the cephalic index) were reponsive to cultural change; Boas had shown that some physical traits of recent immigrants to the

---

[76] See, for fuller discussion, Richards, *Conscience and the Constitution*, 80–89.

[77] See Franz Boas, *The Mind of Primitive Man*, (orig. pub., 1911; rev. ed., Westport, Conn.: Greenwood Press, 1983); George W. Stocking, Jr., ed., *A Franz Boas Reader: The Shaping of American Anthropology, 1883–1911* (Chicago: University of Chicago Press, 1974). For commentary, see Stocking, *Race, Culture, and Evolution*; Carl N. Degler, *In Search of Human Nature: The Decline and Revival of Darwinism in American Social Thought* (New York: Oxford University Press, 1991), 61–83. For a useful recent comparative study of developments in the United States and Britain, see Elazar Barkan, *The Retreat of Scientific Racism: Changing Concepts of Race in Britain and the United States between the World Wars* (Cambridge: Cambridge University Press, 1992).

[78] See Franz Boas, "Race," in Edwin R. A. Seligman, ed., *Encyclopaedia of the Social Sciences* (New York: Macmillan, 1937), 7:25–36; Boas, *The Mind of Primitive Man*, 45–59, 179. For commentary, see Stocking, *Race, Culture, and Evolution*, 192–94.

United States (both Jews and Italians) had changed in response to acculturation.[79]

The crucial factor, heretofore missing from the human sciences, was culture; Boas made this point to Du Bois on a visit to Atlanta University, a visit that "had an impact of lasting importance"[80] for Du Bois's interest in black culture and its sources. Cultural formation and transmission could not be understood in terms of the reductive physical models that had heretofore dominated scientific and popular thinking. In particular, the Lamarckian explanation—having been discredited by Mendelian genetics in favor of random genetic mutation—was not the modality of cultural transmission, which was not physical at all but irreducibly cultural. One generation born into a progressive culture could no more take credit for an accident of birth than a generation could be reasonably blamed for birth into a less progressive culture. In fact, cultures advance often through accident and good luck and through cultural diffusion of technologies from other cultures. Such diffusion has been an important fact in the history of all human cultures at some point in their histories. No people has been through all points in its history the vehicle of the cultural progress of humankind, nor can any people reasonably suppose itself the unique vehicle of all such progress in the future.[81]

Boas's general contributions to the human sciences were powerfully elaborated in the area of race by his students Otto Klineberg[82] and Ruth Benedict.[83] They argued that the explanatory role of race in the human sciences was, if anything, even less important than the judicious Boas might have been willing to grant[84] (Boas's student Margaret Mead suggested that, to some significant extent, much the same might be true of gender).[85]

[79] See Franz Boas, "Changes in Immigrant Body Form," in Stocking, A Franz Boas Reader, 202–14; Boas, The Mind of Primitive Man, 94–96. For commentary, see Stocking, Race, Culture, and Evolution, 175–80.

[80] See Lewis, W. E. B. Du Bois, 352; see also ibid., 414, 462.

[81] See, in general, Boas, The Mind of Primitive Man. For commentary, see, in general, Stocking, Race, Culture, and Evolution.

[82] See Otto Klineberg, Race Differences (New York: Harper & Brothers, 1935).

[83] See Ruth Benedict, Race: Science and Politics (New York: Viking Press, 1945).

[84] See, for example, Franz Boas, "Human Faculty as Determined by Race," in Stocking, A Franz Boas Reader, 231, 234, 242; Boas, The Mind of Primitive Man, 230–31.

[85] See Degler, In Search of Human Nature, 73, 133–37.

But, the most important study of the American race problem was not by an American but by the Swedish social scientist Gunnar Myrdal. His monumental *An American Dilemma*[86] brought the new approach to culture powerfully to bear on the plight of American blacks, who, from the perspective of the human sciences, now were increasingly well understood as victims of a historically entrenched, unjust cultural construction of racism. In effect, the advances in morally independent critical standards of thought and analysis in the human sciences had enabled social scientists to make the same sort of argument that abolitionist theorists of race, such as Lydia Maria Child[87] and Frederick Douglass, had made earlier, largely on ethical grounds.

Previously, the human sciences had been claimed by proponents of the theory of race differences against what they perceived as regressive religion and ethics; now, however, developments in the human sciences had cleared away as so much rationalizing self-deception the false dichotomy between science and ethics and revealed the ethically regressive uses to which even science may be put by politically entrenched epistemologies concerned to preserve the politics of race. Such political epistemologies, a modernist expression of essentially sectarian conceptions of religious and moral truth, cannot legitimately be the basis of political enforcement on society at large. Rather, legitimate political power must be based on impartial standards of reasonable discussion and debate not hostage to entrenched political orthodoxies. An old ethical point—that of the argument for toleration already used by the abolitionists against slavery and racism—was articulated yet again, now used in the service of an articulate argument of public reason against the force that American racism had been permitted to enjoy in the mistaken interpretation of equal protection in cases like *Plessy*. Such cultural criticism made possible public understanding of the naturalization of injustice that supported American racism, namely, that the grounds for abridgment of basic human rights rested on a stereotypical dehumanization of African Americans (as nonbearers of human rights) that reflected not nature but a viciously

[86] See Gunnar Myrdal, *An American Dilemma: The Negro Problem and Modern Democracy*, 2 vols. (orig. pub., 1944; New York: Pantheon Books, 1972). For commentary, see David W. Southern, *Gunnar Myrdal and Black-White Relations: The Use and Abuse of an American Dilemma, 1944–1969* (Baton Rouge: Louisiana State University Press, 1987).

[87] See Richards, *Conscience and the Constitution*, 82–85.

circular cultural injustice that grew out of the abridgment of such rights. Such naturalization of injustice pivotally rationalized racism.

This point of public reason was much highlighted in the American public mind by a comparable kind of racism that had flourished in Europe in the same period in the form of modern anti-Semitism. As I have elsewhere argued,[88] during this period both American racism and European anti-Semitism evolved into particularly virulent political pathologies under the impact of the respective emancipations of American blacks from slavery and of European Jews from various civil disabilities keyed to their religious background. In both cases, the respective emancipations were not carried through by consistent enforcement of guarantees of basic rights (in the United States, despite clear constitutional guarantees).

The characteristic nineteenth-century struggles for national identity led to rather stark examples of the paradox of intolerance, in which the exclusion of race-defined cultural minorities from the political community of equal rights became itself the irrationalist basis of national unity. Strikingly similar racist theorists evolved in Europe to sustain anti-Semitism[89] and in America to sustain a comparable racism against the supposedly non-Aryan.[90] American constitutional institutions were, as a consequence, misinterpreted, but nonetheless, increasingly, they were the vehicle of organized black protest and dissent, including the forms of protest we have already mentioned. Certainly, American institutions did not collapse on the scale of the German declension into atavistic totalitarianism and the genocide of five million European Jews.[91] In both cases, however, the underlying irrationalist racist dynamic was strikingly similar: emancipation, inadequate protection of basic rights, a devastating and humiliating defeat, and a move by the populace to use the excluded minority as an irrationalist scapegoat.

Boas's important criticism of the role of race in the human sciences had, of course, been motivated as much by his own experience of Euro-

---

[88] See ibid., 156–60.

[89] See Houston Stewart Chamberlain, *The Foundations of the Nineteenth Century*, trans. John Lees, 2 vols. (London: John Lane, 1911).

[90] See Madison Grant, *The Passing of the Great Race or the Racial Basis of European History* (New York: Charles Scribner's Sons, 1919).

[91] See Raul Hilberg, *The Destruction of the European Jews* (New York: Holmes & Meier, 1985), 3:1201–20.

pean anti-Semitism as by American racism; Boas as much forged his own self-respecting identity as a Jew against anti-Semitism as Frederick Douglass or Du Bois had defined theirs as African Americans against American racism. The subsequent elaboration of his arguments by Klineberg, Benedict, and Myrdal had further raised the standards of public reason to expose both the intellectual and the ethical fallacies of racism in America and in Europe. As a result of such criticism, the constitutional attack in the United States on the analytic foundations of *Plessy* began well before World War II in the litigation strategy undertaken by the NAACP to question and subvert the racist principle of separate but equal in the area of public segregated education.

But World War II itself, not unlike the Civil War, played an important role in stimulating the development of much more enlightened public attitudes on racial questions than had prevailed theretofore. Not only did the distinguished military service of African Americans in both wars call for recognition of full citizenship but the Allied victory in World War II raised corresponding questions about the state of American constitutionalism prior to the war not unlike those raised by the Reconstruction Amendments about antebellum American constitutionalism. The United States successfully fought in World War II in Europe against a nation that, like the American South in the Civil War, defined its world historic mission in self-consciously racist terms. The political ravages of this racism—both in the unspeakable moral horrors of the Holocaust of five million innocent European Jews and in the brutalities inflicted by World War II on so many others—naturally called for a moral interpretation of that war, again like the Civil War, in terms of the defense of the political culture of universal human rights against its racist antagonists. In the wake of World War II and of its central role in the Allied victory and in the European reconstruction, the United States took up a central position on the world stage as an advocate of universal human rights. America was thus naturally pressed critically to examine, not only at home but also abroad, practices like state-sponsored racial segregation in light of the best interpretation of American ideals of human rights in contemporary circumstances.[92]

World War II thus played a role in American moral and political thought somewhat akin to a kind of Third American Revolution (the

---

[92] See Mary L. Dudziak, "Desegregation as a Cold War Imperative," 41 *Stan. L. Rev.* 41 (1988); Fredrickson, *The Black Image in the White Mind*, 330.

Civil War being the second such revolution).[93] American ideals of revolutionary constitutionalism were tested against the aggression on human rights of a nation, Nazi Germany, that attacked everything the American constitutional tradition valued in the idea and constitutional institutions of respect for universal human rights.[94] The self-conscious American defense of human rights against the totalitarian ambitions of Nazi Germany required Americans, after the war, to ask if their own constitutionalism was indeed adequate to their ambitions.

In fact, the painful truth was what Du Bois and Boas and others had long argued, namely, that America had betrayed the revolutionary constitutionalism of its Reconstruction Amendments in ways and with consequences strikingly similar to the ways in which Germany had betrayed the promise of universal emancipation. Americans did not, however, have to reconstruct their constitutionalism in order to do justice to this sense of grievous mistake. Unlike the question that had faced the nation in the wake of the Civil War, the problem after World War II was not one of a basic flaw in the very design of American constitutionalism. Rather, the issue was a corrigible interpretive mistake. The judiciary had failed to understand and give effect to the moral ambitions fundamental to the Reconstruction Amendments themselves, namely, that the American political community should be a moral community committed to abstract values of human rights available on fair terms of public reason to all persons, rather than a community based on race.

The focus for testing American interpretive practice was, naturally, *Plessy v. Ferguson,* in which the Supreme Court had accepted the exclusion of black Americans from the American community of equal rights. But, the intellectual and ethical foundations of *Plessy,* to the extent it ever had such foundations, had collapsed under the weight of the criticism we have already discussed at some length. The idea of natural race differences had been thoroughly discredited as itself the product of a long American history of an unjust cultural construction of racism, precisely the same way that European anti-Semitism had been discredited. The Supreme Court, which in 1896 in *Plessy* could rationalize itself as merely following nature or history, faced in the early 1950s a wholly

---

[93] I develop this thought at length in Richards, *Conscience and the Constitution.*

[94] See, in general, Hannah Arendt, *The Origins of Totalitarianism* (New York: Harcourt Brace Jovanovich, 1973).

different space for moral choice, which Boasian cultural studies and African American activism had opened up.

Thurgood Marshall, in his argument to the Supreme Court for the NAACP, morally dramatized this choice in terms of the blue-eyed, innocent African American child, indistinguishable in all reasonable respects from other children, playing and living near them, except for the role the Supreme Court would play in legitimating a constructed difference (segregated education) that enforced an irrationalist prejudice with a long history of unjust subjugation.[95] The Supreme Court was compelled to face, on behalf of American culture more generally, a stark moral choice *either* to give effect to a culture of dehumanization *or* to refuse any longer to be complicitous with such rights-denying evil. Moral responsibility for one's complicity with evil could not be evaded. In effect, Marshall, as an African American, stood before the Court in the full voice of his moral personality as a free person and asked the Court to accept its responsibility for either degrading him as subhuman or to refuse any longer to degrade any person. State-sponsored racial segregation, once uncritically accepted as a reasonable expression of natural race differences, now was construed as itself an unjust construction of an irrationalist dehumanization that excluded citizens from their equal rights as members of the political community and was, as such, unconstitutional. In 1954, in *Brown v. Board of Education*,[96] the Supreme Court of the United States articulated this deliberative interpretive judgment for the nation by unanimously striking down state-sponsored racial segregation as a violation of the Equal Protection Clause of the Fourteenth Amendment.

In 1967, in *Loving v. Virginia*,[97] a similarly unanimous Supreme Court struck down as unconstitutional state antimiscegenation laws. Repeating, as it had in *Brown*, that the dominant interpretive judgments of the Reconstruction Congress could not be dispositive on the exercise by the judiciary of its independent interpretive responsibilities, the Court rejected the equal application theory of *Pace v. Alabama*. The Equal Protection Clause condemned all state-sponsored sources of indivious racial discrimination, and, the Court held, antimiscegenation

---

[95] See Anthony G. Amsterdam, "Thurgood Marshall's Image of the Blue-Eyed Child in *Brown*," 68 *N.Y.U. L. Rev.* 226 (1993).

[96] *Brown v. Board of Education*, 347 U.S. 483 (1954).

[97] 388 U.S. 1 (1967); cf. *McLaughlin v. Florida*, 379 U.S. 184 (1964).

laws were one such source. Indeed, the only basis for such laws was the constitutionally forbidden aim of white supremacy.

Antimiscegenation laws had come to bear this interpretation as a consequence of the Court's endorsement of the cultural theory of the rights-denying construction of racism first suggested by Lydia Maria Child in 1833 [98] and importantly elaborated by Ida Wells-Barnett in 1892.[99] Child had examined and condemned both American slavery and racism in light of the argument for toleration: basic human rights of the person were abridged on wholly inadequate sectarian grounds that Child, like other radical abolitionists, expressly analogized to religious persecution. Antimiscegenation laws violated the basic human right of intimate association on such inadequate grounds, thus dehumanizing a whole class of persons as subhuman animals unworthy of the forms of equal respect accorded rights-bearing persons. Ida Wells-Barnett, elaborating the role of the rights-denying sexual dehumanization of African Americans under slavery made clear earlier by Harriet Jacobs,[100] analyzed Southern racism after emancipation as resting on a similar basis, sustained, in part, by antimiscegenation laws. The point of such laws was, Wells showed, not only to condemn all interracial marriages (the focus of Child's analysis) but to deny the legitimacy of all sexual relations (marital and otherwise) between white women and black men; illicit relations between white men and black women were, in contrast, if not legal, socially acceptable. The asymmetry rested on the enforcement at large (through antimiscegenation and related laws and practices, including lynching) of a sectarian sexual and romantic idealized mythology of white women and a corresponding devaluation (indeed, dehumanization) of black women and men as sexually animalistic; illicit sexual relations between white men and black women were consistent with this political epistemology and thus were tolerable; both licit and illicit consensual relations between black men and white women were not tolerable and therefore were ideologically transformed into violent rapes requiring lynching.

---

[98] For citations and commentary, see Richards, *Conscience and the Constitution*, 80–89.

[99] For citations and commentary, see Richards, *Women, Gays, and the Constitution*, 182–90.

[100] For citations and commentary, see Richards, *Women, Gays, and the Constitution*, 117–24.

W. E. B. Du Bois, a lifelong feminist like Frederick Douglass, condemned in related terms the role the idealized image of women (as either virgin or prostitute) played in sustaining not only racism but a sexism that unjustly treated all women:

> The world wants healthy babies and intelligent workers. Today we refuse to allow the combination and force thousands of intelligent workers to go childless at a horrible expenditure of moral force, or we damn them if they break our idiotic conventions. Only at the sacrifice of intelligence and the chance to do their best work can the majority of modern women bear children. This is the damnation of women.
>
> All womanhood is hampered today because the world on which it is emerging is a world that tries to worship both virgins and mothers and in the end despises motherhoood and despoils virgins.
>
> The future woman must have a life work and economic independence. She must have knowledge. She must have the right of motherhood at her discretion. The present mincing horror at free womenhood must pass if we are ever to be rid of the bestiality of free manhood; not by guarding the weak in weakness do we gain strength, but by making weakness free and strong.
>
> The world must choose the free women or the white wraith of the prostitute. Today it wavers between the prostitute and the nun.[101]

American racism, on this analysis, rested on a culturally constructed and sustained racialized sexual mythology of gender (white virgin versus black prostitute); antimiscegenation laws were unconstitutional because of the central role they played unjustly in sustaining this sectarian ideology. Both Harriet Jacobs and Ida Wells-Barnett had analyzed this injustice from the perspective of black women, who had experienced its indignities at first hand.

James Baldwin, one of the greatest American writers of his generation and a black homosexual, brought the same experienced sense of indignity to bear on his later explorations of American sexual racism.[102]

---

[101] See W. E. B. Du Bois, "The Damnation of Women" (1920), in Du Bois, *W. E. B. Du Bois*, 952–53. On the specifically racist use of such an unjust idealization, see ibid., 958: "one thing I shall never forgive, neither in this world nor the world to come: its wanton and continued and persistent insulting of the black womanhood which it sought and seeks to prostitute to its lust."

[102] See, in general, David Leeming, *James Baldwin* (New York: Alfred A. Knopf, 1994).

When he traveled in the South, Baldwin wrote "about my unbelieving shock when I realized that I was being groped by one of the most powerful men in one of the states I visited."[103] He wrote searingly of his indignation from his experience as a black man and what he learned of the way racism fulfilled men's "enormous need to debase other men":[104]

> To be a slave means that one's manhood is engaged in a dubious battle indeed, and this stony fact is not altered by whatever devotion some masters and some slaves may have arrived at in relation to each other. In the case of American slavery, the black man's right to his women, as well as to his children, was simply taken from him and whatever bastards the white man begat on the bodies of black women took their condition from the condition of their mothers: blacks were not the only stallions on the slave-breeding farms! And one of the many results of this loveless, money-making conspiracy was that, in giving the masters every conceivable sexual and commercial license, it also emasculated them of any human responsibility—to their women, to their children, to their wives, to themselves. The results of this blasphemy resound in this country, on every private and public level, until this hour. When the man grabbed my cock, I didn't think of him as a faggot, which, indeed, if having a wife and children, house, cars, and a respectable and powerful standing in that community, mean anything, he wasn't: I watched his eyes, thinking with great sorrow, *The unexamined life is not worth living.*[105]

Baldwin made clear the general role that sexual dehumanization played in American racism as such: the mythological reduction of both black women and men to their sexuality on terms that fundamentally denied their moral personalities and their human rights to respect for conscience, speech, work, and, of course, intimate life, including their right to love on terms of respect (a right, for Baldwin, owed all persons, heterosexual or homosexual, male or female, white or nonwhite).[106]

---

[103] See James Baldwin, *No Name in the Street* (New York: Dell, 1972), 61.

[104] Ibid., 63.

[105] Ibid., 62–63.

[106] For Baldwin's frankest first-person treatment of these issues, see James Baldwin, "Here Be Dragons," in James Baldwin, *The Price of the Ticket: Collected Nonfiction, 1948–1985* (New York: St. Martin's Press, 1985), 677–90; for a much more elliptical, self-hating treatment, see James Baldwin, "The Male Prison," in ibid., 101–5.

African American's rights-based protest against the terms of their unjust subordination led, on grounds of principle, to protests against related forms of structural injustice, as the antisexist arguments of Jacobs, Well-Barnett, and Du Bois and the antihomophobic arguments of Baldwin make quite clear. To challenge the unjust terms of the structural injustice of American racism was, as Du Bois made clear, to demand that one's ethnic and American identity be recognized and acknowledged in a new way, namely, on terms of justice that extended as well to related forms of structural injustice. The moral empowerment of making claims to one's basic human rights in one domain generalizes, on grounds of rights-based principle, to claims calling for the revision of the terms of all identities marred by structural injustice. Such a protest, based on the self-respecting sense of one's humanity as a bearer of human rights, calls for often profound criticism of the cultural forms that have sustained the injustice, including not only political protest but the creation of new cultural forms that make imaginative space for moral and human protest and affirm a self-respecting sense of the creative and critical powers expressive of one's sense of one's human rights.[107] Under the pressure of such criticism, as we have seen, what was supposed to be a fundamentally important physical difference comes reasonably to be regarded as a profoundly unjust construction of difference in service of an indefensible conception of national identity. If there is nothing in the traditional American importance attached to race but culture, then we have ethically responsible choices to make about addressing and rectifying the history and culture that have sustained such choices. The African American struggle is a rights-based narrative of choices made to identify and protest injustice, exposing to the American public mind its ugly nescience and complacency in the face of fundamental injustice rationalized as in the nature of things. Nothing in this dynamic of self-respecting claims to an identity based on justice corresponds to the terms of immutability and salience in which much constitutional theory claims to address this matter. Indeed, it gets it quite perversely wrong, repeating the way of regarding the problem (as a physical fact) that it should protest. The protest is to giv-

---

[107] See, for example, George Hutchinson, *The Harlem Renaissance in Black and White* (Cambridge, Mass.: Harvard University Press, 1995).

ing weight not to immutable and salient facts as such, but to the imposition of a cultural identity of dehumanizing self-contempt that rests,
as we have seen, on structural injustice.

I have suggested that the abridgment of the inalienable right to
conscience should normatively frame our understanding of such injustice, because making self-respecting claims on the basis of this right
addresses the dehumanizing evil both by affirming what the evil
denies and making possible reasonable debate and discourse about the
irrationalist basis on which the evil has been sustained. The perspective
opens up a new way of understanding not only the structural injustice
of racism but the way in which we should interpret that analogy in the
understanding of sexism and homophobia, namely, in terms of the
structural injustice I call moral slavery.

The claim of a rights-based analogy between racism and sexism
was in the similar method of structural injustice inflicted in both cases,
namely, "that others have controlled the power to define one's existence."[108] This structural injustice is marked by two features: first, the
abridgment of basic human rights to a group of persons, and, second,
the unjust rationalization of that abridgment on the inadequate
grounds of dehumanizing stereotypes that reflect a history and culture based on that abridgment. I call this injustice moral slavery (such
a category of persons is so defined to rationalize their servile status
and roles) and believe it can be plausibly argued that its moral condemnation is, properly understood, the abstract normative judgment
of the Thirteenth Amendment of the United States Constitution.[109]
From the perspective of the constitutional condemnation of such
structural injustice, race and gender should be equally suspect as
grounds for state action or inaction, because blacks and women share
a common history of rights-denying moral degradation that continued
with the complicitous support of law long after their formal emancipation and enfranchisement and that powerfully and unjustly persists
today. The guarantee of equal protection in the Fourteenth Amendment was ratified in 1868 but was held inapplicable to women until

---

[108] See William H. Chafe, *Women and Equality: Changing Patterns in American Culture*
(New York: Oxford University Press, 1977), at 77; on the similar methods of repression,
see ibid., at 58–9, 75–6.

[109] See, for extensive defense of this claim, Richards, *Women, Gays, and the Constitution*.

1971[110] and was interpreted until 1954[111] to allow racial segregation. In both cases, the Supreme Court of the United States and the constitutional culture it reflects and shapes acted as powerful agents in the transmission and reinforcement of moral slavery in the domains of gender and race. The betrayal of basic rights expressly guaranteed is functionally often equivalent to the express deprivation of such rights, and may be even less morally excusable or justifiable when this betrayal powerfully reinforces, through the rationalizing power of the paradox of intolerance, the political forces of sexism and racism as forms of moral slavery. Racial apartheid in the United States was an instrument of racial subjugation of blacks, isolating them from their basic rights of fair access on equal terms to public culture on specious racist grounds; as such, it gave powerful political legitimacy to the illegitimate force of racism in American public and private life and thus to a continuing, unjust cultural pattern of moral slavery in the domain of race that persists in various illegitimate forms today.[112] The wholesale failure even to acknowledge the evils of the subjugation of women gave powerful constitutional support to the illegitimate force of sexism in American public and private life and thus to moral slavery in the domain of gender; gender segregation in separate spheres was, as in the case of race, a pivotal institutional mechanism of women's degradation; a still largely unchallenged sexist political epistemology of gender roles, which continues to hold sway in still powerful sectarian religious and moral traditions, undercut the resources of public reason by which these mechanisms might be subjected to criticism and reform. This silencing of the morally independent critical voice of reason rendered unjustly entrenched patterns of gender hierarchy largely unquestioned and unquestionable.

From the perspective of the theory of moral slavery, the constitutional injury of racism and sexism was the unjust cultural burden of contempt placed on identifications important to moral personality. Du Bois made this point in characterizing the struggle of African Americans as two souls in one body, the one an African identity, the other an American, and in describing the struggle to reconstruct both identities on

---

[110] See *Reed v. Reed*, 404 U.S. 71 (1971).

[111] See *Brown v. Board of Education*, 347 U.S. 483 (1954).

[112] See, for example, Massey and Denton, *American Apartheid: Segregation and the Making of the Underclass*.

terms of rights-based justice in the vocabulary of American revolutionary constitutionalism. Betty Friedan, anticipated by Sarah Grimke,[113]
also defined women's struggle on similar grounds as "a problem of
identity,"[114] the struggle to reconstruct American culture on terms of
justice that would reconcile one's identity as a woman and also as a
rights-bearing person and equal citizen. In both cases, the struggle for
constitutional justice would by its nature reconstruct both personal
identity and public (including constitutional) culture; in both cases, the
personal and the political would become inextricably intertwined questions of both personal and moral-constitutional identity.

This perspective clarifies the justice of the remarkable interpretive
development in American public law in the twentieth century that, on
the basis of a radical abolitionist interpretation of the argument for toleration, subjected to increasingly skeptical scrutiny the cultural construction of racism and, later, of sexism.[115] Arguments of toleration and
antisubordination are, on this analysis, not contradictory and, properly
understood, not even in tension. Antisubordination is, on analysis, a
structurally more profound form of cultural intolerance along the two
dimensions of the argument for toleration: identification of certain
basic rights of the moral person and the requirement of a compelling
form of reasonable public justification for the abridgment of these basic
rights. In particular, moral slavery, as I develop that idea, identifies a
structural injustice marked by both its abridgment of basic rights to a
certain class of persons and its unjust enforcement of irrationalist
stereotypical views whose illegitimate force has traditionally degraded
the class of persons from their status as full bearers of human rights.
European anti-Semitism (with its associated ideology of Jews as the
slaves of Christians) is a case study that, in my approach, classically
exemplifies a form of structural injustice along these two dimensions:
it is certainly a species of religious intolerance but, in its European
forms, is a form of unjust subordination, as well. Suspect classification
analysis, on this view, skeptically condemns the expression through
law of the structural injustices that underlie this unjust subordination

---

[113] On this point, see Richards, *Women, Gays, and the Constitution*, at 100.

[114] See Betty Friedan, *The Feminine Mystique* (orig. pub., 1963; repr. ed., London:
Penguin, 1982) at 68.

[115] For further defense of this claim, see, in general, Richards, *Women, Gays, and the
Constitution*.

(reflected in the cultural stereotypes of race and gender that express unjust subordination). Equal protection requires that political power must be reasonably justifiable in terms of equal respect for human rights and the pursuit of public purposes of justice and the common good.[116] Suspect classification analysis enforces this principle by rendering constitutionally suspect grounds for laws that not only lack such public reasons but war against public reason by illegitimately rationalizing, on inadequate grounds, structural injustice. Laws whose irrationalist bases thus war on public reason lack constitutional legitimacy and are, for this reason, subjected to demanding tests of constitutional skepticism. The unconstitutionality of state-sponsored racial segregation and antimiscegenation laws shows the force of this constitutional skepticism in the area of race; the comparable developments in the sphere of gender reflect a comparable skepticism (both in protecting basic rights, including aspects of the right to reproductive autonomy, and in subjecting gender classifications to a constitutional scrutiny increasingly close to that accorded race). All these interpretive developments are systematically clarified and organized by the insights afforded by the theory and practice of rights-dissent of the terms of one's moral slavery.

Finally, the common ground of our concern with racism, sexism, and homophobia is the radical political evil of a political culture, ostensibly committed to toleration on the basis of universal human rights, that unjustly denies a class of persons its inalienable human rights as persons with moral powers on the basis of the structural injustice of moral slavery. Liberal political culture, consistent with respect for this basic right, must extend to all persons the cultural resources that enable them critically to explore, define, express, and revise the identifications central to free moral personality.[117] The constitutional evil, condemned by suspect classification analysis under the Equal Protection Clause of the Fourteenth Amendment, is the systematic deprivation of this basic right to a group of persons, unjustly degraded from their status as persons entitled to respect for the reasonable exercise of their free moral

[116] For the classic statement of equal protection as a form of public reasonableness, see Joseph Tussman and Jacobus tenBroek, "The Equal Protection of the Laws," 37 *Calif. L. Rev.* 341 (1949); cf. Jacobus tenBroek, *Equal under Law.*

[117] For development of this theme, see Will Kymlicka, *Liberalism, Community, and Culture* (Oxford: Clarendon Press, 1989), at 162–78; Tamir, *Liberal Nationalism*, at 13–56.

powers in the identifications central to an ethical life based on mutual respect.[118] To deny such a group, already the subject of a long history and culture of moral slavery, its culture-creating rights is to silence in it the very voice of its moral freedom, rendering unspoken and unspeakable the sentiments, experience, and reason that authenticate the moral personality that a political culture of human rights owes each and every person (including moral powers to know and claim his or her basic rights and to protest injustice on these grounds). Sexual orientation is and should be a fully suspect classification, because homosexuals are today victimized, in the same way African Americans and women are and have been victimized, their claims to basic rights held hostage to irrational political prejudices rooted in this radical political evil, denying them the cultural resources of free moral personality.[119]

Racism, sexism, and homophobia share a common background in moral slavery, which explains both the character and the depth of the political evil they represent, in particular, its imposition of an injustice on the very terms of personal and moral identity, both for the individuals afflicted by such injustice and for the society at large. Both Du Bois and Friedan thus characterized the struggles against racism and sexism, respectively, in such terms, as claims by African Americans and women to forge new identities as blacks and as women but also as claims to alter the roles of race and gender in the constitution of American constitutional identity. By its very rights-based terms, this protest challenged the terms of moral slavery, whose unjust cultural force required abridgment of the basic human rights of conscience and speech; the structural injustice thus under criticism attacked the very making of such criticism, as in, for example, the attempt in antebellum America to silence abolitionist dissent; it was not that the dissent was not conscientious or did not have a perceived basis in justice, but precisely because it was thus conscientious and perceived by many (including slaveowners) as just that it was regarded as so dangerous (inciting slave revolts, for example).[120] Rights-based protests of the cultural terms of homosexuality have a similar character and have excited

---

[118] For further development and defense of this position, see, in general, Richards, *Women, Gays, and the Constitution.*

[119] See, for further development of this position, Richards, *Women, Gays, and the Constitution.*

[120] See, on this point, Richards, *Conscience and the Constitution*, at 59.

a similar repressive response, but one that attacks the very making of such claims as conscientious. Rights-based protests against racism and sexism both challenged and transformed identity, but identity that at least occupied a familiar if embattled cultural space in conscientious public opinion. The structural injustice of homophobia imposes, however, a regime of unspeakability, that is, the denial of any acceptable terms of identity at all. The contemporary reactionary response to rights-based protest of this structural injustice is an attack on the protest itself because of its content, namely, its ethical criticism of the dehumanizing injustice of cultural unspeakability, invisibility, and marginalization.

A politics actuated by such an justice is suspect not only on the same structural grounds as race and gender but also on grounds of the first suspect classification under American public law—religion.[121] Elsewhere, I have argued that many constitutional controversies currently in play correspond to the terms of the analysis proposed. In particular, many of these disputes are best understood as unconstitutionally sectarian attacks on gay and lesbian identity as a conscientious conviction entitled to equal respect. Three cases correspond closely to the terms of this analysis: antilesbian/gay initiatives, the exclusion of homosexuals from the military, and the exclusion of gays and lesbians from the right to marriage.[122] In all these cases, the constitutionally crucial point is that assertions of gay and lesbian identity, including claims to justice made as a gay or lesbian person entitled to the basic human rights accorded all other persons, are specifically targeted for focused disadvantage without any adequate secular basis.

THE RATIONALIZATION OF STRUCTURAL INJUSTICE

The interpretive proposals I have discussed define a normative scope and its associated limits.[123] Not all basic constitutional values and rights can be understood in terms of these proposals, but some can be. In particular, my account focuses attention on the unjust burdens on

---

[121] See, on this point, Richards, *Foundations of American Constitutionalism*, at 260, 280.

[122] See, on this point, Richards, *Women, Gays, and the Constitution*, chs. 7–8.

[123] For further discussion of the limits of these proposals, see Richards, *Women, Gays, and the Constitution*, 371–3.

identity imposed by a background structural injustice of history and culture with two features. First, a class of persons has been denied basic human rights of conscience, speech, intimate life, and work; second, this denial is rationalized in terms of dehumanizing stereotypes that, in a vicious circle of self-entrenching injustice, limit both discussion and speakers to the presumptively settled terms of the denial of basic rights. The model for both the understanding of basic rights and the burden of justification required for their just abridgment arises, I have suggested, from the argument for toleration (so clearly central to our understanding of both religious liberty and free speech); however, the understanding of the structural injustice I describe, while dependent on the argument for toleration, elaborates that argument to condemn an independent constitutional evil, one not limited to unjust abridgment of one right but involving abridgment of all rights on grounds that remove a class of persons from the category of bearers of human rights. Some cases of religious intolerance are rooted in this structural injustice as well (in my view, anti-Semitism and homophobia), but that fact requires special explanation in terms of a background history and culture of particularly focused and aggressively dehumanizing intolerance.

Both the burdens on identity and the background structural injustice inform a principled understanding of the constitutional condemnation of racism, sexism, extreme religious intolerance, and homophobia. In all these cases, the background structural injustice imposes unjust terms of identity on a subjugated group. Though the structural injustice may radiate out to encompass as well material and related disadvantages, merely remedying the latter disadvantages, without doing more, does not address the roots of the problem, which is a distinctive injury to moral personality.

The idea of identity, in the sense relevant to our concerns here, is not the philosophical problem of identity (in terms of the criteria of mind and / or body for identifying a person as the same over time and space) or the broadly sociological question of our multiple roles and statuses, many of which are uncontroversially socially ascribed. It would, thus, trivialize the evil of the burdens on identity to condemn any and all social ascriptions on identity. A rights-based struggle against structural injustice does not renegotiate all the terms of personal identity; one's identity as a person is never either infinitely malleable or even desirably regarded as entirely open to choice. Cultural assumptions must always be taken as given if any reasonable criticisms and reforms, including those based on rights-based protest of structural injustice, are to go forward sensibly.

But, structural injustice, marked by the two features earlier described, inflicts an injury on aspects of our identity and identifications that are organizing features of our understanding of ourselves as persons and moral agents; this is the narrower sense of contestable and contested identity that is my concern here. The important feature that structures the character of the injustice is its abridgment of basic human rights in general and of the inalienable rights to conscience and intimate life in particular, that is, the denial of the very moral powers in terms of which we come to understand and protest basic injustice. Abridgment of conscience and intimate life play the role they do in inflicting this evil because they are so intimately tied up with the sense of ourselves as persons with the moral powers of rational choice and reasonable deliberation over the convictions and attachments that give shape and meaning to our personal and ethical lives, as lives lived responsibly from conviction. The dehumanization of people on grounds of race or gender or religion or sexual orientation imposes objectifying stereotypes of identity (in terms of race or gender or gendered sexuality) that deny these moral powers, indeed, that are rationalized in terms of this denial. In consequence, these stereotypes take on significance in our lives in terms dictated by the underlying injustice, reducing not only life chances but self-conceptions to their terms.

The depth of this genre of injustice is seen in the double consciousness that its most probing critics (like Du Bois and Friedan, anticipated by Sarah Grimke)[124] identified as among its worst consequences. The imposition of unjust stereotypes of race or gender thus rationalized the abridgment of conscience, imposing on the very terms of blacks' and women's sense of themselves as African Americans or women a devalued self-image of subhumanity. Such a lack of free conscience rendered protesting thoughts unthinkable, thereby entrenching such stereotypes in the consciousness of oppressed and oppressor alike. Blacks' and women's awakening sense of injustice was thus understandably articulated in the terms of double consciousness, the inward sense of oneself both in terms of the dominant stereotype and in yet undefined

---

[124] On this point, see Richards, *Women, Gays, and the Constitution*, at 100.

terms of oneself made possible by challenge to the uncritical force the stereotype had enjoyed.

We need a deeper critical understanding of the common grounds used to rationalize such dehumanization if we are to confront the force that it has enjoyed and continues to enjoy over public and private life. Two such important grounds are patterns of dehumanizing sexual stereotyping and the distortion of the public/private distinction. It is a virtue of the study of gay rights that it advances our understanding of the role played by both grounds in the support of the structural injustice that is our concern here. Study of the case for gay rights confronts and criticizes the role that stereotypical images of sexuality and gender play not only in the dehumanization of homosexuals but in the rationalization as well of the structural injustice that underlies racism, sexism, and anti-Semitism. The issue pervades all the forms of structural injustice examined in often interlinking ways.

American racism was importantly constructed in terms of dehumanized images of black sexuality expressed, under slavery, by laws that abridged blacks' rights of marriage and custody of children, reducing black slaves to the terms of marketable cattle (reproduction being understood and defined in terms that advanced their market utility for the slaveowner). After slavery, laws against miscegenation were enforced to police the color line between black men and white women but not that between white men and black women, thus imposing, often through lynchings, a racialized conception of gender (white women on their idealized pedestal, black women as sexually available prostitutes) that rationalized the dehumanization of African American men (as sexual predators) and women (as prostitutes).[125]

The same racialized conception of gender supported American sexism as well, a point cogently noted by Sojourner Truth in her famous speech pointing out that the alleged gender differences that supported unjust treatment of (white) women appealed to an idealizing pedestal of delicacy that was belied by the experience of black women.[126] American feminism would address this problem only when, in the spirit of the abolitionist feminism of Sojourner Truth and others, it critically examined the unjust role that uncritical conceptions of gen-

---

[125] See, for full discussion of these points, Richards, *Women, Gays, and the Constitution*, in particular, at 183, 224, 229, 244, 293, 423, 447.

[126] For excerpts, see Richards, *Women, Gays, and the Constitution*, at 116–7.

der roles (including their racialized character) had been permitted to enjoy in determining the terms of public and private life. Importantly, this realization was crystallized for many American feminists by their own roles in forging stronger antiracist principles as participants in the civil rights movement.[127] Such interracial cooperation was interpreted by the parents of these white women as a degradation of their identities as white women (one such father angrily accused his daughter "of being a whore and chased her out of the house in a drunken rage, shouting that she was disowned").[128]

Questioning images of gender and sexuality in this way naturally led as well to a comparable critical understanding of the unjust enforcement through law of gendered conceptions of sexuality that had abridged basic human rights of thought, speech, intimate life, and work. Such abridgments had been traditionally defended in terms of the idealizing pedestal of women's superior character and roles. But, in the wake of serious criticism of the racist character of the pedestal, criticism of its sexist character shortly followed. The pedestal was, from this perspective, a cage,[129] dehumanizing women in terms of stereotypical conceptions of their roles solely in terms of the sexual and reproductive interests of men. Second-wave American feminism importantly stated and elaborated the consequences of this criticism in terms of demands for equal respect for the basic human rights of women to conscience, speech, intimate life, and work, whose abridgment was not supported by compelling secular purposes.[130]

Extreme forms of religious intolerance like anti-Semitism were rationalized in terms of images of sexuality and gender drawn from the roles of such stereotypes in both racist and sexist discourse. Religious intolerance was thus rationalized in racist terms of describing the designated group's alleged propensities to be sexual predators or prostitutes, and in sexist terms that feminized Jews in the same terms as homosexuals (as women, and fallen women at that).[131]

[127] See, on this point, Richards, *Women, Gays, and the Constitution*, at 228.
[128] Sarah Evans, *Personal Politics: The Roots of Women's Liberation in the Civil Rights Movement and the New Left* (New York: Vintage Books, 1979), at 44.
[129] See, on this point, Richards, *Women, Gays, and the Constitution*, at 257, 462.
[130] For full discussion of these developments, see Richards, *Women, Gays, and the Constitution*.
[131] See Richards, *Women, Gays, and the Constitution*, 293, 333–4, 461.

Introduction of the case for gay rights into a serious study of the forms of structural injustice compels attention to the pervasive force of dehumanizing images of gender and sexuality in the rationalization of such injustice. The powerful populist resistance to this relatively new human rights struggle crucially takes the stereotypical form of a dehumanizing obsession with homosexuality solely in terms of a rather bleakly impersonal interpretation of same-gender sex acts in general, or, as Leo Bersani has observed,[132] some such same-gender sex acts in particular (in particular, sexual penetration of a man), an interpretation that deracinates these sex acts from the life of a person who is recognizably human or humane. The background of this unjust sexualization was the dominant stereotype of the homosexual as a fallen woman, as a prostitute; the terms of such stereotyping are, of course, unjust to sex workers,[133] but they are unjust to homosexuals, as well. In the case of homosexuals, this objectification of sex acts crucially isolates them from any of the familiar narratives of mutual love and tender concern through which we normally frame our understanding of the role and place of sex acts in a human life, as if homosexuality *could not* be as much (or as little) about sexuality as heterosexuality. Rather, the culture limits the discussion of homosexuality, in contrast to heterosexuality, to one and only one genre—a clinical focus on sex acts historically associated with the trade of sex workers, namely, pornography.[134]

Another feature of the various forms of structural injustice is usefully clarified by the case for gay rights. A structural injustice like racism and sexism is an affront to human rights, in both the public and the private spheres, that is often rationalized in terms of protecting the values of intimate personal life (one's slave or one's wife as intimately oneself).[135] The

---

[132] See Leo Bersani, "Is the Rectus as a Grave?" in Douglas Crimp, *Cultural Analysis/Cultural Activism* (Cambridge: MIT Press, 1988), 211 2, 222.

[133] See David A. J. Richards, "Commercial Sex and the Rights of the Person: A Moral Argument for the Decriminalization of Prostitution," 127 *U. Penn. L. Rev.* 1195 (1979); on the scapegoating of prostitutes, see Richards, *Women, Gays, and the Constitution*, 164, 166–7. 169–71. 178. 296. 310. 321–2; on gender stereotyping of prostitutes, see ibid., 175–6, 185, 295–6.

[134] On these historical and related issues, see David A. J. Richards, "Free Speech and Obscenity Law: Toward a Moral Theory of the First Amendment," 123 *U. Penn. L. Rev.* 45 (1974).

[135] For fuller discussion, see Richards, *Women, Gays, and the Constitution*, 253, 273–74, 347–8, 367–8.

sphere of women was thus defined as fixed and limited to private life, and the sphere of African Americans segregated to an appropriately servile sphere that did not extend to public rights and responsibilities. There is an intimacy to the kinds of despotic control thus rationalized, for the control was often over intimate services in the home, including sexual availability. This structural injustice was constructed in terms of a distorted interpretation of the public/private distinction, and its remedy required a recasting of this distinction. For example, issues previously regarded as private (e.g., spouse and child abuse) became matters of legitimate public concern.[136]

The structural injustice of homophobia raises the same general issue, but at another, perhaps deeper level that advances our understanding of the political dynamics that support structural injustice in general. Homophobia does not limit homosexuality to a private sphere (as with gender) or to a servile sphere (race); it offers no legitimate sphere of activity at all, a sphere defined by its unspeakability. This structural injustice inflicts a deeper injury to moral personality than even injustices related to race and gender, in the sense that it grants no legitimate cultural space at all to the thoughts, feelings, and actions that express spontaneous erotic feelings and attachments deeply rooted in one's sense of self as a person, let alone to the integration of that sense of self into the fabric of convictions about enduring personal and ethical value in living.

THE SOUTHERN ITALIAN EMIGRATION AND AMERICAN RACISM, 1890–1920

We have already discussed at some length the Italian background of the massive Southern Italian emigration of 1890–1920, in particular, identifying the moral insult of the irrationalist racist degradation of Southern Italians as one among the multitude of motives that led the people of the South to leave Italy for the United States, a racism expressed in Corra-

---

[136] See, for example, *People v. Liberta*, 64 N.Y.2d 152, 474 N.E.2d 567 (N.Y. Ct. App. 1984) (rape in marriage no longer exempt from criminal liability). See, for an important exploration of the normative considerations that motivate the growing legal concern with violence in private life, Jane Maslow Cohen, "Regimes of Private Tyranny: What Do They Mean to Morality and for the Criminal Law?" 57 *U. Pitt. L. Rev.* 757 (1996).

dini's statement (in justifying Italian imperialism in Africa) that "the difference between North and South is the difference between Europe and Africa."[137] We must now complement our earlier analysis with a discussion of the American experience of this first generation of Southern Italian immigrants, who faced in the United States prejudice comparable to that experienced in Italy. The distinctive form of Italian American multicultural identity was initially forged under such unjust circumstances, which accordingly must be closely examined.

The terms of American racism had, as we have seen, been largely developed as a rationalization of the race-based enslavement of African Americans. American racism, however, not only did not end with the abolition of slavery; it worsened. The background of this development lay in the roots of the Equal Protection Clause of the Fourteenth Amendment in antebellum abolitionist argument and the degree to which such argument set the moral ambitions for the nation in the wake of the Civil War that it was unprepared to meet. The consequence, as we shall see, was a structurally flawed liberal nationalism not dissimilar from the sort the people of the South had experienced in Italy. We must now examine in greater depth how and why this reactionary political racism developed as background for our understanding of how it came to be targeted at the new immigrants to the United States in the late nineteenth and early twentieth centuries. On this basis, our inquiry can clarify why the people of the South not unreasonably found in the American form of racism a better balance of justice over injustice and how their accommodation to its injustice shaped their sense of themselves as Italian Americans.

The normative theory of equal protection arose in the historically contextualized criticism by the abolitionists of slavery and its underlying political pathology, racism. This criticism focused on white's denial of blacks' basic capacity even to be eligible to be bearers of the rights that were central to the moral identity of the culture: conscience, free speech, intimate personal and family life, free labor, and the like. These rights are, in their nature, culture-creating rights, forms of moral creativity through which people authenticate themselves, the larger meaning of their lives, and the culture of public reason required for the exercise of their moral powers as persons. The systematic denial of

---

[137] Quoted in Foerster, *The Italian Emigration of Our Times*, at 498. See, for illuminating commentary, Gambino, *Blood of My Blood*, 65–8.

these rights to any group by the dominant culture condemns that group to cultural death and deformed marginality, a form of denationalization.[138] The condition of the national identity of dominant white America was the construction of a negative identity (what an American is not) by means of a culturally defined image of a race-defined people accorded lower moral status on grounds that various rights were not to be theirs because of their underlying incapacity. Both Roger Taney and Alexander Stephens thus had argued that white supremacy was constitutive of American constitutional identity.[139]

Under American slavery, the image of blacks as subhuman was constructed on the basis of their alleged incapacities that disqualified them from basic rights. These included putative incapacities of moral reflection and deliberation (no right to conscience), lack of reasoning skills such as literacy (no right of free speech), incapacity for responsible sexual intimacy and moral education of young (lack of privacy rights of sexual autonomy and family integrity), and lack of rational powers for many forms of work that call for the independent exercise of rational powers (no right to free labor).[140] The underlying image of incapacity, constructed on the basis of the abridgment of these rights, was then alleged to be the reasonable basis (natural race differences) for American slavery. Only in this way could some Americans square their belief in human rights with the forms of total control that American slavery—in contrast to that in Latin America—peculiarly involved (including abridgments of legal rights to religious liberty, free speech, and family life and restrictions on man-

---

[138] For a related mode of analysis, see Orlando Patterson, *Slavery and Social Death* (Cambridge, Mass.: Harvard University Press, 1982).

[139] See, for pertinent citations, Richards, *Conscience and the Constitution*, 25, 113.

[140] On these features of American slavery, see Stanley M. Elkins, *Slavery: A Problem in American Institutional and Intellectual Life*, 3d ed. (Chicago: University of Chicago Press, 1976); Kenneth M. Stampp, *The Peculiar Institution: Slavery in the Ante-Bellum South* (New York: Vintage Books, 1956); Eugene D. Genovese, *Roll, Jordan, Roll: The World the Slaves Made* (New York: Vintage Books, 1974); Eugene D. Genovese, *The World the Slaveholders Made: Two Essays in Interpretation* (Middletown, Conn.: Wesleyan University Press, 1988); John W. Blassingame, *The Slave Community: Plantation Life in the Antebellum South*, rev. ed. (New York: Oxford University Press, 1979); Herbert G. Gutman, *The Black Family in Slavery and Freedom 1750–1925* (New York: Vintage Books, 1976). For a leading proslavery justification of many of these features of the institution, see Thomas R. R. Cobb, *An Inquiry into the Law of Negro Slavery in the United States of America* (orig. pub., 1858; New York: Negro Universities Press, 1968).

umission).[141] A group thus supposedly by nature not entitled to the basic rights constitutive of American nationality could not, by definition, be part of American nationality.

The abolitionist criticism of American racism observed that the same definition of national identity that had rationalized slavery in the South also supported racial discrimination against free blacks both in the South and in the North.[142] In the North the alleged inferiority of blacks could not perhaps justify slavery, but it could justify deprivations of rights aimed at excluding blacks from the political community. For example, states forbade blacks from entering[143] and passed various discriminatory measures regarding voting rights, access to education, and the like that encouraged free blacks to leave.[144] Abolitionists like Garrison and Maria Child clearly saw that the natural expression of this view was the advocacy, from Jefferson to Lincoln, of abolition on terms of colonization abroad, confirming the basic racist image of the terms of

[141] See works cited in previous note, especially Elkins, *Slavery*; see also Herbert S. Klein, *Slavery in the Americas: A Comparative Study of Virginia and Cuba* (Chicago: Elephant Paperbacks, 1989). It remains controversial, however, whether on balance slaves were treated worse in British than Latin America. See, for example, David Brion Davis, "The Continuing Contradiction of Slavery: A Comparison of British America and Latin America", in Ann J. Lane, ed., *The Debate Over Slavery: Stanley Elkins and His Critics* (Urbana: University of Illinois Press, 1971), at pp. 111–36; Herbert S. Klein, "Anglicanism, Catholicism, and the Negro Slave", *id.*, at pp. 137–90. For an important general study, see Carl N. Degler, *Neither Black Nor White: Slavery and Race Relations in Brazil and the United States* (Madison: University of Wisconsin Press, 1986).

[142] On the South, see Ira Berlin, *Slaves without Masters: The Free Negro in the Antebellum South* (New York: Pantheon Books, 1974). On the North, see Leon F. Litwack, *North of Slavery: The Negro in the Free States 1790–1860* (Chicago: University of Chicago Press, 1961); V. Jacque Voegeli, *Free but Not Equal: The Midwest and the Negro during the Civil War* (Chicago: University of Chicago Press, 1967). But, for a balanced account of the improving treatment of blacks in the North prior to the Civil War, see Paul Finkelman, "Prelude to the Fourteenth Amendment: Black Legal Rights in the Antebellum North," 17 *Rutgers L.J.* 415 (1986).

[143] Three states—Illinois, Indiana, and Oregon—incorporated such anti-immigration provisions in their state constitutions, which were overwhelmingly approved by white state electorates. See Litwack, *North of Slavery*, at 70–74.

[144] By 1840, some 93 percent of Northern free blacks lived in states that either completely or as a practical matter excluded them from the right to vote. See Litwack, *North of Slavery*, at 74–5. Although some white schools admitted blacks, especially before 1820, most Northern states either excluded them from schools altogether or established racially separate and unequal schools for them. See ibid., at 114.

American national identity. The theorists of radical antislavery drew the remedial inference that blacks must be fully included in the terms of a national citizenship that extended equal protection of basic rights to all.

Abolitionist analysis of the evil of racism focused on the corruption of public reason that its defense required. Its defense, by the nature of the evil to be defended, required the denial of the basic rights of whites as well as blacks, for example, to free debate about the evils of slavery and racism. The abolitionists—the only consistent advocates of the argument for toleration in antebellum America—were for this reason path-breaking moral and constitutional dissenters of conscience from and critics of the stifling tyranny of the majority of Jacksonian America. The ethical impulse that motivated abolitionists was the corruption of conscience that slavery and racism, like religious persecution, had worked on the spiritual lives of Americans. To sustain these practices and institutions, proslavery theorists had, consistent with the paradox of intolerance, repressed criticism precisely when it was most needed. Instead, they fostered decadent standards of argument in the use of history, constitutional analysis, Bible interpretation, and even in science, whose effect had been to corrupt the public sense of what ethics was. For abolitionists like Garrison and Child, such attitudes could, consistent with respect for human rights, no more legitimately be allowed political expression than could religious intolerance, with its analogous corruption of public reason.[145]

The original abolitionist aim was an ethical transformation of these public attitudes from their decadent to a more critically informed sense of the requirements of ethical impartiality; the abolitionists sought to accomplish this goal by making public arguments that would deliberately persuade and enlighten the public conscience. In response to the brick wall of repression that met them, they retained as their overriding aim ethical persuasion. The abolitionists' commitment to nonviolence reflects this approach; only very late in the antebellum period did rational despair lead some of them (Theodore Parker and Henry David Thoreau,[146] for example) to support the armed revolution of John Brown. Most aboli-

---

[145] See, for further discussion and citations, Richards, *Conscience and the Constitution,* 80–89.

[146] On Parker, see, in general, Henry Steele Commager, *Theodore Parker* (Boston: Little, Brown, 1936); on Thoreau, see, for a good general treatment on this point, Daniel Walker Howe, "Henry David Thoreau on the Duty of Civil Disobedience," an Inaugural Lecture delivered before the University of Oxford on 21 May 1990 (Oxford: Clarendon Press, 1990).

tionists turned to politics as the best way effectively to make their ethical case, to forge through democratic politics a new moral consensus around sound ethical principles.

The task of the Reconstruction Amendments was not only, however, to set the terms of a desirable ethical transformation of American public opinion. It was also to undertake a rather more difficult task in which its abolitionist forebears had not taken much interest and that some expressly disavowed, namely, to enforce constitutional standards of respect for rights against those who would flout them.[147] The aims of ethical transformation of public attitudes and constitutional enforcement of respect for rights were not necessarily coincident, at least in the short term. Indeed, one abolitionist, Maria Child, had prophetically worried, twenty-three years before the Thirteenth Amendment was ratified, about their possible antagonism:

> Great political changes may be forced by the pressure of external circumstances, without a corresponding change in the moral sentiment of a nation; but in all such cases, the change is worse than useless; the evil reappears, and usually in a more aggravated form.[148]

Those committed to the abolitionist ethical vision would have universally preferred that Americans, in both the North and the South, had been persuaded to assent to the vision that condemned both slavery and racism. But, the Reconstruction Amendments were passed at a time when there was a moral chasm in public opinion between the moral revolution the Civil War had worked in the North and a counterrevolution in the South of which the freedmen were the unjust victims.[149]

[147] The leading criticism of the abolitionists, for not properly preparing the ground for what the Reconstruction Amendments required, is that of Stanley Elkins; see Stanley Elkins, *Slavery*, at 140–206; for response to his criticism, see Aileen S. Kraditor, "A Note on Elkins and the Abolitionists," in Lane, *The Debate Over Slavery*, at pp. 87–101. For a good collection of essays that explore the issue, see Martin Duberman, ed., *The Antislavery Vanguard: New Essays on the Abolitionists* (Princeton: Princeton University Press, 1965).

[148] Cited in Kraditor, "A Note on Elkins and the Abolitionists", in Lane, *The Debate over Slavery*, at 100–1.

[149] See, in general, Leon F. Litwack, *Been in the Storm So Long: The Aftermath of Slavery* (New York: Vintage Books, 1979). See also C. Vann Woodward, *The Strange Career of Jim Crow*, 3d rev. ed. (New York: Oxford University Press, 1974); *Origins of the New South 1877–1913* (Baton Rouge: Louisiana State University Press, 1971); *The Future of the Past* (New York: Oxford University Press, 1989).

The moral revolution in American public opinion in the North worked by the Civil War rendered the abolitionist arguments, regarded as so marginally radical in the antebellum period, the basic conservative principles of American revolutionary constitutionalism embodied in the Reconstruction Amendments.[150] The stark contrast between blacks' contribution to the Civil War and the South's intransigent attempts to return freedmen to the functional equivalent of slavery enabled the congressional leadership of the Republican Party to forge a public opinion in the nation—despite a resisting president— that supported the central principles of the Reconstruction Amendments.[151] Black Americans were included in the American political community on terms of principles that guaranteed them equal protection of their basic human rights. The abolitionist vision of equal rights was realized.

Of course, it was not realized. A president of the exquisite political skill and moral principle and capacity for moral growth of a Lincoln might have stood some chance of bringing the nation (North and South) into some enduring consensus of principles about respect for the constitutional rights of black Americans.[152] But Andrew Johnson lacked both skill and principle, so polarizing the nation by his tragically misguided encouragement of Southern racist resistance to the Fourteenth Amendment that "the South was united [on racism] as it had not been on slavery."[153] The constitutional abolition of slavery and guarantee of equal rights of citizenship to black Americans would, however, have been dead letters without some effective constitutional protection of the rights of black Americans against the populist racism that now flourished in the defeated South as the terms of Southern sectional identity. The Reconstruction Amendments stood for an ethical vision of *national* identity based on respect for the human rights of all

---

[150] See, in general, James M. McPherson, *The Struggle for Equality: Abolitionists and the Negro in the Civil War and Reconstruction* (Princeton: Princeton University Press, 1964).

[151] For good general studies, see Eric L. McKitrick, *Andrew Johnson and Reconstruction* (New York: Oxford University Press, 1960); Michael Les Benedict, *A Compromise of Principle: Congressional Republicans and Reconstruction 1863–1869* (New York: W. W. Norton, 1974).

[152] See LaWanda Cox, *Lincoln and Black Freedom* (Urbana: University of Illinois Press, 1985).

[153] C. Vann Woodward, "Emancipations and Reconstructions: A Comparative Study," in Woodward, *The Future of the Past* (New York: Oxford University Press, 1989).

persons (liberal nationalism). Southern attempts to perpetuate racist subjugation through law (the Black Codes) were inconsistent with respect for human rights for all people and could not legitimately be allowed expression through public law.

The Equal Protection Clause of the Fourteenth Amendment afforded a nationally applicable constitutional guarantee and enforcement power designed to protect American citizens against subjugation based on race. The task now was the novel one, not really anticipated by the abolitionists, of how such guarantees were to be understood, interpreted, and implemented against those who would unconstitutionally abridge the rights of Americans to equal standing before the law. If the abolitionists (with their historical mission of persuasion by appeal to conscience) were unprepared for the task before them, the nation at large had even less understanding of what was required reasonably to achieve its publicly avowed constitutional aims to rectify the American heritage of both slavery in the South and the cultural construction of racism nationwide.

The interpretive task required a theory of what counts or should count as racist subjugation, couched in the terms of moral community, namely, what kinds of abridgments of equal standing have been pivotally responsible for the unjustifiable cultural construction of the subhuman status of a class of persons not eligible to be regarded as bearers of human rights. The transformation of religious persecution into racial degradation should be the key to this analysis.

The racist subjugation of blacks took root in America under the circumstances of the American institution of slavery combined with the denial that blacks, as "heathens," were within the ambit of the argument for toleration.[154] Religious persecution here took the form of enforcement at large of a politically entrenched view of religious truth that condemned "heathen" forms of cultural life as not reasonably entitled to respect. In effect, a political orthodoxy (concerned to maintain slavery as an institution) both imposed on the "heathens" sectarian standards of what counted as reasonable thought and inquiry and

---

[154] See, for example, Winthrop D. Jordan, *White over Black: American Attitudes toward the Negro, 1550–1812* (New York: W. W. Norton, 1977), 91–98; Edmund S. Morgan, *American Slavery American Freedom: The Ordeal of Colonial Virginia* (New York: W. W. Norton, 1975), at 77; David Brion Davis, *The Problem of Slavery in Western Culture* (Ithaca: Cornell University Press, 1967), at 170, 195, 207–8, 214, 246–7, 281, 473.

degraded them from the status of persons capable of exercising moral powers reasonably.

Religious persecution became racist subjugation when the sectarian enforcement of the political orthodoxy unreasonably interpreted the "heathens" not merely as willfully blind to religious truth (as Augustine supposed the Donatists to be),[155] but as incapable of the moral powers that entitle one to be regarded as a bearer of rights at all. The central mechanism of the cultural construction of racism was the radical isolation (through the institution of slavery and practices of racial discrimination) of a race-defined people from the culture-creating rights extended to all others. Such unjust exclusion from these rights (to conscience, free speech, education, family life, and labor) was the unreasonable basis for condemning their culture and, ultimately, them as irrationally subhuman.

The normative theory of equal protection, when contextualized to this history, interpretively explains racist degradation as a constitutional evil, an insult to the status owed persons in a political community founded on equal human rights. The argument for toleration has played a central role in the analysis of this evil because the evil arose as a form of intolerance and was identified and attacked as an evil in such terms by its most acute critics. For the same reason sectarian conviction could not be the measure of religious liberty, racist subjugation could not be the measure of the community of human rights. In both cases, attitudes inconsistent with respect for human rights must be denied expression through public law, and constitutional guarantees, rooted in respect for rights, must debar the legitimacy of laws and policies rooted in such attitudes.

The principles of the Reconstruction Amendments could probably have been effectively realized only by a continuing national commitment to the ongoing federal enforcement of constitutional rights in the South; such federal programs would have included land distribution and integrated education for the freedmen (of the sort suggested by Thaddeus Stevens in the House[156] and Charles Sumner in the Senate)[157] and active and ongoing federal protection of black voting rights.

[155] See Richards, *Toleration and the Constitution*, at 86–8.

[156] On Stevens's abortive proposals for confiscation and distribution of Southern plantations to the freedman, see Eric Foner, *Reconstruction: America's Unfinished Revolution 1863–1877* (New York: Harper & Row, 1988), at 222, 235–6, 237, 245–6, 308–9, 310.

[157] On Sumner's proposals for federally sponsored land distribution and integrated education for the freedmen, see Foner, *Reconstruction*, at 236, 308.

Mainstream antebellum abolitionists, aside from radicals like Stevens and Sumner, were unprepared for the task that reconstruction of the South would pose,[158] and the rest of the nation was even less prepared. The government's failure to accord the needed protection exposed the freedmen to the hostile environment of the South, now committed with redoubled fury to the cultural construction of racism as the irrationalist symbol of Southern sectional unity in defeat. Southern racism now evolved into a politically aggressive racism that the victory of the Union had, if anything, worsened. But even the inadequate federal congressional and executive commitment to black rights that existed (protecting voting rights and prosecuting the Ku Klux Klan) effectively ceased in 1877.[159]

The judiciary, for its part, did little better. It effectively aborted some of the central principles of the Reconstruction Amendments (notably, in its narrow and quite mistaken construction of the Privileges and Immunities Clause of the Fourteenth Amendment[160] and of state action under the Equal Protection Clause of the same amendment),[161] and it misinterpreted the guarantee of equal protection itself as applied to state-sponsored racial segregation. The theory of illegitimate racist degradation, central to the understanding of equal protection, must be interpreted and applied in light of the circumstances relevant to its terms of reasonable justification of state power. The pivotal interpretive issue should be whether some law or policy by act or omission gives expression to an unreasonable exclusion of black Americans from one of the culture-creating rights central to the American public constitutional culture of equal rights.

One such issue should surely be state-sponsored racial segregation, which perpetuates and reinforces the image of black Americans as outcasts from the common culture of the larger society—a point Charles Sumner (pointing to the analogy of European anti-Semitism)

---

[158] The key to much abolitionist thought during this period was the guarantee of voting rights to the freedmen (eventually realized through the Fifteenth Amendment), which would, it was hoped, accord them sufficient political power to defend themselves without the need for more extensive federal intervention in the South to protect them. See, in general, McPherson, *The Struggle for Equality*; Benedict, *A Compromise of Principle*.

[159] See C. Vann Woodward, *Reunion and Reaction: The Compromise of 1877 and the End of Reconstruction* (New York: Oxford University Press, 1966).

[160] See *Slaughter-House Cases*, 16 Wall. 36 (1873).

[161] See *Civil Rights Cases*, 109 U.S. 3 (1883).

forcefully made.[162] Illegitimate racist degradation should be understood against the background of the cultural intolerance fundamental
to the social construction of American racism, in particular, the historical exclusion of the disfavored group from any of the rights of conscience, free speech, family life, and work that have been accorded
other persons and the cultural groups with whom those in power identified. The task of equal protection, construed against that background,
must be to refuse public recognition and enforcement of the attitudes
of unjust exclusion on the basis of which racist degradation was rationalized. But state-sponsored racial segregation was precisely so motivated, expressing and legitimating a social construction of isolation
and exclusion of the disfavored race-defined people that perpetuated
the underlying evil of moral subjugation.[163]

The mission of the Reconstruction Amendments was and should
have been the inclusion, on terms of equal rights, of black Americans
into the American political community now understood to be a moral
community of free and equal citizens, rather than two nations
divided by a culturally constructed chasm of intolerance and subjugation supported by law.[164] In *Plessy v. Ferguson*,[165] the Supreme
Court of the United States held state-sponsored racial discrimination
to be consistent with the Equal Protection Clause of the Fourteenth
Amendment, one of the more egregious examples of grave interpretive mistake in the Court's checkered history. The Supreme Court in

---

[162] See Charles Sumner, "Equality before the Law," in Charles Sumner, *His Complete
Works*, vol. 3 (New York: Negro Universities Press, 1969), at pp. 51–100; for the analogy
to anti-Semitism, see his discussion of the construction of anti-Semitism on the basis of
compulsory segregation in ghettoes, at 88; see also Charles Sumner, "The Question of
Caste," in ibid, vol. 17 (New York: Negro Universities Press, 1969), at 133–183; on anti-
Semitism, see 158. For commentary on Sumner's attacks on racial segregation through-
out his career, see David Donald, *Charles Sumner and the Coming of the Civil War* (New
York: Alfred A. Knopf, 1960), at 180–1; David Donald, *Charles Sumner and the Rights of
Man* (New York: Alfred A. Knopf, 1970), at 152, 246–7, 298, 422.

[163] See, in general, Woodward, *The Strange Career of Jim Crow*; for an interesting com-
parison of the comparable development of state-sponsored segregation in the United
States and South Africa, see George M. Fredrickson, *White Supremacy: A Comparative
Study in American and South African History* (Oxford: Oxford University Press, 1981).

[164] On the continuing power of this cultural construction today, see Andrew
Hacker, *Two Nations: Black and White, Separate, Hostile, Unequal* (New York: Charles Scribner's Sons, 1992).

[165] See *Plessy v. Ferguson*, 163 U.S. 537 (1896).

this opinion itself powerfully advanced the cultural construction of American racism.

The interpretive issue in *Plessy* was whether there was a reasonable basis for the racial distinction that the state law used. The Court's decision can be plausibly explained, as Charles Lofgren has recently shown,[166] against the background of the dominant racist social science of the late nineteenth century. The American ethnologists had already usefully offered such science to support antebellum proslavery thought.[167] The later development of this alleged science of natural race differences measured moral capacity through alleged physical differences (physically measured by brain capacity or cephalic indices).[168] These measures afforded a putatively scientific basis for making the allegedly reasonable judgment that the separation of races was justified. Segregation in transportation (the issue in *Plessy*) might thus discourage forms of social intercourse that would result in degenerative forms of miscegenation; segregation in education would reflect race-linked differences in capacity best dealt with in separate schools, as well as usefully discourage social intercourse, and so on.

The abolitionists had offered plausible objections to the scientific status of American ethnology,[169] and similar objections were available at the time *Plessy* was decided in 1896. For example, Boas had already published his early paper debunking the weight to be accorded race in the social sciences.[170] It is striking that the putative reasonable basis for *Plessy* was not, in fact, critically stated or discussed in the opinion but rather conclusorily assumed. Even in the circumstances of the state of the human sciences at the time of *Plessy*, the interpretive argument in the decision did not meet the standards of impartial public reason

[166] See Lofgren, *The Plessy Case.*

[167] See, in general, Stanton, *The Leopard's Spots: Scientific Attitudes Toward Race in America 1815–59.*

[168] For good general treatments, see Stephen Jay Gould, *The Mismeasure of Man* (New York: W. W. Norton, 1981); Gossett, *Race: The History of an Idea in America*; Fredrickson, *The Black Image in the White Mind*; John S. Haller, Jr., *Outcasts from Evolution: Scientific Attitudes of Racial Inferiority, 1859–1900* (New York: McGraw-Hill Book Company, 1971); Reginald Horsman, *Race and Manifest Destiny: The Origins of American Racial Anglo-Saxonism* (Cambridge, Mass.: Harvard University Press, 1981).

[169] See, for further discussion, Richards, *Conscience and the Constitution*, 87–8.

[170] See Franz Boas, "Human Faculty as Determined by Race," originally published 1894, reprinted in George W. Stocking, Jr., *A Franz Boas Reader*, at 221–42.

surely due all Americans. Americans have a right to expect more of their highest court than the conclusory acceptance without argument of controversial scientific judgments hostage to an entrenched political epistemology that protected the increasingly racist character of the American South. One justice (Justice Harlan, a Southerner) powerfully made precisely this point in his dissent in *Plessy*.

It is surely not without importance that Southern blacks had during this period been left by the federal government almost wholly at the mercies of Southern state governments; these governments had (in violation of the spirit of the Fifteenth Amendment) effectively disenfranchised them, certainly not afforded them adequate educational opportunity, and cast a blind eye on, when they did not actively support, the informal forms of terrorism used to intimidate blacks from challenging their subjugated economic, social, and political position.[171] The Supreme Court, abandoning abolitionist ethical impartiality, supinely surrendered any semblance of morally independent critical testing in order to take instruction from bad and politically corrupt science to legitimate the further degradation of this already unconstitutionally victimized group. The consequence was what betrayal of the argument for toleration has taught us to expect. The political identity of the postwar South, like its antebellum predecessor, immunized itself from serious discussion of its greatest evil[172] and constituted its sense of political identity in racist subjugation. Consistent with the paradox of intolerance, such a failure of reason projectively fed on forms of political irrationalism (myth, factual distortion, deprivation of basic rights of conscience and free speech) based on the racist subjugation of its victims. A great shift in American public opinion correspondingly took place from the era of Radical Republicans to the Progressive Era, a fact shockingly visible in a speech by Charles Francis Adams, Jr., to Virginians in 1908. Adams first reminded the audience that he was the great-grandson of John Adams (who had signed the Declaration of Independence), grandson of John Quincy Adams (who had defeated the gag rule),[173] son of the

---

[171] See, in general, Woodward, *Reunion and Reaction; The Strange Career of Jim Crow; Origins of the New South 1877–1913*.

[172] See, in general, Cash, *The Mind of the South*.

[173] See, on this important historical event in the antislavery struggle and John Quincy Adams's important role in it, William Lee Miller, *Arguing about Slavery: The Great Battle in the United States Congress* (New York: Alfred A. Knopf, 1996).

ambassador to Britain who had kept Britain from siding with the Confederacy, and "an old antislavery man" who had fought "four long years" as a Union officer. Nonetheless, Adams announced that the nation's "archaic" political theory based on "the equality of men" had "broken down." It must be replaced by a modern "scientific" understanding of blacks in place of "scriptural" accounts of human equality. Reconstruction now seemed "absurd," "worse than a crime," a "political blunder, as ungenerous as it was gross."[174] The inclusive moral vision of one of America's greatest political families had thus been shrunk to the measure of what in the United States, as in Italy (chapter 3), was taken to be progressive thought, the pseudoscientific racism of a Madison Grant.[175]

The consequences of this common view for the nation at large were felt not only in racist aspects of America's increasingly imperialist foreign policy[176] but in the racist immigration restrictions on Asians and, after World War I, on Southern and Eastern Europeans.[177] If race and culture were in this period so unreasonably confused, it is not surprising that American intolerance, to the extent it was legitimated by betrayal of constitutional principles, should turn from blacks to non-Christian Asians or Catholic Latins or Jewish Slavs, whose cultures appeared, to nativist American Protestant public opinion, so inferior and (equating culture and race) therefore peopled by the racially inferior.

The massive Southern Italian emigration to the United States (1890–1920) thus took place during a period of resurgent political racism (*Plessy*, which expresses and indeed legitimates this development, was decided in 1896). There is, of course, no reason in logic why American racism, bad as it was when applied to African Americans or

---

[174] Quoted in Smith, *Civic Ideals*, at 417.

[175] For Madison Grant on the blunder of the Reconstruction Amendments, see Madison Grant, *The Passing of the Great Race*, 82; on reading the Declaration of Independence as extending only to Anglo-Saxons and revising it in light of modern science, see ibid., xx–xxi, 263.

[176] See, on this point, Smith, *Civic Ideals*, at 429–33; for useful background, see also Horsman, *Race and Manifest Destiny*.

[177] See, for a good general treatment, John Higham, *Strangers in the Land: Patterns of American Nativism 1860–1925* (New Brunswick: Rutgers University Press, 1988). See also Ronald Takaki, *Iron Cages: Race and Culture in 19th-Century America* (New York: Oxford University Press, 1990); Ronald Takaki, *Strangers from a Distant Shore* (New York: Penguin, 1989); Horsman, *Race and Manifest Destiny*; Gossett, *Race: The History of an Idea in America*.

Native Americans or Asian Americans,[178] should have been applied to European, visibly white peoples. But, American racism arose not from reasoned deliberation but from the attempt, by Jefferson among others,[179] to rationalize entrenched structural injustices that were conspicuously dissonant with the principles and promises of liberal nationalism. After the Civil War and the abolition of slavery, the tension, as we have seen, remained, as America first constitutionally made liberal nationalistic promises of equal citizenship to African Americans and then inconsistently legitimated racist institutions of segregationist and antimiscegenationist policy. Irrationalist political racism took on the implacable cultural force it did in the United States during this period because, consistent with the paradox of intolerance, its pseudoscience of race so conveniently suppressed both the persons and the views (namely, the dehumanized group) that might confront the American public mind with reasonable doubts about its fundamental justice and decency as a people now constitutionally committed to liberal nationalism. But, such political irrationalism, once thus legitimated, could not be cabined. Its force extended, as it clearly did in this period, to the cultural racialization of the new European immigrants, including Jews and the Southern Italians, who might otherwise challenge on equal terms the powerful racist orthodoxy whose force depended on suppressing the speakers and views who might contest it; Southern Italians, for example, during this period were thus culturally regarded as blacks[180] or as Asians.[181]

These groups were a target of American racial anxiety because their growing presence raised precisely the kinds of questions about legitimate cultural difference and moral pluralism (including, in the case of the Italians and Jews, religion, language, history, and lifestyle) that challenged the terms of the racist orthodoxy that had been formed

---

[178] See, for illuminating historical background about the application of American racism to these groups, Takaki, *Iron Cages*; Horsman, *Race and Manifest Destiny*.

[179] On Jefferson's important role in American racist thought, see Richards, *Conscience and the Constitution*, 86–8.

[180] See Foerster, *The Italian Emigration of Our Times*, 383, 407–8, 437–8, 504–5; Gambino, *Blood of My Blood*, 107–16; DeConde, *Half Bitter, Half Sweet*, 98–103, 116–19.

[181] See Higham, *Strangers in the Land*, 164–5, 175; Grant, *The Passing of the Great Race*, at 148–66. For illuminating background on the racist stereotyping of Asians, see Edward W. Said, *Orientalism* (Vintage: New York, 1978); Edward W. Said, *Culture and Imperialism* (New York: Alfred A. Knopf, 1993).

and sustained, as we have seen, on the basis of religious and then cultural degradation of African Americans and others; Italian Americans and Jews, like African Americans before them, were scapegoats of Americans' self-doubt about their liberal nationalism. The very fact, for example, that Italian Americans did not display the usual American prejudices against blacks (dealing with them economically on equal terms)[182] and, reflecting long-standing Italian traditions of tolerance (shown in popular resistance to the persecution of the Jews during World War II),[183] did not share the dominant American pattern of Christian anti-Semitism[184] raised reasonable questions that had to be suppressed. The means of suppression of Italian Americans included the terroristic tactic of lynching (often because of their willingness to do business with blacks), which was also used to suppress African Americans,[185] as well as the xenophobic excesses that accompanied the political intimidation of anyone who suggested that cultural differences might be legitimate (let alone supported ideological dissent)—for example, the overwrought Palmer raids brought by President Wilson's attorney general, A. Mitchell Palmer, under a 1920 federal law providing for deportation of enemy aliens and anarchists (which led to the deportation of politically dissident immigrants) and the nativist injustices in the trial, conviction, and electrocution of Sacco and Vanzetti on the basis of weak circumstantial evidence of homicide (both of whom were despised as political anarchists);[186] the repressive crusade of "100 percent Americanization" also made clear that no cultural divergences from American views and values were tolerable, let alone of value.[187] Threatening cultural differences were during this period explicitly racialized by the American racist theorist Madison Grant, in whatever

---

[182] See, on this point, DeConde, *Half Bitter, Half Sweet*, at 125.

[183] On the striking history of the Italians, in not persecuting and sometimes pro tecting Jews both in Italy and in the territories occupied by Italy, see Zuccotti, *The Italians and the Holocaust*; Michaelis, *Mussolini and the Jews*; and Steinberg, *All or Nothing*.

[184] See DeConde, *Half Bitter, Half Sweet*, 117; Rudolf Glanz, *Jew and Italian: Historic Group Relations and the New Immigration (1881–1924)* (New York: Shulsinger Bros., 1970), at 72–3.

[185] See, on this point, Foerster, *The Italian Emigration of Our Times*, 408; DeConde, *Half Bitter, Half Sweet*, 121–6; Gambino, *Blood of My Blood*, 109–11; Higham, *Strangers in the Land*, 169, 264.

[186] See DeConde, *Half Bitter, Half Sweet*, 164–8; Gambino, *Blood of My Blood*, 108–12.

[187] See, on this point, Higham, *Strangers in the Land*, 234–63.

ways entrenched the alleged superiority of the Aryan, Anglo-Saxon race over the new immigrants, "the broken and the mentally crippled of all races."[188] Whatever might distinguish Italian culture was thus conclusorily dismissed; the political and cultural achievements of Rome, while conceded, *could not* have been produced by people of the same race as the Italian immigrants.[189] Italian distinction in the visual arts was made a badge of dishonor in contrast to the alleged Anglo-Saxon achievements in the hard sciences (the sciences on which Grant notably depended to rationalize his racism).[190] Consistent with the paradox of intolerance, facts and values were suppressed or inverted in whatever ways confirmed "true race consciousness,"[191] which was, of course, threatened by the continued immigration of peoples who could not, because of their racial inferiority, be improved by American culture.[192] Such racialized views were specifically used against Italian Americans, prominently by Senator Henry Cabot Lodge of Massachusetts, urging exclusion of "the criminals and anarchists of foreign countries."[193] Consistent with the standard racist confusion of culture and nature, Lodge urged the use of literacy tests as a condition for immigration on the ground that such tests would weed out the lower races "most alien to the great body of the people of the United States," including "the Italian, Russians, Poles, Hungarians, Greeks, and Asiatics" (including Jews); in contrast, Lodge observed, English speakers, Germans, Scandinavians, and the French would be affected "very lightly or not at all."[194] In effect, the long tradition of depriving Italian people of the South of their basic rights of conscience and speech and associated educational opportunities (which resulted in their illiteracy, not to mention their lack of English-language literacy) was, in the vicious circularity characteristic of both American and European racism, taken to define their permanent subhumanity.[195] In October 1915, former President Theodore Roosevelt gave a speech in New York

[188] See Grant, *The Passing of the Great Race*, 89.
[189] See ibid., 153–4.
[190] See ibid., 229.
[191] See ibid., 57.
[192] See ibid., 89–94.
[193] Quoted in Gambino, *Blood of My Blood*, at 110.
[194] Quoted in Smith, *Civic Ideals*, at 364.
[195] On the background of Southern Italian illiteracy, see Foerster, *The Italian Emigration of Our Times*, at 95–6.

City's Carnegie Hall, in which he announced, "There is no room in this country for hyphenated Americans. . . . There is no such thing as a hyphenated American who is a good American"; Woodrow Wilson concurred, in 1915, that "hyphenated Americans . . . have poured the poison of disloyalty into the very arteries of our national life . . . such creatures of passion, disloyalty and anarchy must be crushed out."[196] Such blatant political racism, directed against Italian Americans among other recent immigrants, became American public policy in the "massively racist and ideologically repressive restriction" on immigration from Southern and Eastern Europe that was introduced in 1924, in the National Origins Quota system.[197]

Southern Italians had experienced, under an Italy ostensibly unified on the basis of liberal nationalism, a political racism that they now experienced under the liberal nationalism of the United States as well. Both forms of racism had similar characters and were rationalized, as Croce in Italy and Boas in the United States clearly saw, in the same uncritical way (the confusion of the unjust consequences of culture with nature). After comparing life under both forms of defective liberal nationalism, many (though by no means all) of the Southern Italians reasonably reviewed their comparative experience of life in both nations and opted for the United States. Why?

Their choice of Italy or the United States was, in either case, unlikely to be influenced by rhetorical claims of either nationalism or liberal nationalism; as we observed (chapter 3), both their culture and history did not support a sense of themselves as members of the Italian nation, and their more recent experience under a unified Italy gave them good reason to be skeptical about all such claims. That experience had taught them to bring to their assessment of such claims a cool and practical intelligence, skeptical perhaps of political idealism[198] but not of the idealism of family life and devotion.[199]

Their journey to the United States was a choice to take risks.[200] They needed to weigh, as we saw (chapter 3), an Italy rooted in its sense of its past against an America that reasonably seemed to them, on bal-

[196] Quoted in Gambino, *Blood of My Blood*, at 108–9.
[197] See Smith, *Civic Ideals*, 443.
[198] See Foerster, *The Italian Emigration of Our Times*, 424–6.
[199] See ibid., 428–9.
[200] See ibid., 417–8.

ance, much more justly open. The experience of American racism would have seemed, to this realistic people, at least from their perspective, no worse than Italian racism and, in the balance of justice, in several ways less unjust.

First, American racism was at its worst in the American South, in which African Americans were subject to the state-imposed racist institutions of segregationist and antimiscegenationist policy. Italian Americans, for very good reasons, largely chose not to live in the South, indeed, chose not to pursue the largely agricultural lives they had known in Italy.[201] Work in agriculture in Southern Italy was associated with living in towns, not, as in America, on isolated farms (more people lived in towns Southern Italy than in any other part of the country),[202] and the American pattern of agriculture was not culturally congenial to the Italian immigrants. The emigration to the United States was a movement of this socially gregarious people not only away from agriculture and rural towns but to urban centers;[203] most Italian Americans settled in the already diverse urban areas of New York, New Jersey, Pennsylvania, and southern New England.[204] This choice of a more cosmopolitan lifestyle must be understood against the background of Gramsci's analysis of the defective elitism of Italian liberal nationalism: Italy's cosmopolitan artistic, scientific, and literary traditions, including those of the Risorgimento, were so limited to a small elite that they never democratically engaged or energized the minds and lives of most Italians as the basis of a popularly supported liberal tradition. Part of what Italian Americans experienced as the more just openness of America was the possibility that they might find in America a cosmopolitanism more democratically open to them and their children. The emigration, undertaken by many as an alternative to revolution against the illegitimacy of the Italian state,[205] might reasonably make available to them and their children what Italy had never afforded the Italian people: a democratic experience of the Renaissance comparable to the Protestant Reformation. American racism might reasonably be endured if it, in contrast to Italian racism, made such an opportunity available.

[201] See ibid., 371–2.

[202] See ibid., 62.

[203] See ibid., 418–9.

[204] See Nelli, "Italians," in Thernstrom, *Harvard Encyclopedia of American Ethnic Groups*, at 547.

[205] See Foerster, *The Italian Emigration of Our Times*, 102.

Second, the burdens placed by American racism on Italian Americans might, from the perspective of their history, be regarded as less onerous than they might at first seem. As we have seen, American racism arises from two features: the abridgment of basic human rights of conscience, speech, intimate life, and work and the dehumanizing stereotypes on the basis of which that abridgment is rationalized. The abridgment of rights of conscience and speech is especially pivotal because it enforces the dominant racist orthodoxy by suppressing the speakers and views who might most reasonably contest it; but, as we have seen (e.g., the Palmer raids), any form of political dissent by immigrants during this period was repressed under threat of deportation, and the judicial protection of such dissent was during this period quite undeveloped (serious judicial protection of free speech largely developed after World War II).[206] Some of the more excessively repressive measures of the crusade for Americanization (for example, laws forbidding the teaching of foreign languages to young children and others requiring all children to be educated in public schools) were struck down as unconstitutional.[207] But, the dominant message to the new immigrants was quite clear: their views, to the extent they were conscientiously critical of America or its policies, were not to be tolerated; indeed, the crusade for Americanization indulged the racist assumption that the immigrants' ethnic culture and history had nothing of value to contribute and required that they be "100 percent Americanized," as the phrase went.[208] In addition, the first generation of Italian Americans, largely illiterate and not yet adept in English, was also functionally disabled from asserting its rights of conscience and speech; discourse about Italians was thus, by force both of American law and of background culture and experience, limited to the measure

[206] For discussion of these much more protective judicially enforceable principles of free speech, see Richards, *Toleration and the Constitution* 165–227; and in general David A. J. Richards, "Constitutional Legitimacy, the Principle of Free Speech, and the Politics of Identity," forthcoming, *Chicago-Kent Law Review.*

[207] See Higham, *Strangers in the Land*, 260. See, for example, *Meyer v. Nebraska*, 262 U.S. 390 (1923) (state law prohibiting the teaching of foreign languages to young children held unconstitutional); *Pierce v. Society of Sisters*, 268 U.S. 510 (1925) (state law requiring all students to be educated in public schools held unconstitutional).

[208] On the crusade to Americanize the immigrants (some of it struck down as unconstitutional), see Higham, *Strangers in the Land*, 234–63; on 100 percent Americanization, see ibid., 242.

of the dominant racist view of them. Italian Americans might have regarded this form of injustice as less grave because it was so historically familiar to them in their traditional experience as people of the South; they had traditionally accommodated themselves to such an injustice by regarding interest in culture or political history as not within their sphere.[209] More important, whatever sense of injustice they might have experienced about these basic rights (which were abridged also in Italy) was a price worth paying because of what they may have regarded as the greater access to other basic rights that they enjoyed in America compared to Italy. Italian Americans, when they became American citizens, could and did vote and thus could exercise control over the unjustly racist balance of benefits and burdens that had been a major grievance in Italy; they were free, for example, of compulsory military service[210] and could exercise at least some control over levels of taxation imposed for policies (including imperialism) of which they disapproved. American constitutional traditions of the rule of law, including the accountability of politicians, was, for the people of the South, an enormous advance over the endemic corruption of Italian politics and the large and small political tyrannies so culturally familiar to and despised by them.[211] In addition, substantially better employment opportunities were available in the United States than in Southern Italy, even for the illiterate, so much so that the racial discrimination that Italian Americans faced in some forms of employment may not have had the significance it would otherwise have had.[212] Indeed, having experienced the traditional contempt for physical labor that is part of Southern Italian culture, the American work ethic must have struck the people of the South as dignifying their work, indeed, valuing and rewarding their traditions of "helot-like" hard physical work in groups.[213] In America, their associated frugality and propensity to saving would also be valorized consistent with the nation's capitalist

---

[209] See Foerster, *The Italian Emigration of Our Times*, 424–7.

[210] See ibid., 6, 12, 100, 465–7.

[211] For an important treatment of the issue of political tyranny (including its corruption of independent moral judgment) in an influential and popular Italian novel, see Alessandro Manzoni, *The Betrothed*, trans. Bruce Penman (London: Penguin, 1972), at 361–5, 370.

[212] See Foerster, *The Italian Emigration of Our Times*, 360.

[213] See ibid., 401; see also ibid., 424, 438–9.

ethos.[214] In short, the ostensible vices of Southern peasants which were held in contempt in Southern Italian culture, were the mainstream virtues of the great American middle class, in which the Italian Americans saw themselves as, in time, taking their rightful place. America, in contrast to Italy, thus addressed and ameliorated both the moral and the economic sources of Southern Italian *misèria*.

Third, and perhaps most important for this first generation of Italian Americans, American racism, at least that form of it targeted at them, did not compromise the traditional functions of the institution that more than any other organized the meaning of their lives and even ideals—the Southern Italian family.[215] In contrast to the long history of American racist abridgment of African Americans' basic human right to intimate and family life,[216] the circumstances of American life, in the areas where Italians chose to settle, usually as communities similar to those they had left in Southern Italy,[217] left space for the forms of Southern Italian family life, rooted in pagan Magna Graecia,[218] that had meaningfully sustained them, as a people, against the political despotisms and tyrannies they had lived under for millenia. Indeed, if it is true, as I have elsewhere argued at length, that American recognition of the basic human right to intimate life appeals to the same grounds as its recognition of the basic human right to conscience,[219] Italian Americans may have found both the theory and the practice of such liberal respect for the right to intimate life intuitively very close to their sense of what gave enduring moral and even religious value to living. Southern Italian religiosity combined skepticism about the Catholic Church as a *political* institution (arising from its often repressively illiberal role in the politics of Italy)[220] with a syncretic integration of ancient pagan rituals and Christian symbols, creating a family-centered religious piety organized around the change of

[214] See ibid., 422–3.

[215] See ibid., 428–9; Covello, *The Social Background of the Italo-American School Child*, at 149–238.

[216] See, on this point, Richards, *Conscience and the Constitution*, at 224–32.

[217] See Lopreato, *Italian Americans*, at 36–55.

[218] See Covello, *The Social Background of the Italo-American School Child*, at 65–238.

[219] See, for extended defense of this position, Richards, *Toleration and the Constitution*, 231–81; see also Richards, *Identity and the Case for Gay Rights: Race, Gender, Religion as Analogies* (forthcoming, University of Chicago Press, 1999).

[220] See, on this point, Gambino, *Blood of My Blood*, 209–16.

seasons and a corresponding sense of the humane values of the seasons of intimate personal life in the transcendent mysteries of birth, love, and death.[221] The people of the South, who had learned from painful experience the need for skepticism about political and religious ideas and ideals,[222] were, nonetheless, idealists about the family.[223] We may see the power of the human right of intimate life in Italian culture in Alessandro Manzoni's influential novel, *The Betrothed*,[224] in which the operative metaphor for the larger issues of political tyranny under discussion in the novel is the interference of the local noble thug, supported by the quintessentially evil tyranny of the Unnamed,[225] in the love and projected marriage of a young couple; such abridgment of the central human right of intimate associational decisions was, for Manzoni's Italian audience, a kind of interpretive paradigm for the politically illegitimate exercise of abusive power, namely, tyranny. Italian opera of the nineteenth century, with its deep expressive roots in the personal and political aspirations of the Italian people, also often coded its politically liberal messages in terms of the price political tyranny unjustly exacted in disrupting and even corrupting attachments of romantic love.[226] The American respect for inti-

---

[221] See, for an illuminating discussion of Southern Italian religiosity, Covello, *The Social Background of the Italo-American School Child*, at 103–45; on family life, see ibid., at 149–238; Lopreato, *Italian Americans*, 87–93.

[222] See Foerster, *The Italian Emigration of Our Times*, 424–6.

[223] See ibid., at 428–9.

[224] See Manzoni, *The Betrothed*.

[225] See ibid., at 361–5.

[226] The theme is powerfully operative, for example, in the operas of both Gaetano Donizetti and Giuseppe Verdi. For Donizetti, see, among other operas, *Gabriella di Vergy* (heroine forced to marry man she doesn't love) (see, for relevant commentary, William Ashbrook, *Donizetti and His Operas* [Cambridge: Cambridge University Press, 1982], at 297–8, 540–1); *Anna Bolena* (Anna, pressured by her brother to abandon the man she loves for a royal marriage, disastrously marries king of England, who grows to despise her) (see, for relevant commentary, ibid., at 317–21); *Parisina* (wife forced, for familial and political reasons, to marry husband she doesn't love) (see, for relevant commentary, ibid., at 341–44); *Lucrezia Borgia* (Lucrezia, seeking revenge for insults to family honor, kills her own son) (see, for relevant commentary, ibid., 348–57); *Gemma di Vergy* (loving wife divorced by husband because she had no children to sustain his dynasty) (see, for relevant commentary, ibid., 365–8); *Lucia di Lammermoor* (sister forced by brother for dynastic reasons to marry man she doesn't love) (see, for relevant commentary, ibid., 375–82; *Roberto Devereux* (queen forces Sara, her confidante, to marry man she does not

mate life and associations, as an important source of enduring value in living, thus corresponded to Italians' experience and to their sense of personal as well as legitimate political values. It also made more bearable the relentless demands of hard work in America, valorizing Italian immigrants' often remarkable frugality, saving, and self-deprivation as occurring in credible service of a better life for their families.[227] This religious devotion to family life also may have made more bearable the racist discrimination inflicted on Italians, enabling them, in the name of devotion to family life, to curtail their ambition and to choose lines of work (like the civil service) that were relatively free of discrimination and that also allowed more space for family life. It also rationalized Italians' traditional social and political habits of keeping a low profile,[228] which had, as we shall see, important consequences for the enduring sense of Italian American identity in subsequent generations.

ITALIAN AMERICAN IDENTITY AND AMERICAN RACISM

Italian American identity was pivotally formed, as we have seen, under circumstances of injustice based on American racism. Henry James

---

love, betraying her love for Roberto, whom the queen loves) (see, for commentary, ibid., 400–409); *Caterina Cornaro* (daughter forced by leaders at Venice for political reasons to marry man she doesn't love) (see, for relevant commentary, ibid., 478–87. For Verdi, see, among other operas, *Luisa Miller* (young girl forced to promise to marry man she despises) (see, for relevant commentary, Julian Budden, *The Operas of Verdi*, vol. 1 [New York: Oxford University Press, 1973], at 419–46); *Rigoletto* (young girl's pure love abused by corrupt duke) (see, for relevant commentary, ibid., at 475–510); *La Traviata* (former courtesan, in love with young man for first time in her life, forced by his father to give him up) (see, for relevant commentary, ibid., vol. 2 at 113–66); *Simone Boccanegra* (young man, separated by her politically antagonistic family from the woman who loves him as well as from their child) (see, for relevant commentary, ibid., 243–334); *La Forza del Destino* (woman separated by her racist father and brother from Amerindian prince she loves) (see, for relevant commentary, ibid., 425–521); *Don Carlos* (princess of France, promised to and in love with son of Spanish king, forced to marry his father) (see, for relevant commentary, Julian Budden, ibid., vol. 3 at 3–157); *Aida* (Ethiopian princess, held in slavery in Egypt, separated from man she loves and whom her father, for political reasons, demands she betray) (see, for relevant commentary, ibid., 159–259).

[227] See, on this point, Sowell, *Migrations and Cultures*, at 140–74.

[228] See Gambino, *Blood of My Blood*, 128, 143–4, 247, 278.

conveys some measure of the human dimension of this development when he compares his experience of Italians in the Italy he loved with his experience of the Italians he encountered in his native New York, which he revisited as an expatriate settled in Britain:

> There are categories of foreigners, truly, meanwhile, of whom we are moved to say that only a mechanism working with scientific force could have performed this feat of making them colourless. The Italians, who, over the whole land, strike us, I am afraid, as, after the Negro and the Chinaman, the human value most easily produced, the Italians meet us, at every turn, only to make us ask what has become of that element of the agreeable address in *them* which has, from far back, so enhanced for the stranger the interest and pleasure of a visit to their beautiful country. They shed it utterly, I couldn't but observe, on their advent, after a deep inhalation or two of the clear native air; shed it with a conscientious completeness which leaves one looking for any faint trace of it. "Colour," of that pleasant sort, was what they had appeared, among the races of the European family, most to have. . . .[229]

James's discourse is quite self-consciously racialized: the racial stereotype of "the Negro and Chinaman," drained of all individuality ("the human value most easily produced"), is the mechanical model for the Italian in America; this new species of Italian has been drained of what the Italian in Italy possessed for the traveler, "that element of the agreeable address in *them*," "colour." The model for this change in Italians is, for James, the contrast between "the ancient graces"[230] of European cities and the New York urban development of the skyscraper, sinking all life "in the common fund of mere economic convenience,"[231] with human life "almost in the likeness of an army of puppets."[232] James's sense of horror[233] at this development (echoing Henry

---

[229] Henry James, *Collected Travel Writings: Great Britain and America* (New York: Library of America, 1993), "The American Scene," 353–736, at 462.

[230] See ibid., 432.

[231] See ibid., 432.

[232] See ibid., 444.

[233] James, in an inner voice, addresses himself thus: "You *care* for the terrible town, yea even for the 'horrible', as I have overheard you call it"; ibid., 445.

Adams's similar contrast of the virgin and the dynamo)[234] should be contrasted with the very different perspective of the Italian immigrant cited at the end of the previous chapter; where the immigrant perceives the skyscraper as a metaphor for a new life less burdened by a confining history, James identifies the loss of Italian history, culture, and personality under the exigent pressure of a relentlessly dehumanizing routinization. James points to "the great assimilative organism"[235] as the force behind this remarkable development and wonders, prophetically, about both its permanence and its point:

> The "American" identity that has profited by their sacrifice has meanwhile acquired (in the happiest cases) all apparent confidence and consistency; but may not the doubt remain of whether the extinction of qualities ingrained in generations is to be taken for quite complete? Isn't it conceivable that, for something like a final efflorescence, the business of slow comminglings and makings-over at last ended, they may rise again to the surface, affirming their vitality and value and playing their part?[236]

James's complaint about the price America has exacted of its Italian immigrants (both for them and for America) strikingly echoes Du Bois's similar argument about the injustice inflicted on African Americans' identity; Du Bois's argument about African American double consciousness bears repeating:

> The history of the American Negro is the history of this strife,—this longing to attain self-conscious manhood, to merge his double self into a better and truer self. In this merging he wishes neither of the older selves to be lost. He would not Africanize America, for America has too much to teach the world and Africa. He would not bleach his Negro soul in a flood of white Americanism, for he knows that Negro blood has a message for the world. He simply wishes to make it possible for a man to be both a Negro and an American, without being cursed and spit upon by his fellows, without having the doors of Opportunity closed roughly in his face.[237]

---

[234] See Henry Adams, *The Education of Henry Adams*, in Ernest Samuels and Jayne N. Samuels, eds., *Henry Adams* (New York: Library of America, 1983), 717–1181, at 1066–76.
[235] See James, *The American Scene*, 461.
[236] See ibid., 463.
[237] Ibid., 365.

The cultural character and effects of the dynamics of American culture are vivid for James in the case of Italian Americans in a way they are not for "the Negro and the Chinaman"; but, to do justice to James, he at least is taking objection to the dominant popular view, reflected in Madison Grant among others, of racist Anglo-Saxonism that subordinated racially not only Africans and Asians but Italians and Jews as well.[238] Because of his expatriate experience as an American abroad and well traveled in Italy and knowledgeable about its people and culture, James points to a cultural process, "the great assimilative organism," by which a people he knew in Italy as all too colorfully personal became a stereotype, a kind of puppet. But, in light of the argument about the cultural evil of American racism made earlier, we may now understand the cultural process, which James only sketches, as an aspect of a larger cultural pattern applicable to "the Negro and the Chinaman" as well as to Italian Americans and Jews—the unjust entrenchment of the structural injustice of American racism.

Du Bois offered his classic examination of double consciousness as a way of understanding, from within the experience of American structural injustice, the grounds for its moral protest, namely, the unjust devaluation of African American identity and the need, correspondingly, for African Americans to forge a sense of their identity both as blacks and as Americans free of such structural injustice. Racial prejudice is an invidious political evil because it is directed against significant aspects of a person's cultural and moral identity on irrationalist grounds of subjugation because of that identity. As we earlier saw, choosing to pass as white was rejected by many African Americans because it would cut them off from intimately personal relationships to family and community that nurture and sustain self-respect and personal integrity;[239] the price of avoiding racial prejudice is an unreasonable sacrifice of basic resources of personal and ethical identity that they will not accept. In effect, one is to avoid injustice by a silencing of one's moral powers to protest injustice, degrading moral integrity into silent complicity with evil. The same terms of cultural degradation apply to all victims of racism, whether visibly or nonvis-

---

[238] See, on this point, Smith, *Civic Ideals*, at 353–6, 364–5, 369–70, 430–1, 446–8; Higham, *Strangers in the Land*.

[239] Davis, *Who Is Black?* at 56–57.

ibly black—the demand of supine acceptance of an identity unjustly devalued.

The formation of Italian American identity under the circumstances of injustice earlier described placed them among the victims of racism that were nonvisibly black. The extension of racism to this class of persons shows, as I earlier argued, that its irrationalist object is not some brute fact (e.g., the color of one's skin) that cannot be changed but that it is directed at important aspects of moral personality: in particular, "the way people think, feel, and believe, not how they look"—the identifications that make them "members of the black ethnic community."[240] Racial prejudice, thus analyzed, shares common features with certain forms of religious intolerance. In particular, racism and anti-Semitism share a common irrationalist fear: *invisible blackness* or the *secret Jew*, persons who can pass as white or Christian but who are allegedly tainted by some fundamental incapacity fully to identify themselves as authentically a member of the majoritarian race or religion.[241] Such an incapacity is ascribed to persons on the basis of "perceived attitudes and social participation rather than on . . . appearance or lineage."[242] On this basis, any dissent from the dominant racist or anti-Semitic orthodoxy, let alone sympathetic association with the stigmatized minority, is interpreted as evidence of membership in the defective minority, thus imposing a reign of intellectual terror on any morally independent criticism of racial or religious intolerance and encouraging a stigmatized minority to accept the legitimacy of subordination.[243]

As I earlier argued, it is an important feature of the structural injustice of moral slavery (which underlies the constitutional condemnation, properly understood, of racism, sexism, and homophobia) that it must conceal its cultural character by rationalizing structural injustice as based in a natural fact (whether race or gender or gendered sexuality). Otherwise, persons would have to acknowledge and take responsibility for their complicity in a structural injustice condemned by now constitutionally acknowledged principles of liberal nationalism. As Rogers M. Smith has recently made clear in his magisterial study of this ques-

---

[240] Ibid., at 179.

[241] Ibid., at 55–56, 145.

[242] Ibid., at 145.

[243] For exploration of this phenomenon, in the form of Jewish anti-Semitism, see, for example, Sander L. Gilman, *Jewish Self-Hatred*; Lerner, *The Socialism of Fools*.

tion,[244] American constitutional culture has throughout its history had two conflicting strands: first, principles of liberal nationalism that, in principle, extend basic human rights to all persons consistent with the argument for toleration, and, second, patterns of structural injustice (racism, sexism, and homophobia) that structure national identity in terms of this same injustice. As Smith is at pains to show, liberal principles have not always been in the ascendant; instead, liberal progress (e.g., the Civil War and the Reconstruction Amendments) has been followed by some of the most reactionary periods of political racism in our history, including during the so-called Progressive Era.[245] Americans concealed these ugly facts from themselves by the naturalization of structural injustice, the claim that such injustice is not something for which they have any moral responsibility but rather is differential treatment rooted in nature. To challenge this naturalization of injustice was to question nothing less than national honor. Thus, the terms of 100 percent Americanization patriotically precluded any such challenge.

If I am right about this, any form of structural injustice will be most threatening when its terms are most conspicuously likely to challenge the naturalization of injustice. The victims of racism that I earlier called the nonvisibly black raised this issue acutely, particularly when they came from European cultures that were, in the way of thinking typical of late-nineteenth-century Americans, at least not obviously inferior to American culture. Their subordination rested not on the usual obvious natural fact (skin color) taken to be an apodictic marker of subordination but rather on cultural differences (including more tolerant religious and racial attitudes) that conflicted with dominant American views. The very existence of such groups in America, at least if conceived as equals of other groups, thus reasonably raised the issue that the naturalization of injustice requires not to be raised, namely, the cultural entrenchment of structural injustice. What was obvious to Henry James about the cultural processes that had transformed Southern Italians into Italian Americans threatened the whole structure of American racism: if this was true about Italian Americans (or Jews), it might be true of "the Negro and the Chinaman" as well, and Americans would have to face moral responsibilities that their uncritical racism, as Croce had acutely observed (chapter 3), had enabled them to avoid (supposing that what

[244] See, in general, Smith, *Civic Ideals*.
[245] See ibid., 347–469.

was, in fact, complicity with cultural injustice was required by nature). Such groups, whose very existence as equals challenged the legitimacy of American racism, *must* thus be degraded as racist inferiors unworthy of attention, and their Americanization required that they be "100 percent Americanized,"[246] in effect, suppressing any suggestion of the equal dignity, let alone political value of their cultural traditions.

Structural injustice arises, as we have seen, from the abridgment of basic human rights of conscience and speech, which limits speakers and speech to the terms compatible with the underlying injustice. The non-visibly black class of victims of racism might, by protest of the structural injustice, conspicuously make clear its cultural character, reasonably debunking in its own voice the unjust cultural stereotypes that had naturalized injustice. To avoid such a devastating ideological threat to the sense of American nationalism, racist pressure was unjustly imposed on victims uncritically to accept the flawed terms of American nationalism and certainly not to protest it; both the political repression of any suggestion of dissent (drawing on alternative cultural traditions) and the crusade of Americanization made this quite repressively clear to the new immigrants. Such a Faustian bargain was perhaps particularly easy to accept in a historical period when the unjust construction of American racism was so little publicly understood, let alone discussed. Dominant American views might thus easily be accepted, particularly when such attitudes allowed a nonvisibly black group at least to experience uncritically some sense of racial privilege over the visibly black,[247] a form of what Du Bois called a "public and psychological wage."[248] This sense of privilege was supported by ostensible legal doctrines about who could count as "white" for purposes of naturalization (Italians were white for this purpose, although not, after 1924, for purposes of immigration).[249] The price, however, for this privilege over

---

[246] See Higham, *Strangers in the Land*, at 242.

[247] See, on this point, Ann Douglas, *Terrible Honesty: Mongrel Manhattan in the 1920s* (New York: Farrar, Straus and Giroux, 1995), 303–309; see, on the importance of racial privilege in the construction of American racism, Flagg, *Was Blind But Now I See*.

[248] See Du Bois, *Black Reconstruction in America 1860–1880*, at 700. For illuminating development of this analysis, see David R. Roediger, *The Wages of Whiteness: Race and the Making of the American Working Class* (New York: Verso, 1991).

[249] See, for illuminating discussion of this body of law, Ian F. Haney Lopez, *White by Law: The Legal Construction of Race* (New York: New York University Press, 1996), esp. 104–6.

people of color was often the acceptance of a range of opportunities on discriminatory terms, including, as we have seen, the willingness to forgo the exercise of basic rights of conscience and speech. As Frederick Douglass had earlier put the same point about the Irish,

> Every hour sees us elbowed out of some employment to make room for some newly-arrived emigrant from the Emerald Isle, whose hunger and color entitle him to special favor. These white men are becoming houseservants, cooks, stewards, waiters, and flunkies. For aught I see they adjust themselves to their stations with all proper humility. If they cannot rise to the dignity of white men, they show that they can fall to the degradation of black men. . . . In assuming our avocation, [the Irishman] has also assumed our degradation.[250]

Sometimes, complicity took the form, as in performances by Irish Americans as blackface minstrel entertainers, of affirming a common whiteness, even during periods of anti-immigrant hysteria, by indulging racist stereotypes of African Americans.[251] In general, we may understand the unjust terms of the Americanization of immigrants to include such patterns of complicity with and accommodation to American racism. The minstrel phenomenon (white skins wearing black masks) exemplifies a more general dynamic of acculturation: white skins wearing masks (concealing and suppressing multicultural identity) to affirm, rather than challenge, the unjust privilege of whiteness under American cultural racism.

This process has, I believe, enormously impacted the identity of first- and second-generation Italian Americans as an ethnic group for reasons related to the factors that led them to conclude that America offered a less unjust way of life than did Italy. As we have seen, for Italian Americans, the great appeal of America was twofold: first, it afforded, rewarded, and valorized hard work, even if on discriminatory terms; second, it allowed space for the values Italian Americans placed on family life. There were, of course, changes in both work and family

---

[250] Quoted in Ignatiev, *How the Irish Became White*, at 111.

[251] See, for probing commentary on this phenomenon of white skins and black masks, Roediger, *The Wages of Whiteness*, 116–127. On the comparable phenomenon of black skins and white masks, see Frantz Fanon, *Black Skin, White Masks*, trans. Charles Lam Markmann trans. (New York: Grove Weidenfeld, 1967).

life. Italian Americans no longer worked in agriculture and lived largely in or near urban centers.[252] Also, the traditional balance between husband and wife in the Southern Italian family[253] changed as women became interested in work, first inside and later outside the home, leading to a corresponding growth in their independence.[254] Traditional relations between parents and children also underwent change, for example, under the impact of American compulsory education, which Southern Italian parents sometimes resisted (following the agrarian tradition that children worked in the father's occupation, for which he supplied all the needed education).[255] The resulting basic orientation to work and family life reinterpreted yet continued their lives in Italy in ways that better addressed and relieved the economic and moral sources of Southern Italian *misèria* than did life in the old country.

Consistent with both their Southern Italian culture and history and their experience in America, Italian Americans made a Faustian bargain on American racism that was, for many in both the first and the second generations, easier to accept (or at least to acquiesce in) than it otherwise might have been. The Italian culture and history imparted to them by their parents had taught them not only skepticism about moral and political ideals but the wisdom of keeping a low profile, focusing on issues of work and family as the main business of living.[256] The largely illiterate way of life in Southern Italy in which children worked in the family business and life was based on humane codes of living communicated by parents to children,[257] shaped later generations that were resistant to higher education, particularly those forms of it that seemed to them conspicuously nonutilitarian;[258] certainly, little or no cultural support was extended to those interested in such education,[259]

---

[252] See Lopreato, *Italian Americans*, 36–55.

[253] See, on this point, Covello, *The Social Background of the Italo-American Child*, 149–238.

[254] See, on this point, Foerster, *The Italian Emigration of Our Times*, 349, 381, 459; Lopreato, *Italian Americans*, 58–9.

[255] See, on this point, Covello, *The Social Background of the Italo-American Child*, 242–391.

[256] See Gambino, *Blood of My Blood*, 128, 143–4.

[257] See ibid., 247.

[258] See ibid., 240–4, 247; Lopreato, *Italian Americans*, 154–61; DeConde, *Half Bitter, Half Sweet*, 335–6.

[259] See, on this point, Gambino, *Blood of My Blood*, 241–4.

as "intellectual curiosity and originality were ridiculed or sup-pressed"[260] and the aspiration to achievement kept within conventional bounds.[261] Their American experience (including both the repressive terms of Americanization and the stark censorship of dissent moti-vated by American racism), if anything, rationalized these tendencies as requisite terms of the Faustian bargain of Americanization: not only was a low profile to be kept on issues of public life (silencing the exer-cise of critical conscience and speech in public dissent),[262] but forms of education that might cultivate independent moral and intellectual standards of thought and inquiry, including reflection on uncritically accepted traditional codes of behavior, were to be held in disfavor.[263] There was even an applicable Southern Italian proverb at hand to ratio-nalize this view: *"Fesso chi fa i figli meglio di lui"* (Stupid and con-temptible is he who has children better than himself).[264] The Italian Americans, after comparing their experiences in Italy and in the United States, regarded America as a superior form of liberal nationalism, indeed, came to experience a rational love for America as a nation that largely delivered on the modest promises it made, in contrast to the empty rhetorical promises of Italian nationalism. This realistic and skeptical people, idealistic about the family but not about politics, regarded the terms of the American Faustian bargain as the best poli-tics available to them. They would hold up their part of the bargain, submitting to its demands as, on balance, better than any realistic alter-native available to them.

Both their Italian cultural background and their American experi-ence thus led to a relentless dedication to hard, often physical work, what the Italian American novelist Pietro di Donato described as "an ancient mighty athlete of Job,"[265] with the consequent reduction of human individuality to a common routinized measure: "men seem-

---

[260] Nathan Glazer and Daniel P. Moynihan, *Beyond the Melting Pot: The Negroes, Puerto Ricans, Jews, Italians, and Irish of New York City* (Cambridge, Mass.: MIT Press, 1970), 199.

[261] For illuminating commentary on this point, see Lopreato, *Italian Americans*, 149–65.

[262] See Gambino, *Blood of My Blood*, 128, 143–4.

[263] See ibid., 247.

[264] Cited in Covello, *The Social Background of the Italo-American Child*, at 257.

[265] See Pietro di Donato, *Christ in Concrete* (Indianapolis: Bobbs-Merrill, 1939).

ingly all alike in olympic contest for living with Job."[266] Di Donato thus observed from within the reflective experience of an Italian American the impact of American culture on the Italian immigrants that Henry James had noted as an astute student of comparative Italian and Italian American culture; di Donato discussed this impact in terms that echo those of James:

> Before the grace of morning properly rises over earth, before Christians can gather their senses and stretch upward to God's heaven in joy of living, they are bent and twisted into unfeeling reds and grays of Job. . . .
>
> They were the bodies to whom he would be joined in bondage to Job. Job would be a brick labyrinth that would suck him in deeper and deeper, and there would be no going back. Life would never be a dear music, a festival, a gift of Nature. Life would be the torque of Wall's battle that distorted straight limbs beneath weight in heart and rain and cold.
>
> No poet would be there to intone meter of soul's sentence to stone, no artist upon scaffold to paint the vinegary sweat of Christian in correspondence with red brick and gray mortar, no composer attuned to the screaming movement of Job and voiceless cry in overalls.[267]

I earlier argued that the structural injustice that underlay political racism was made possible by two cultural processes: first, the enforcement of dehumanizing stereotypes as the measure of the persons and issues worth hearing; second, its privatization. The Italian American withdrawal from public discourse served both processes.[268]

First, as is still true to a remarkable extent, stereotypical images of the Mafia were the measure of public discussion of Italian American life.[269] The dominance of such stereotypical images enforced a dehu-

---

[266] See ibid., at 234.

[267] See ibid., 187–9.

[268] See, on this withdrawal, ibid., 278, 330.

[269] See Higham, *Strangers in the Land*, at 65, 66, 160. On the dominance of these images in the American cinema, perpetuated in part by Italian American directors, see Carlos E. Cortes, "The Hollywood Curriculum on Italian Americans: Evolution of an Icon of Ethnicity," in Tomasi, Gastaldo and Row, *The Columbus People*, at 89–108.

manizing image of lawless public and private violence, rooted in a psychopathically amoral view of sexuality and gender and sense of family, that unjustly dehumanized the personal and moral life of the overwhelming number of Italian Americans for whom, whatever may have been the appeal of such criminal groups in the circumstances of the legitimacy crisis of late-nineteenth-century Italy, they had no legitimate appeal in America.[270] There have, of course, been important novels that dealt more fairly with Italian American life,[271] but only a few,[272] and none of them culturally influential.[273] There was nothing remotely comparable, for example, to the rights-based cultural dissent of the Harlem Renaissance.[274] The growing material success of Italian Americans thus largely accommodated itself to the terms of American racism.[275]

Second, and more fundamental, Italian Americans' withdrawal from public discourse privatized the issue of their identity, rendering their protesting voices and perspectives on Italian American identity unspoken and unspeakable.[276] This was sustained both by the political stick of stark repression of any suggestion of ideological dissent (the Palmer raids,[277] the trial of Sacco and Vanzetti,[278] and the terms of the

[270] See, on this point, Gambino, *Blood of my Blood*, 250–84; DeConde, *Half Bitter, Half Sweet*, 342–50, 380–1.

[271] See, for example, Pietro di Donato, *Christ in Concrete*; Mario Puzo, *The Fortunate Pilgrim* (London: Heinemann, 1965); Josephine Gattuso Hendin, *The Right Thing to Do* (Boston: David R. Godine, 1988); Robert Viscusi, *Astoria* (Toronto: Guernica, 1995). See, in general, Mangione and Morreale, *La Storia: Five Centuries of the Italian American Experience*.

[272] Cf. Gay Talese, "Where Are the Italian American Novelists?" in Tomasi et al., *The Columbus People*, 464–74.

[273] Strikingly, the novels by a gifted Italian American writer that did enjoy popularity and influence, consistent with the cultural stereotype, were those dealing with the Mafia as the locus of Italian American life. Contrast, in this regard, Puzo, *The Fortunate Pilgrim*, with his much more popular Mafia novels, Mario Puzo, *The Godfather* (New York: Signet, 1969); and *The Last Don* (New York: Ballantine Books, 1996).

[274] See, for a good general study, Hutchinson, *The Harlem Renaissance in Black and White*.

[275] On this success, see Lopreato, *Italian Americans*, 141–65.

[276] See, for similar developments of this theme, Richard D. Alba, "Identity and Ethnicity among Italians and Other Americans of European Ancestry," in Tomasi et al., *The Columbus People*, 21–44, at 31; Gay Talese, "Where Are the Italian American Novelists?" in ibid., at 464–74.

[277] On the abusive use of these raids against political dissent, see Higham, *Strangers in the Land*, at 229–30.

[278] See DeConde, *Half Bitter, Half Sweet*, at 164–8; Gambino, *Blood of My Blood*, at 108–12.

crusade for Americanization)[279] and by the carrot of a routinized work life and flourishing family life; both the carrot and the stick discouraged higher education and cumulatively rationalized the sense of privatization as in the nature of things.

It clarifies the dimensions and importance of this silence about Italian American identity that, as part of the Faustian bargain, Italian Americans played but a small role in the development of the serious antiracist public discourse, earlier described, that led to the judicial overturning of cases like *Plessy v. Ferguson*.[280] The terms of the bargain, which required them not to contest the terms of Italian American identity, also required them not to contest the larger pattern of American racism, a pattern that applies, as we have seen, to both the visibly and the nonvisibly black. Italian Americans did not contest American racism in general for the same reasons they did not contest the unjust treatment of their own ethnic group in particular. The consequence was that American racism targeted them as it did Asian Americans in the internments undertaken during World War II. About 1,600 Italian citizens were interned, and about ten thousand Italian Americans were forced to move from their houses in California coastal communities to homes further inland. Italian immigrants were thus caught up, albeit in a milder form (consistent with their racial privilege over the more visibly black), in the racist hysteria that swept the West Coast after the Japanese attack on Pearl Harbor on December 7, 1941. While all the interned Italians were citizens of Italy, about two-thirds of the interned Japanese were American citizens. The anti-Japanese measures lasted the length of the war (about 110,000 were interned in a network of camps), while the anti-Italian restrictions ended for the most part after less than a year.[281]

---

[279] See, on this point, Higham, *Strangers in the Land*, at 234–63.

[280] See, on this lack of participation, DeConde, *Half Bitter, Half Sweet*, at 339–41.

[281] In addition, in this sweep of people suspected of sympathy with enemies of the United States, 10,905 Germans and German Americans as well as a few Bulgarians, Czechs, Hungarians, and Romanians were interned. Interestingly, while Italian Americans have increasingly tried to bring public attention to bear on this internment, German American organizations are generally silent about the internment for fear of dredging up old emotions linking Germans and Nazis. Italian Americans may be more willing to protest the internment because they see it, not unreasonably, as linked to the racism of the Japanese internments; the German internment, not having this basis for protest, has not been analogously pursued. See, on all these points, James Brooke, "After Silence, Italians Recall the Internment," *New York Times*, August 11, 1997, A10.

This privatized sense of Italian American identity should be contrasted with the very different sense of both African American and Jewish American identity that resulted from the important roles both
groups played in the development of the antiracist discourse earlier
described. African Americans, consistent with the terms of Du Bois's
analysis of the problem of double consciousness discussed earlier,
protested both the terms of the structural injustice that oppressed them
(namely, the debased sense of themselves as blacks) and the defective
conception of American nationality that rested on that debasement.
Their rights-based protest transformed both their ethnic identity and
their sense of American identity. Similarly, many Jewish Americans
protested both the religious intolerance of anti-Semitism and the
related evil of racism and thus forged a new sense of Jewish identity
(both religious and cultural) and a correspondingly inclusive sense of
American nationality; from this perspective, Louis Brandeis could
insist that his Jewish American identity was importantly enhanced by
his Zionism, since both were based on corresponding principles of
antiracist justice.[282] American nationality, on this view, included, on
grounds of principle, both blacks and Jews; on such grounds, leading
Jewish intellectuals, like Franz Boas and others, advanced the critical
understanding of antiracist discourse.[283] And the issues and understanding of this American antiracist discourse importantly connected
to the modernist nightmare of European anti-Semitism and the allied
victory in World War II, challenging America to reconsider and criticize its own cultural racism. The alliance between blacks and Jews in
the protest against American racism has been so profound that some
recent disagreements between them have been troubling to members
of both groups.[284]

The contrast between the Italian Americans and the Jews is particularly informative from my perspective. Both groups came to the

---

[282] See Louis Brandeis, "The Jewish Problem and How to Solve It," reprinted in
Arthur Hertzberg, *The Zionist Idea* (New York: Atheneum, 1959), at 517–23. See, for an
important recent study of Zionism, Geoffrey Wheatcroft, *The Controversy of Zion: Jewish
Nationalism, the Jewish State, and the Unresolved Jewish Dilemma* (Reading, Mass.: Addison-
Wesley, 1996).

[283] See, on this point, Gossett, *Race: The History of an Idea in America*, 449–50.

[284] See, for a good general discussion of this point and its background, Paul Berman,
ed., *Blacks and Jews: Alliances and Arguments* (New York: Delacorte Press, 1994).

United States in roughly the same historical period, shared strong family traditions and an experience of European racism, and lived and worked with each other in the United States with a sense of mutual respect,[285] even admiration[286] (Italians were much less anti-Semitic than other Christian groups[287] and, despite their ostensibly common Catholicism, were often at odds with the earlier Catholic immigrants, mostly Irish Americans, who dominated the hierarchy of the American Catholic Church.)[288] Both the Italians and the Jews were also nonvisibly black victims of American racism, the targets of the National Origins Quota system instituted in 1924.[289] While Italians and Jews shared a common orientation to work and family, the cultural tradition of European Jews promoted much higher rates of literacy and greater interest in higher education and the professions than did that of the Italians.[290] Unlike the Italians, the Jews did not withdraw from public discourse, many of them rather becoming active participants in both the theory and the practice of rights-based protest against an American racism that they regarded as directed at themselves as well as at African Americans.[291] They understand all too well, as Franz Boas clearly saw, the relationship of such discourse to the need to criticize and resist resurgent European anti-Semitism in Hitler's Germany. Italian Americans, in contrast, often uncritically supported Mussolini[292] (of course, many others, including Winston Churchill, were also "a little simpleminded" in regard to Italian fascism.)[293]

The elaboration of antiracist principles earlier discussed (including

[285] See, for an informative general study of the relations between the two groups, Glanz, *Jew and Italian.*

[286] See ibid., 107–12, 148.

[287] See, on this point, ibid., 72–3.

[288] See ibid., 86–7; Gambino, *Blood of My Blood,* 214–8; DeConde, *Half Bitter, Half Sweet,* 92–4, 336–7.

[289] See Smith, *Civic Ideals,* at 442–3.

[290] See Glanz, *Jew and Italian,* 66–72.

[291] See Takaki, *A Different Mirror,* at 406–8. On the impact, for example, of Boas on the Harlem Renaissance, see George Hutchinson, *The Harlem Renaissance in Black and White,* at 62–77. For an important example of the associated emergence of Jewish literature on the immigrant experience, see Henry Roth, *Call It Sleep* (orig. pub., 1934; New York: Noonday Press, 1991).

[292] See DeConde, *Half Bitter, Half Sweet,* 182–246.

[293] See Albert S. Lindemann, *Esau's Tears: Modern Anti-Semitism and the Rise of the Jews* (Cambridge: Cambridge University Press, 1997), at 477.

their judicial validation in important Supreme Court decisions like *Brown v. Board of Education*), as well as the related development of judicially enforceable principles of free speech,[294] led to a quite different situation for Italian Americans of later generations, including a revived interest among Italian Americans of the third and later generations in their identity as Italian Americans. Such interest reflects a general sociological phenomenon, described by Marcus Lee Hansen as the problem of the third-generation immigrant: "the almost universal phenomenon that what the son wishes to forget the grandson wishes to remember."[295] But, the shape of this revival among Italian Americans of interest in their identity was, I believe, importantly framed by the civil rights movement and its impact on the larger American culture; clearly, this development facilitated the repeal in 1965 of the national origins formula that had been approved in 1924 as a racist restriction on further immigrations from Southern and Eastern Europe.[296] It was against this background that the two most critically important interpretive studies by Italian Americans, as well as a related sociological study, were thus published in the 1970s; they reflect the period's interests in identity as the basis of rights-based protest against the unjustly stigmatized terms of identity.[297]

My aim here has been to understand, interpret, and advance the increasingly public discourse on Italian American identity as a discourse that builds upon and elaborates the antiracist principles of the civil rights movement in the same way that, as we earlier saw, antisexist and antihomophobic movements built on and elaborated those principles. My claim is that such public discourse is, consistent with the argument earlier advanced about the basis of suspect classification analysis, the perhaps long overdue but wholly just rights-based protest by Italian Americans against the unjustly stigmatized terms of their identity as nonvisibly black. The issue, for those who undertake such protest, is, like the comparable protest of nonvisibly black African Americans or Jews, a

---

[294] See, on this development, Richards, *Toleration and the Constitution*, 165-227.

[295] See Marcus Lee Hansen, "The Problem of the Third Generation Immigrant," reprinted in Werner Sollors, ed., *Theories of Ethnicity: A Classical Reader* (London: Macmillan, 1996), 202–15, at 206.

[296] See DeConde, *Half Bitter, Half Sweet*, 173–81, 316–18, 364–5.

[297] For the sociological study, see Lopreato, *Italian Americans* (1970); for the interpretive studies, see DeConde, *Half Bitter, Half Sweet*; Gambino, *Blood of My Blood*.

refusal to pass and thus mask one's stigmatized identity precisely because such a refusal cuts them off from intimately personal relationships to family and community that nurture and sustain self-respect and personal integrity. For Italian Americans, such a refusal has a peculiar poignancy and depth, as it calls for a public discourse that makes clear both to others and to themselves the humane struggle of grandparents and parents under circumstances of injustice that were often concealed from them (as if the Faustian bargain required loss of memory). For each Italian American in particular, recovery of memory not only, consistent with ancient humane values, rightly honors earlier generations, but makes clear who one is and what one's ethical options and responsibilities are and might be in contemporary circumstances.

This protest also importantly valorizes in public discourse the strands of multicultural identity that were previously unjustly privatized. Indeed, the very terms of the protest require cultural empowerment in two related ways. First, the very act of protesting on the grounds of one's basic human rights empowers a multicultural voice, using and developing strands of the previously stigmatized tradition in public discourse. Second, this culturally empowered voice makes possible reasonable criticism of the terms of the unjust stigma of multicultural identity. No criticism is more reasonably powerful than that which not only reveals the humane values of the tradition but uses and elaborates them in the criticism of the entrenchment of structural injustice in American institutions and values. If the racist targeting of Italian Americans turned on their Americanization on terms of injustice, their reasonable rights-based protest must in its nature reforge the sense of American identity, their own and others'. Their multicultural identity, previously unjustly confined to private life, must find its reasonable public voice and scope as a valuable resource for an improved discourse of democratic constitutionalism.

Such a voice and scope must, in light of the unjust privatization of Italian American identity, include more humane public understanding of the value *onore della famiglia*,[298] which culturally sustained Italian Americans for so many centuries against the larger and smaller tyrannies of Italian life and, more recently, against the injustices of American life. In particular, such rights-based protest importantly makes possible reasonable discourse that rebuts the stereo-

---

[298] Covello, *The Social Background of the Italo-American School Child*, 152.

types that have dehumanized Italian American life, in particular, their family life in terms of the stereotype of a violent, psychopathic amoral familism. The reality of Italian American family life (with its sense of abundant love, responsibility, hard work, and ethical rigor) has been not only culturally unrepresented but misrepresented in terms that fail to understand its humane place as a basis for moral independence against a history of political abuse and injustice. To do justice to this truth, public discourse must insist on a larger sense of interpretive history (of both Italy and the United States)[299] as the background for understanding the reasonable choices made by the Italian immigrants, in light of revolutionary constitutionalism, to reject Italian for American liberal nationalism as less unjust and more promising. It demands the recognition of their courage and intelligence, their integrity and humanity, as they attempted to realize these values against the background of a certain context of their own Italian history and culture and the circumstances of American racism; it also suggests that a reasonable sense of contemporary Italian American identity be forged to realize those values against the background of a quite different context, requiring correspondingly different ethical choices.[300] Italian American identity must, of course, change; change is already under way. No longer transmitted in privatized codes that minimize critical understanding,[301] the identity must be publicly and reasonably defended as Italian Americans refuse to accept, as an acceptable price to be paid for American identity, a silencing of their moral powers to protest injustice, thereby degrading moral integrity into silent complicity with racist evil. In so doing, Italian Americans do not compromise but vindicate the humane values, including the sense of personal dignity, that led their ancestors to take such risks and undertake such sacrifices for their future. The first generation of Italian immigrants, for example, was notable for its religious and racial tolerance. Such defensible values are better served by an interpretation of ethnic identity that advances these humane ends and by a refusal complacently to accept the Faustian bargain of the Americanization of one's identity in return for complicity with or at least acquiescence in American racism.

---

[299] See, on this point, Gambino, *Blood of My Blood*, 37, 100, 143–5, 175.

[300] See, on this point, ibid., 190.

[301] See, on this point, ibid., 247

If I am right about this, public discourse about Italian American identity should, as Du Bois urged, transform both one's sense of ethnic identity and one's sense of American identity in ways beneficial to both. Henry James painfully noted the burden of stereotypes that America had placed on the Southern Italian immigrants now so drained of "colour," compelled to wear masks to hide their multicultural identity, and he wondered, in words that bear repeating, whether this demand might not sometime be lifted to the reasonable benefit of both America and the Italians:

> The "American" identity that has profited by their sacrifice has meanwhile acquired (in the happiest cases) all apparent confidence and consistency; but may not the doubt remain of whether the extinction of qualities ingrained in generations is to be taken for quite complete? Isn't it conceivable that, for something like a final efflorescence, the business of slow comminglings and makings-over at last ended, they may rise again to the surface, affirming their vitality and value and playing their part?[302]

We must now further explore what, in light of our argument, he should reasonably be taken to mean.

I have argued that the burden placed on the Italian immigrants was, in fact, an aspect of American racism, naturalizing (as based on a brute fact of race) the structural injustice of abridging basic human rights on grounds of dehumanizing stereotypes that arose from that abridgment. Public discourse about Italian American identity must, in its nature, deconstruct the terms of that structural injustice, showing how its cultural construction has unjustly been permitted to rationalize itself.

To deal with this question, the public discourse must be multiculturally Italian and American and thus advance a comparative perspective, of the sort developed in the argument of this book, on the promises and betrayals of liberal nationalism. As I have argued, the emigrants from Southern Italy were leaving a unified Italy that had, in their reasonable judgment, betrayed the promises of liberal nationalism of the Risorgimento. Unification had accorded them not equality with all other Italians as had been promised to them, but racism, a new

---

[302] See ibid., 463.

insult to their human dignity that directly flouted the humane values of liberal nationalism. America also had a tradition of liberal nationalism, recently reaffirmed and reformed in the wake of the Civil War and the Reconstruction Amendments; it also had traditions of racism, which, if anything, worsened in the period of the massive Italian immigration and indeed turned on the recent immigrants. In both Italy and the United States, racism was rationalized by a positivist pseudoscience; its unjust confusion of culture and nature had been subjected to searching criticism by Italian (e.g., Croce) and American (e.g., Boas) liberal intellectuals. Such a rich discourse advances understanding not only of the continuities of the Italian American experience with that of American blacks and Jews but of the larger themes of liberal nationalism and racism reflected in the experience of other nations and peoples. It thus advances understanding of the universal values of and threats to liberal constitutionalism.

The cosmopolitanism of this public discourse draws fruitfully on both American and Italian cultural themes in ways that illuminate both. Not only do American and Italian liberal nationalism share a common cosmopolitan discourse (the six ingredients of revolutionary constitutionalism, see chapters 2–3), but the aspirations that brought millions of the people of Southern Italy to the United States were framed by that discourse. The cultural tradition of Italy, as both Croce and Gramsci make clear, was always multicultural and cosmopolitan in both its secular and its religious dimensions. Its contributions to art and learning, as well as science, constituted, in contrast to its balkanized politics, a universal culture nourished by artists, intellectuals, and scientists who were at home anywhere;[303] its humanistic traditions integrated complex elements of ancient Greek and Roman, as well as Christian, theory and practice and later European thought; its trade and exploration spanned the world.[304] Such a culture naturally gives expression to a universalistic moral ideal of the dignity of the free mind, expressed in Pico Della Mirandola's *Oration*,[305] whose imaginative moral powers resist preordained scripts or orders of being but rather reasonably reflect upon and discriminate among the

---

[303] See Braudel, *Out of Italy.*

[304] See ibid.

[305] See Giovanni Pico Della Mirandola, *Oration on the Dignity of Man,* trans. A. Robert Caponigri (Chicago: Henry Regnery Co., 1956).

various options available and construct a sense of humane meaning and value accordingly. However, as Gramsci observed, this cosmopolitan culture appealed basically to aristocratic, family-centered elites and did not democratically address or energize the lives and minds of the great mass of the Italian people.[306] Italian political culture could not, Gramsci argued, sustain an enduring reasonable consensus on revolutionary constitutionalism until its Renaissance was democratized in the spirit of the Protestant Reformation, the cultural background of British and American revolutionary constitutionalism. The racist degradation of the people of Southern Italy in an Italy ostensibly reunified on the basis of liberal nationalism importantly expressed and reinforced this general problem in Italian political culture. It is against this background that we may sensibly interpret the culturally revolutionary character of the great Italian emigration as the people of the South, after intelligent comparative experience of life in the two nations, chose the political culture that could much better afford them the democratized cosmopolitanism promised and betrayed by Italian liberal nationalism. Italian Americans came to feel more politically at home in the United States than in Italy because they found here a culture that was, from their perspective, at once more cosmopolitan and more liberally democratic than the culture they had left. However, both their experience of reasonable choice among cultures and their cosmopolitan grounds for that choice suggest, as well, that their culture and history, reasonably understood as the roots of their ethnic identity, afford impartial intellectual and ethical standards in terms of which both the promises and betrayals of American liberal nationalism may reasonably be assessed to the benefit of all Americans and all free peoples moved, as Italians certainly were, by both its experience and its ideals.

I have in mind, of course, the experience of the Italian immigrants with racism in both Italy and America as a crucially formative aspect of Italian American identity. If the unjust privatization of that identity required a collective forgetting of these matters, a reasonable public discourse about such identity must recover and interpret closely this forgotten history and bring to bear on any interpretation a sense of both

---

[306] See, for an illuminating general study of the power of these elites throughout Italian history, Philip Jones, *The Italian City-State: From Commune to Signoria,* (Oxford: Clarendon Press, 1997).

the injustice of the construction of American racism and the ways it may reasonably be both exposed and discussed.

Some of the most important resources for such an emancipatory public discourse may lie at hand in the forms of Italian culture implicit in the distinctive character of Italian American identity. It is surely significant, as I noted in my earlier discussion of Italian constitutionalism (chapter 3), that the interpretive turn was literally invented by the Neapolitan Vico and importantly put to use by another Neapolitan, Croce, to understand the cosmopolitanism of Italian culture (against chauvinistic fascism) and the irrationalism of the Italian racist degradation of the people of the South. Such a tradition, not unlike the background of the Scottish Enlightenment,[307] arose not only from the interpretive problems faced in making sense of the diversity of cultures within Italy but from the need to integrate the diverse historical layers of secular and religious culture (Greek, Roman, Christian) that were self-consciously synthesized in the formation of Italian culture in all its forms; Italian culture was, from this perspective, profoundly and self-consciously multicultural, which may explain why Italians felt so culturally at home with American cultural pluralism. The interpretive process thus arose in Italy from the need to ascribe meaning to multicultural, cosmopolitan sources of authority and to take seriously the universal competence of persons and of their cultures (however unfamiliar) to ascribe meaning in addressing the problems of living. What Croce found so unacceptable in Italian racism was its failure to even attempt to make interpretive sense of the ways in which the people of the South had, as moral agents, ascribed meaning to living against a background of injustice. Italian racism thus avoided facing its own interpretive responsibility for perpetuating and enforcing this injustice by its indulgence of dehumanizing racist stereotypes, rationalized in terms of positivistic pseudoscience, that confused culture and nature.

This fact gives a particularly sinister character to Madison Grant's rationalization of his racist degradation of the Italian immigrants in

---

[307] See, on this background, R. H. Campbell and Andrew S. Skinner, *The Origins and Nature of the Scottish Enlightenment* (Edinburgh: John Donald Publishers, 1982); Istvan Hont and Michael Ignatieff, eds., *Wealth and Virtue: The Shaping of Political Economy in the Scottish Enlightenment* (Cambridge: Cambridge University Press, 1983); Ronald L. Meek, *Social Science and the Ignoble Savage* (Cambridge: Cambridge University Press, 1976).

terms of "superiority" "[i]n the field of art" but inferiority in the much more important "scientific research and discovery,"[308] for it was Grant's conception of hard science that rationalized his racism. Of course, as one would expect in such a self-deceiving ideologue, Grant gets the facts conspicuously wrong ("Galileo is after all the linchpin in the history of basic research"),[309] but his interpretive blunders are even more egregious. His misunderstanding of good human science is of a piece with his denigration of good art: he fails, as both Boas and Croce make clear, to understand, let alone give weight to, the role of culture and the interpretation of culture in human life. American racism crucially achieved the political power it unjustly did by its appeal to such anti-interpretive, positivistic pseudoscience, and part of its uncritical power rested on its denigration, as by Grant, of the interpretive powers of art. Any reasonable deconstruction of such racism must involve the exercise of such interpretive powers and refuse to marginalize the forms of what may seem to be nonutilitarian education and higher education that cultivate the critical exercise of such powers. From this perspective, conventional Italian American marginalization of such education must be critically understood and evaluated as integral to their Faustian bargain with American racism.

There was a gap, as I earlier observed, between Italian cosmopolitan elite culture and its political culture. But, the cosmopolitan forms of Italian culture in all their dazzling profusion connected to and expressed the interpretive life of its people and the ways in which they attached meaning to living in both private and public life. Music, for example, was "the only free and autonomous sign of the artistic life of the Italian people;"[310] theatrical forms like commedia del l'arte were rooted in Neapolitan popular satire,[311] and the Italian invention of opera, combining innovations in music and theater and spectacle,[312] had deep popular roots and impact on Italian culture (including, notably in the operas of Giuseppe Verdi, the aspirations of the Italian

---

[308] See Grant, *The Passing of the Great Race*, at 229. Madison also claims that Italians are less accomplished in literature. None of Madison's factual claims, including the superiority of non-Italian science, is defensible.

[309] Braudel, *Out of Italy*, 122. See, for elaboration of this point, Michael Sharratt, *Galileo: Decisive Innovator* (Cambridge: Cambridge University Press, 1994).

[310] Quoted in Fernand Braudel, *Out of Italy*, at 130; for discussion, see ibid., 130–6.

[311] See ibid., 139–46.

[312] See ibid., 149–57.

Risorgimento).[313] When Henry James characterized the impact of America on the Italians he encountered in New York City in terms of a loss of "colour," he described the effects of the relentlessly mechanical regime of work in America on Italians, displacing and even stigmatizing many of the cultural forms that had sustained their sense of the emotional richness and the moral complexity of public and private life (reflected in the human range and depth of artistic representation, both comic and tragic) , including the proper role of spontaneity and the play of the artistic and sensual imagination.[314] Such interpretive dimensions of the meaning of life withdrew to the privatized sphere of Italian American identity; life outside that sphere was to be conducted on rigidly productive, routinized American terms. Family life thus took on the extraordinary value it did for many Italian Americans because only in the family could life express these inward interpretive dimensions.

If we properly understand the withdrawal as a compromise with the injustice of American racism, an appropriate way of engaging in the required public discourse of Italian American identity is not only to insist on the importance and legitimacy of such cosmopolitan cultural forms in general but to bring to bear both on that discourse and on the larger discourse challenging the terms of what I earlier called moral slavery (including racism, sexism, and homophobia) the interpretive traditions they reflect, including those of Vico and Croce, which take seriously the universal competence of persons and of their cultures (however unfamiliar) to ascribe meaning in addressing the problems of living. This book, which is very much in the spirit of Croce's conception of interpretive history, attempts to illustrate how this project might reasonably be understood. We have at hand, however, other illustrations of such powers, for example, in the distinctive interpretive contributions Italian Americans have made to antiracist discourse (understanding the power and vitality of African American culture to resist

---

[313] See, for a good general discussion, Philip Gossett et al., *The New Grove: Masters of Italian Opera* (New York: W. W. Norton, 1983). On Verdi in particular, see Frank Walker, *The Man Verdi* (London: J. M. Dent, 1962); Mary Jane Phillips-Matz, *Verdi: A Biography* (New York: Oxford University Press, 1993); on his operas, see Budden, *The Operas of Verdi.*

[314] On the dark side of this public baroque culture, enforcing a cultural regimentation, see Barzini, *The Italians,* 299–328.

the dehumanizing ravages of slavery),[315] as well as antisexist and anti-homophobic discourse (understanding the cultural complexities of the representation of gender and sexuality).[316]

Public discourse on Italian American identity may interact particularly fruitfully with the comparable discourse on issues of gender and sexuality. The former discourse must in its nature reasonably contest the dehumanizing stereotypes in terms of which Italian American life has been construed, stereotypes that render unspoken and unspeakable the humanity, ethical rigor, hard work, and loving devotion characteristic of much Italian American life. No aspect of such life has been more subject to such obfuscating stereotypes than the area of their lives on which Italian Americans have traditionally placed such ultimate value—intimate family life. There is accordingly no story more difficult to tell truthfully, for such stories, subverting stereotypes, will be not popular.

Mario Puzo's career as a novelist illustrates my point. His remarkable interpretive study of an Italian American family, the novel *The Fortunate Pilgrim*,[317] captures the dense web of Italian American family life, including the pivotal moral character, devotion, and practical intelligence of an Italian mother (particularly, as in the case of my own maternal grandmother, when deprived of her husband) in trying to sustain and support her children to become responsible adults. The mother, the novel's heroine, is described sometimes in terms of a divine watchfulness, more usually in heroically Napoleonic terms:

> Luca Santa Angeluzzi-Corbo, a beleaguered general, pondered the fate and travails of her family, planned tactics, mulled strategy, counted resources, measured the loyalties of her allies.[318]

Puzo's novel, as good as it is, however, cuts against stereotype. His great popularity and success rest on a later novel that, in contrast, plays

---

[315] See, for example, Genovese, *Roll, Jordan, Roll*.

[316] See, for example, Camille Paglia, *Sexual Personae: Art and Decadence from Nefertiti to Emily Dickinson* (New York: Vintage, 1991); Richards, *Women, Gays, and the Constitution.* See also Michelangelo Signorile, *Queer in America: Sex, the Media, and the Closets of Power* (New York: Random House, 1993); Gabriel Rotello, *Sexual Ecology: AIDS and the Destiny of Gay Men* (New York: Dutton, 1997).

[317] See Puzo, *The Fortunate Pilgrim*.

[318] See ibid., 177.

to stereotype, in which the dominant figure of the godfather rules a mafia family in which women barely exist as personalities; the character of the godfather, in fact, was based on Puzo's mother, which gives some sense of the distortions that the force of dominant stereotypes required as the price to be paid for novelistic popularity.[319] The considerable popular success of Italian American artists has thus largely required accommodation, certainly not challenge, to dominant stereotypes.[320] It is surely paradoxical that Italian Americans, whose life has so centered on devotion to the family, should feel compelled, in public discourse, to so misrepresent it, finding it necessary, as in the case of Puzo's popular novel, even to change the genders of important characters in order to appeal to an American audience. That sense of compulsion rests on the continuing force of a largely uncontested form of American racism directed against Italian Americans as nonvisibly black.

It has often been non–Italian American artists, such as Arthur Miller, who have more truthfully and painfully investigated the impact of Americanization on Italian American identity, as in his portrayal of the tragic conflict of Eddie Carbone, an acculturated longshoreman working the docks of New York, with the illegal recent immigrant Rodolfo in Miller's play *A View from the Bridge*.[321] The tension between the two men arises from Eddie's unacknowledged feelings for his niece, Catherine, who falls in love with Rodolfo (as well as possibly from Eddie's suppressed homoerotic feelings for Rodolfo), but it is expressed by Eddie's homophobic outbursts at Rodolfo's very Italian love of music and singing,[322] culminating in Eddie's insulting kiss of Rodolfo before his niece.[323] Eddie's relentlessly American devotion to family and work has alienated him not only from the imaginative resources of Italian culture but, tragically, from himself. The very hos-

[319] See Puzo, *The Godfather*; on Puzo's basing Don Corleone on his mother, see Camille Paglia, "At Home With: Mario Puzo; It All Comes Back to Family," *New York Times*, May 8, 1997, section C, p. 1, col. 1; Camille, Paglia, "Questions for : Mario Puzo," *New York Times Magazine*, Sunday, March 30, 1997, section 6, p. 15.

[320] See, on this point, Carlos E. Cortés, "The Hollywood Curriculum on Italian Americans: Evolution of an Icon of Ethnicity," in Tomasi et al., *The Columbus People*, at 89–108.

[321] See Arthur Miller, *A View from the Bridge* (New York: Penguin, 1977).

[322] See ibid., 26–29, 41–7.

[323] See ibid., 62–4.

tility of the Americanized Italian American to the culture of the recent, notably illegal Italian immigrant shows the unacceptable sacrifice of multicultural resources that America unjustly exacted, making possible Eddie's loss of his moral compass as he betrays the illegal immigrants to the authorities. For Miller, who was reflecting on the populist sources of the ugly impulses of the McCarthy witchhunts against the allegedly un-American, Eddie's alienation from Italian culture reflects the moral vacuum that leads to the betrayal of the best values of both Italian and American culture.[324] This alienation deforms the humane character and values of Italian American family life, which are, in consequence, not brought critically to bear on the many areas of public discourse that would profit from such contributions. There are a number of such relevant contributions in the areas of sexuality and gender, that are well worth exploring.

First, Italian traditions of sexual love are continuous with those of the ancient Greco-Roman pagan world. Stable sexual relations are intrinsically a great human good; even the peasant who returns home in the evening after a hard day's work wants the *venerem facilem parabilemque* (easy and accessible love) of Horace.[325] This sense of life's legitimate earthly goods, including food and drink and sex, critically resists the American perfectionist ideology that has persistently devalued the place of such goods in human life, often motivated by nativist rejection of the way of life of recent immigrants (as in Prohibition).[326]

Second, the influential Italian theory of love, articulated by Marsilio Ficino, characterizes such love in suitably abstract terms as a transformative moral passion:

> But when the loved one loves in return, the lover leads his life in him. Here, surely, is a remarkable circumstance that whenever two people are brought together in mutual affection, one lives in the other and the

---

[324] See, for useful commentary, Arthur Wertheim, "A View from the Bridge," in Christopher Bigsby, ed., *The Cambridge Companion to Arthur Miller* (Cambridge: Cambridge University Press, 1997), at 101–14.

[325] Quoted in Gramsci, *Prison Notebooks*, at 304.

[326] See, on this and related points, David A. J. Richards, *Sex, Drugs, Death and the Law: An Essay on Human Rights and Overcriminalization* (Totowa, N.J.: Rowman and Littlefield, 1982); on American prohibitionism in the area of alcohol and drugs, see ibid., 157–95.

other in him. In this way they mutually exchange identities; each gives himself to the other in such a way that each receives the other in return. . . .

The truth must rather be that each has himself and has the other, too. A has himself, but in B; and B also has himself, but in A. When you love me, you contemplate me, and as I love you, I find myself in your contemplation of me; I recover myself, lost in the first place by own [sic] neglect of myself, in you, who preserve me. You do exactly the same in me. And then this, too, is remarkable: that after I have lost myself, as I recover myself through you, I have myself through you, and if I have myself through you, I have you sooner and to a greater degree than I have myself. I am therefore closer to you than I am to myself, since I keep a grasp on myself only through you as a mediary.[327]

Importantly, for Ficino, the gender of the object of love is not specified. Ficino's view (interpreting a similar doctrine in Plato)[328] suggests, if anything, that loving bonds between men realize the full moral meaning of reciprocal human love between equals, as, in Ficino's words, "they mutually exchange identities." Of course, the same tradition (Ficino, again following Plato) condemns as unnatural, indeed, unspeakable, same-sex relations as such. For Ficino, like Plato, the issue was resolved apparently by the acceptability, indeed, the ideal-

---

[327] Marsilio Ficino, *Commentary on Plato's Symposium*, trans. and intro. Sears Reynolds Jayne (Columbia: University of Missouri, 1944), 144–45. This aspect of Ficino's account should be distinguished from other elements of it that are less defensible, including his sharp distinction between love and physical union (ibid., 130) and his condemnation of the immoderate desire for copulation and unnatural sex (ibid., 143). On Ficino's as well as Pico della Mirandola's possible motives in legitimating forms of homosexual love, see Giovanni Dall'Orto, "'Socratic Love' as a Disguise for Same-Sex Love in the Italian Renaissance," in Kent Gerard and Gert Hekma, *The Pursuit of Sodomy: Male Homosexuality in Renaissance and Enlightenment Europe* (New York: Harrington Park Press, 1989), at 33–65, especially 37–38, 41–44.

[328] See Plato, *Phaedrus*, in *Collected Dialogues of Plato*, ed. Edith Hamilton and Huntington Cairns; trans. R. Hackworth (New York: Pantheon, 1961), at 476; Plato, *Symposium*, trans. Michael Joyce, in ibid., 527. Plato appears to have had a highly developed, idealized concept of romantic homosexual love that required that it rarely, if ever, be consummated. Plato, himself homosexual and a celebrant of aim-inhibited romantic homosexual love, appears to have condemned actual homosexual relations, introducing, for the first time anywhere, philosophical arguments for its unnaturalness. Plato, *Laws*, Book 7, trans. A. E. Taylor, *835d–42a, in ibid. 1226, 1401–6. For illuminating discussion

ization of homoerotic love, as the model for love, but not of sex.[329] If, however, we find the grounds for condemnation of same-sex relations unacceptable in contemporary circumstances, presumably we may reasonably interpret Ficino's argument to legitimate both gay sex and love.[330] Even when Baldesar Castiglione used Ficino's model of love in idealizing heterosexual courtly love,[331] the idealization of gender in sexual relations remained highly labile; the qualities of the gentlemen must not exclude, on the grounds that they are feminine, a cultivated love of the arts, such as music, because "the man who does not enjoy music can be sure that there is no harmony in his soul,"[332] and the attempt to exclude women from the powers and virtues admired in men is contested at length.[333] If the place of gender in love is culturally labile in these ways, the interpretation of intimate relations is obviously much more culturally open to the possibility, depending on circumstances, of shifting and complementing gender roles (including, as in a great artist like Titian, critical perspectives on such gender roles).[334] That is a cultural resource that may today be usefully harnessed to serve our growing sense of justice in matters of both gender and sexuality.[335]

Third, the moral power of women in Italian American culture has been more frankly acknowledged in Italy than the United States: "in reality, a crypto-matriarchy" involving "the vast, obscure, courageous, and awe-inspiring activities of Italian women of all times to keep their men on their feet, their families safe and the country func-

---

of Plato's insistence that romantic love be aim-inhibited and of the question whether Plato believed consummated homosexual acts themselves to be unnatural, see Gregory Vlastos, "The Individual as an Object of Love in Plato," in Vlastos, *Platonic Studies* (Princeton: Princeton University Press, 1973), 3, 22–28.

[329] See previous notes for fuller discussion of and references to Ficino's and Plato's views on this issue.

[330] See, for development of this argument at length, Richards, *Women, Gays, and the Constitution*.

[331] See Baldesar Castiglione, *The Courtier* George Bull trans. (London: Penguin, 1967), at 324–45.

[332] See ibid., 95.

[333] See, for example, ibid., at 211–7, 218–20, 221–3.

[334] See, on this point, Rona Goffen, *Titian's Women* (New Haven: Yale University Press, 1997).

[335] See, in general, Richards, *Women, Gays, and the Constitution*.

tioning at all."[336] The importance of Catherine of Siena in the formation of Italian political and religious as well as literary identity
bespeaks this cultural power.[337] This culture combines both pagan
and Christian elements (including the cult of the Madonna)[338] and
expresses itself in the special intensity of the mother-child bond[339] (as
an intimately indissoluble unit so that "every son is a 'mother's son'
[*figlio di mamma*]").[340] American Puritanism may have lost something
important in understanding humane moral and religious values, as
Henry Adams certainly believed,[341] by devaluing the role of Mary in
Christian theory and practice.[342] The interpretation of Mary's role has
been and is various; some interpretations may have served misogy-
nist ends,[343] but others may have offered empowering models for
women who identified "with her humility, yes, but also with her defi-
ance and with her victory: '*Deposuit potentes de sedibus suis, et exaltavit
humiles; esurientes implevit bonis, et divites dimisit inanes*—He hath put
down the mighty from their seats and exalted them of low degree; he
hath filled the hungry with good things, and the rich he hath sent

[336] See Barzini, *The Italians*, 202–3.

[337] See, for Catherine's importance in the development of Italian literature as well
as politics and moral theology, Peter Brand and Lino Pertile, eds., *The Cambridge History
of Italian Literature* (Cambridge: Cambridge University Press, 1996), at 124–5; Mary
O'Driscoll, O.P., *Catherine of Siena: Passion for the Truth Compassion for Humanity: Selected
Spiritual Writings* (Hyde Park, N.Y.: New City Press, 1993); Catherine of Siena, *The Dialogue of the Seraphic Virgin*, trans. Algar Thorold (Rockford, Ill.: Tan Books and Publishers, Inc., 1974).

[338] See, on this point, Covello, *The Social Background of the Italo-American School Child*,
at 118–22.

[339] See, on this point, Lopreato, *Italian Americans*, 50–1.

[340] See Allum, *Politics and Society in Post-War Naples*, at 57.

[341] See Henry Adams, *Mont Saint Michel and Chartres*, in Adams, *Henry Adams*,
337–695, at 596–7.

[342] For some sense of the range of conflicting views on this question, see Marina
Warner, *Alone of All Her Sex: The Myth and Cult of the Virgin Mary* (London: Picador, 1990);
Jaroslav Pelikan, *Mary through the Centuries: Her Place in the History of Culture* (New
Haven: Yale University Press, 1996); Caroline Walker Bynum, *Jesus as Mother: Studies in
the Spirituality of the High Middle Ages* (Berkeley and Los Angeles: University of California Press, 1982); Caroline Walker Bynum, *Holy Feast and Holy Fast: The Religious Significance of Food to Medieval Women* (Berkeley and Los Angeles: University of California
Press, 1987); Caroline Walker Bynum, *Fragmentation and Redemption: Essays on Gender and
the Human Body in Medieval Religion* (New York: Zone Books, 1991).

[343] See, for elaboration of this point, Warner, *Alone of All Her Sex*.

away.'"[344] Adams made his interpretive point about Mary rather starkly in his autobiography by contrasting civilizations founded on the Virgin and those based on the dynamo; American civilization, as a dynamo, needed a humane standpoint of resistance to its relentless exigency, namely, the humane values represented by the Virgin:

> The idea survived only as art. There one turned as naturally as though the artist were himself a woman. Adams began to ponder, asking himself whether he knew of any American artist who had ever insisted on the power of sex, as every classic had always done; but he could think only of Walt Whitman; Bret Harte, as far as the magazines would let him venture; and one or two painters, for the flesh-tones.[345]

Adams's view echoed, as I earlier noted, his friend Henry James's horrified vision of the effects of Americanization on the Italian immigrants. But, even under such acculturation, the very privatization of Italian American culture has sustained the kind of alternative standpoint that Adams calls for, one that certainly (as I earlier noted) affirmatively values human sexuality in general and the sexuality of women in particular and that might, in public discourse, critically sustain such a reasonable position. The work of Camille Paglia exemplifies one way that an alternative public discourse might be fruitfully elaborated, suggesting, as does Adams, that "America's sex problem began with the banishment of the maternal principle from Protestant cosmology."[346] It may be part of what James hoped for from Italian American multicultural identity that it might in this and other ways bring such a standpoint into public life and discourse. Such a standpoint may support an alternative understanding of gender that may be elaborated in ways that will advance the aims of rights-based feminism, in particular, a feminism that importantly valorizes sexuality on terms of justice.[347] Italian American women may have much to contribute to such critical discourse.[348] The story is still largely untold of how America's

[344] See Pelikan, *Mary through the Centuries*, 219.

[345] See Adams, *The Education of Henry Adams*, in Adams, *Henry Adams*, at 1071.

[346] See Paglia, *Sexual Personae*, 572.

[347] On the character of such rights-based feminism, see, in general, Richards, *Women, Gays, and the Constitution*.

[348] See, for example, Camille Paglia, *Sexual Personae*.

more liberal feminist ethos impacted on these strong, highly intelligent, industrious, courageous women as they moved out of the home and into the workplace. By far the most difficult change for them, as for similarly situated men, would be the realization of aspirations to higher education and to an intellectual life, both devalued by their culture as nonutilitarian. Such women (and men) still enjoy little cultural support or understanding among Italian Americans,[349] when, consistent with my argument of the need for morally independent public discourse about Italian American identity and related issues, they most deserve it.

If Italian Americans are now more willing and able to contest the terms of their privatized Italian American identity than ever before in their history in the United States, they must be willing to contest it in the most reasonable terms available to them. Such discourse will enable us to forge not only a new Italian American identity that is more truthful to our experience and sense of life (expressing in public life what James called our "colour") but an American identity more worthy of our allegiance. Our multicultural identity, thus acknowledged, will, I hope, better enrich both ourselves and the nation in ways that bear comparison to the role other claims of identity have played in advancing the values of liberal nationalism. To be clear on these points, we must explore the general question of how these questions of identity arise and what contribution they make to the discourse of American constitutionalism.

---

[349] See, on this point, Glazer and Moynihan, *Beyond the Melting Pot*, at 216; for an illuminating novel dealing with the struggle of an Italian American women for such education, see Hendin, *The Right Thing to Do*.

5

Multicultural Identity
and Human Rights

QUESTIONS OF MULTICULTURAL identity have been discussed in the recent philosophical literature largely in terms of Will Kymlicka's defense of what he calls multicultural citizenship.[1] Kymlicka raises only to set aside what he calls the question of "polyethnicity and the American ethnic revival"[2] in order to discuss what is of interest to him: the place in a liberal polity such as Canada of claims by national minorities such as the Amerindians and Québécois to legal guarantees that enable them to sustain their distinctive cultures. Kymlicka regards ethnic claims made by American-style immigrant populations as grounded quite differently. Immigrants, as distinct from refugees, choose to leave their own culture and know that their success depends on integration into the institutions of the national culture of the country to which they emigrate; the expectation of integration is not unjust as long as that integration does not express prejudice; the American ethnic revival itself valorizes ethnic culture but in a context that calls for "a revision in the terms of integration, not a rejection of integration."[3] He distinguishes from both groups (national minorities and immigrants) the situation of African Americans, who were neither allowed to maintain their earlier languages and culture nor integrated into American culture.[4] For Kymlicka, multicultural citizenship, properly understood, describes the coexistence of national minorities, with quite distinct cultures, in a liberal polity. American-style ethnic identity is not multicultural citizenship in his sense because American

---

[1] See Will Kymlicka, *Multicultural Citizenship: A Liberal Theory of Minority Rights* (Oxford: Clarendon Press, 1995). See also Kymlicka, *Liberalism, Community, and Culture*; Kymlicka, *The Rights of Minority Cultures*.

[2] See Kymlicka, *Multicultural Citizenship*, 61.

[3] See ibid., 98.

[4] See ibid., 24–5.

immigrants have ostensibly waived their membership in a foreign nationality[5] and lack "the territorial and institutional prerequisites for self-government."[6]

My focus in this book has been a topic that is not central to Kymlicka's concerns, namely, American-style ethnic identity as an important issue in both liberal nationalism in general and American liberal nationalism in particular. I regard the topic as more central and more interesting than Kymlicka does because, according to my view and in refutation of Kymlicka's view, African American rights-based discourse has pivotally asserted its claims against an unjustly racialized conception of American national identity[7] (claims of feminist and gay and lesbian identity have protested comparably flawed unjust conceptions of American national identity; see chapter 4). Kymlicka quite artificially isolates antiracist discourse from claims of ethnic identity in ways that distort both. The unjust political entrenchment of American racism thus worked its havoc, as I have argued, not only on African Americans and Native Americans and Asians but on Jews and Italians, and the corresponding terms of rights-based protest of American racism included, on grounds of principle, claims of ethnic identity as well.

Multicultural identity is an important constructive resource in rights-based protest in all its forms. Such protest is, I have urged, best understood as a challenge to what I call the terms of one's moral slavery. Such slavery has two features: first, the abridgment of basic human rights of conscience, speech, intimate life, and work; second, its rationalization in terms of dehumanizing stereotypes (defining the group in question as nonbearers of human rights) that limit views and speakers to the terms of the stereotype. Accordingly, rights-based protest of the terms of moral slavery challenges it, first, by claiming the rights denied in one's own voice and, second, engaging in reasonable discourse that challenges the dominant stereotype in terms of which one's group has been dehumanized. Both elements of this protest importantly denaturalize the way in which the structural injustice of moral slavery has been rationalized (in terms of an ostensible fact such as race or gender

---

[5] See ibid., 96.

[6] See ibid.

[7] See, for a similar view, Patterson, *The Ordeal of Integration: Progress and Resentment in America's "Racial Crisis."*

or gendered sexuality). The very fact of protest humanizes the pro-
tester, transforming her or him from a stereotype into a person, and the
terms of the protest bring to bear on public discourse the experience of
the forms of culture that often nurtured and sustained resistance to the
dehumanizing terms of one's moral slavery. It is thus no accident that
the most fully developed and articulated American movement of
protest, African American dissent, included the emergence into public
discourse of the dignity and power of an African American culture that
had been unjustly stigmatized and the creation of new cultural forms
more adequate to the dignity of that culture (the Harlem Renaissance).[8]
Protest of the terms of one's moral slavery is, in its nature, both culturally expressive and creative. Claims of African American identity in
these terms importantly expressed, affirmed, and creatively elaborated
a cultural history and tradition that were entitled to respect at the same
time that they challenged the justice of a conception of American
nationality that had required their dehumanizing subordination.
African Americans' emerging sense of multicultural identity as both
ethnically African and American was the bipolar basis for their constructive identification of and challenge to the contradictions in fundamental American constitutional principles and ideals that had allowed
them to be dehumanized. Their sense of themselves as having such a
legitimate multicultural identity was not peripheral but essential to
their protest. It was because American constitutional principles and
ideals were so profoundly implicated in the structural injustice of
racism that they had to forge a morally independent sense of ethnic
identity, one that expressed and elaborated their culture (including its
history of unjust treatment), that would make possible the remarkable
impartiality and profundity of their challenge to American liberal
nationalism.

The point can be generalized, I believe, to include all the forms of
rights-based protest to moral slavery earlier discussed (chapter 4).
Women, as well as gays and lesbians, have had to develop, express,
and elaborate a sense of shared history and culture in terms of which
they could both understand and articulate their rights-based protest of
the terms of their moral slavery. The sense of having and elaborating a
history and culture affords the requisite morally independent critical
standpoint from which, as a woman or as gay or lesbian, one expresses,

---

[8] See, on this development, Hutchinson, *The Harlem Renaissance in Black and White*.

affirms, and creatively elaborates a cultural tradition that is entitled to respect at the same time that one challenges the fundamental justice of a sense of American nationality based on one's subordination. Such a sense of identity, arising from rights-based protest of the terms of one's moral slavery, as much interprets as it constructs such a sense of identity. Certainly, for women as well as for gays and lesbians, the very act of making rights-based claims in public importantly contested the conventional terms of their gender and sexual identities, which had required their silence. The refusal to be silent was thus the basis for forging a new sense of identity, which was facilitated by the reasonable discourse it made possible about the terms of their moral slavery. Such discourse included often the recovery of dissident traditions that had been marginalized in mainstream historical research, enabling, as it had for African American dissenters, the development of a sense of alternative cultural traditions with which one could choose to identify in the reconstruction of one's previously stigmatized identity on terms of justice.[9] Such alternative traditions take on their critical force as ways of reasonably opposing and protesting the previously hegemonic cultural force of the dominant orthodoxy on matters of race or gender or sexual preference, in particular, the dehumanizing stereotypes in terms of which structural injustice of moral slavery was rationalized. All such alternative traditions are, in the terms of my argument, the constructively interpretive identification and creative elaboration of multicultural resources through which one gives voice to the humanizing protest of the injustice of the dominant orthodoxy that previously was viewed as alone occupying the legitimate space of public culture.

The sense of the American tradition as, in this sense, importantly multicultural is a major achievement of rights-based protest of the terms of moral slavery. It is such resources that allow us to understand the voices and experiences of others as persons struggling against the cultural terms of the structural injustice inflicted on them. Put another way, the structural injustice of moral slavery has had the force it has had because American national identity, ostensibly founded and then reforged, after the Civil War, on the basis of liberal nationalism, has wrongly imagined itself to be justly monocultural, silencing the discourse of alternative traditions that might reasonably have challenged

---

[9] See, for a discussion of such discourse at length, Richards, *Women, Gays, and the Constitution*.

its fundamental coherence as liberal nationalism. If such protest (whether antiracist or antisexist or antihomophobic) has made possible moral progress in the coherence of American liberal nationalism, as it certainly has (see chapter 4), it has been through the legitimation of multicultural traditions through which groups previously subject to the structural injustice of moral slavery have forged a self-respecting sense of identity as bearers of human rights against a hegemonic tradition that dehumanized them by attempting to crush and silence the voice and mind through which they could imagine themselves as persons with the inalienable human right to protest injustice. Multiculturalism, understood from this perspective, has been a condition of progress in the fundamental justice and legitimacy of American liberal nationalism.

Consistent with this perspective, Joseph Rhea has recently shown how identity politics has confronted the American public mind with its historical injustices to Native Americans, Asian Americans, Latinos, and blacks,[10] injustices often based on manifestations of American cultural racism. Such dissent has quite rightly demanded that the representation of American history include its history of injustice, thus responsibly bringing into public discourse and debate our contemporary responsibilities ethically to confront and rectify the cultural entrenchment of racism through hegemonically enforced narratives that failed to acknowledge the internal contradictions in American liberal nationalism.

My attempt in this work has been further to elaborate this new perspective to comprise as well the larger moral and constitutional importance of one strand of what Kymlicka calls "polyethnicity and the American ethnic revival."[11] I have urged a certain interpretation and critical evaluation of the gradual emergence of serious public discourse about Italian American identity as a way of reforging such identity on terms of justice. The interest of my account is its focus on the Italian American experience of liberal nationalism in Italy and in the United States as the background for both the interpretation and the critical evaluation of Italian American identity. My view of this form of identity, like the related rights-based claims of identity earlier discussed,

---

[10] See Joseph Tilden Rhea, *Race Pride and the American Identity* (Cambridge, Mass.: Harvard University Press, 1997).

[11] See Kymlicka, *Multicultural Citizenship*, 61.

calls self-consciously for a heightening of the sense of multicultural identity—interpreting, expressing, and elaborating cultural strands of the Italian American experience on the basis of which Italian Americans, previously subject to unjust stigma as nonvisibly black, may forge a self-respecting sense of identity against a dominant tradition that dehumanized them by compelling privatization of their multicultural identity.

My earlier suggestions about the critical uses of Italian American culture as a self-consciously multicultural identity were along these lines (chapter 4) and should be understood accordingly. The object of rights-based protest is the refusal to live in both public and private life as a stereotype. To undertake such a protest requires what initially may seem to be a personally threatening alienation from familiar guidelines. But the protest of the terms of a distorting stereotype, one based on structural injustice, empowers personal and ethical life in three related ways. First, it dignifies a culture previously unjustly stigmatized; second, it investigates the terms of the abridgment of basic human rights on which the stigma rests; third, it makes available reasonable voice and discourse to rebut the stereotypes in terms of which the unjust abridgment was rationalized.

Rights-based protest thus by its very terms makes clear the humane values of the Italian American culture previously unjustly stigmatized along every evaluative dimension. These dimensions include, as we have seen, its traditions of humane tolerance of religious and racial difference, its humanistic interpretive integration of pluralistic secular and religious sources and their associated sense of history, its distaste for the political corruption of religion and its ethical interpretation of what is valuable in religion, its insistence on moral independence in intimate life and its valuation of sexual love and intimacy, its emphasis on the role of the arts and the cultivation of our imaginative moral powers, and its valuation of dignity as a personal, ethical, and political value. It was cultural values of these sorts that sustained the Italian Americans in their struggle against injustice in both Italy and the United States and their courageous search to construct a way of life more consistent with these values.

Such protest advances our understanding as well of the cultural terms of the structural injustice inflicted on Italian Americans both in Italy and in America, in particular, the terms of the abridgment of basic human rights that stigmatized their identity. We have noted the traditional failure democratically to extend to the people of the South the value of the right of conscience and speech (including educational opportunities), and the ways in which such abridgments continued in the United States; American racism precisely rested on silencing moral powers of dissent and protest, leading to the privatization of Italian American identity, as well as the associated devaluation of higher nonutilitarian education that sustained this privatization. We have also noted how this unjust privatization sustained and was sustained by an unjust limitation in the kinds of work available and in associated ambitions, rationalized in terms of a withdrawal into family life that privatization unjustly required and sustained.

Finally, such protest makes possible reasonable discourse that may rebut the terms of the dehumanizing stereotypes in terms of which the injustice has been sustained. For Italian Americans in particular, the distorting stereotypes of the psychopathic amoralism of the Mafia family could no longer reasonably be imposed on the hard work and ethical rigor in fact characteristic of Italian American public and private life. Indeed, the very terms of the stereotype would be dissolved in wider public understanding of its roots in the cultural injustice that led to the privatization of Italian American identity. It is the injustice of such privatization and its associated crude and dehumanizing stereotypes that should be the object of public concern, scrutiny, and debate. Italian American multicultural identity, properly understood and elaborated, thus offers cultural resources by which such a humanizing discourse might proceed on terms of justice.

If I am right about this, such discourse may critically raise and illuminate not only Italian American identity and other forms of multicultural ethnic identity but larger issues about the past and present relationship of American and European forms of liberal nationalism that are, in the wake of World War II, perhaps of more interest now than they have been since the end of the eighteenth century (chapter 2). In particular, multiculturalism may be as useful here as it has been elsewhere in advancing the theory and practice of liberal nationalism both in the United States and abroad.

As we earlier saw, the problem of racism has been as much a European problem (in the form of a racist interpretation of anti-Semitism; see chapter 2) as an American one, and the experience of World War II and the defeat of Nazi racism undoubtedly had a major impact on

America's willingness more critically to address and remedy its cultural racism (chapter 4). The multicultural legacy of European immigrants to the United States understandably touches on these issues directly, as is seen, for example, in the longstanding interest of Irish Americans in Irish liberal nationalism.[12] Of course, as the Irish American example makes clear, such an interest does not, in and of itself, advance critical understanding of internal defects in American liberal nationalism.[13] But, some forms of such interest may and do, notably, the interests of American Jews shaped by a certain understanding of their European background and its ongoing relevance to the critical evaluation of American liberal nationalism.

In the late nineteenth century, European Jews increasingly despaired of the feasibility of any enduring form of liberal nationalism that would protect their basic human rights. When Theodor Herzl made the case for political Zionism, he argued as a secular Jew facing, as he saw it, growing evidence (e.g., the Dreyfus affair)[14] that anti-Semitism debarred the acceptance of Jews anywhere:

> The Jewish question still exists. It would be foolish to deny it...The Jewish question exists wherever Jews live in perceptible numbers. Where it does not exist, it is carried by Jews in the course of their migrations. We naturally move to those places where we are not persecuted, and there our presence produces persecution. This is the case in every country, and will remain so, even in those highly civilized—for instance, France—until the Jewish question finds a solution on a political basis.[15]

Herzl analyzed anti-Semitism as an ugly political fact of life, compounded "of vulgar sport, of common trade jealousy, of inherited prejudice, of religious intolerance, and also of pretended self-defence."[16] His analysis serves a purpose very like that of Madison's theory of fac-

---

[12] See Patrick J. Blessing, "Irish," in Thernstrom ed., *Harvard Encylopedia of American Ethnic Groups*, 536–8; McCaffrey, *The Irish Catholic Diaspora in America*, 138–68.

[13] See, in general, Ignatiev, *How the Irish Became White*.

[14] See Theodor Herzl, *The Jewish State*, trans. Sylvie d'Avigdor (New York: Dover, 1988), at 34–5.

[15] See Herzl, *The Jewish State*, 75.

[16] See ibid.

tion in his constitutional constructivism,[17] namely, to state those facts of political psychology that any constitutional thinker had to take seriously in making institutional proposals intended to apply to the group activities characteristic of political life. Anti-Semitism should, Herzl insisted, be regarded as "a national question,"[18] that is, as imposing fixed limits on what people could be included in a European sense of nationality. In light of Hitler and the Holocaust, his pessimism about Europe seems, if anything, understated.[19]

Herzl's pessimism extended, however, not just to Europe but to a nation whose traditions he understood much less well—the United States.[20] It is striking, however, that many of the American Jews who disagreed with him about this point nonetheless supported political Zionism and its eventual expression, the State of Israel.[21] As we earlier saw (chapter 4), Louis Brandeis, both deeply committed to America and a Zionist, indeed argued that commitment to Zionism desirably preserved the multicultural integrity of American Jewry. Identifying the Zionist movement with Mazzini's liberal nationalism,[22] both Zionism and the Jewish emigration to and settlement in the United States rested on this moral ideal. Commitment to Zionism and to America were consistent, since they sustained a multicultural identity more supportive of this ideal:

> Let no American imagine that Zionism is inconsistent with Patriotism. Multiple loyalties are objectionable only if they are inconsistent. A man is a better citizen of the United States for being also a loyal citizen of is state, and of his city; for being loyal to his family, and to his profession or trade; for being loyal to his college or his lodge. Every Irish American who contributed toward advancing

[17] See, on this and related points, Richards, *Foundations of American Constitutionalism.*
[18] See ibid., 76.
[19] For the full range of Zionist arguments, including those of Herzl, see Arthur Hertzberg, ed., *The Zionist Idea: A Historical Analysis and Reader* (New York: Atheneum, 1959).
[20] See Herzl, *The Jewish State,* 75, 108, 123.
[21] See, in general, Wheatcroft, *The Controversy of Zion.* On doubts about the liberal nationalism of Israel, see Zeev Sternhell, *The Founding Myths of Israel,* trans. David Maisel (Princeton: Princeton University Press, 1998).
[22] See Louis Brandeis, "The Jewish Problem and How to Solve It," in Hertzberg, *The Zionist Idea,* 517–23, at 518.

home rule was a better man and a better American for the sacrifice he made. Every American Jew who aids in advancing the Jewish settlement in Palestine, though he feels that neither he nor his descendants will ever live there, will likewise be a better man and a better American for doing so.[23]

For Brandeis, rights-based protest of the terms of the traditional moral slavery of the Jews was "the laborious task of inculcating self-respect, a task which can be accomplished only by restoring the ties of the Jew to the noble past of his race, and by making him realize the possibilities of a no less glorious future."[24] American Jewish support for Zionism expressed, sustained, and elaborated a long tradition of dissenting struggle against the stereotypical dehumanization of the Jews and thus helped preserve a sense of multicultural Jewish American identity that was similarly capable of such protest on terms of justice in the United States (for example, the role of Franz Boas and others in advancing antiracist principles).

The mingling of European and American concerns about racist anti-Semitism is conspicuous in Israel Zangwill's expansive hopes for the impact of Jewish American identity on American liberal nationalism expressed in his influential play *The Melting-Pot*,[25] (a play conspicuously dedicated to the public man who much admired it, Theodore Roosevelt),[26] which gave a name and a rationale to the meaning of America for the European immigrants to the United States of 1880–1920. The main protagonist of the play, David Quixano, argues with his more pessimistic uncle, Mendel, who, like Herzl, questions whether America can overcome its cultural anti-Semitism and treat Jews as persons; if his uncle were right, Zionism would, David argues, be the only responsible alternative.[27] Zangwill certainly accepts that there exists one strand of the American tradition that he calls "the anti-Semitism of American uncivilisation";[28] indeed, he embodies such attitudes in one of the blue-blood Americans in the play, Quincy Daven-

---

[23] See ibid., 519–20.
[24] See ibid., 521.
[25] See Israel Zangwill, *The Melting-Pot* (New York: Macmillan, 1922).
[26] See ibid., v, 201.
[27] See ibid., 42.
[28] See ibid., 204.

port, Jr. However, David rejects Davenport's attitudes in this revealing exchange:

> DAVID: Not for you and such as you have I sat here writing and dreaming; not for you who are killing my America!
>
> QUINCY: *Your* America, forsooth, you Jew-immigrant!
>
> VERA: Mr. Davenport!
>
> DAVID: Yes—Jew-immigrant! But a Jew who knows that your Pilgrim Fathers came straight out of his Old Testament, and that our Jew-immigrants are a greater factor in the glory of this great commonwealth than some of you sons of the soil. It is you, freak-fashionables, who are undoing the work of Washington and Lincoln, vulgarising your high heritage, and turning the last and noblest hope of humanity into a caricature.
>
> QUINCY [*Rocking with laughter*]: Ha! Ha! Ha! Ho! Ho! Ho! [*To Vera*] You never told me your Jew-scribbler was a socialist!
>
> DAVID: I am nothing but a simple artist, but I come from Europe, one of her victims, and I know that she is a failure; that her palaces and peerages are outworn toys of the human spirit, and that the only hope of mankind lies in a new world. And here—in the land of to-morrow—you are trying to bring back Europe—
>
> QUINCY [*Interjecting*]: I wish we could!—

The America imagined by David Mendel is self-consciously not the real America such immigrants faced but a moral possibility and responsibility that the new immigrants, on the basis of their multicultural identity, can and should make more probable. American Jews, for example, bring to such debates both a moral heritage and an historical experience that may and should remind Americans of the precious normative heritage of "the Pilgrim fathers" and of the seminal American constitutional promise of a secular republic based on respect for the inalienable right to conscience.[29]

For Zangwill, America's treatment of its immigrants would be an important normative test for the coherence of its liberal nationalism. If it could be pressed better to meet this test, as Zangwill believes it could

---

[29] See, for example, ibid., 97, 208–9.

reasonably be expected to be, it might make possible in the United States a humane sense of moral community unimaginable in Europe. The metaphor for this moral possibility is the mutual love of David Mendel, a Russian Jew whose parents were killed in a progrom, and Vera Revendal, the estranged daughter of a Russian noble who (as it turns out) ordered the program that killed David's family. America may make possible, Zangwill suggests, common grounds of principle (bespeaking a sense of brotherhood and even love) between David and Vera. Whether America can meet this test (symbolized by the question, with which the play ends, whether David's and Vera's love can survive) is left open, as, for Zangwill, it must be. The very fact that such cross-cultural intimacy could be an open question (in America, in contrast to Europe) suggests the important role the immigrants might play in making it probable. Indeed, if ought implies can, such a normative responsibility might be incumbent on American immigrants, since only here (where such intimacy is at least culturally possible) could such ethical obligations be feasibly acted on.

Zangwill's thought is that American identity and the identity of its recent immigrants can, properly understood, develop together in a way that benefits both, in terms of achieving a more coherent and principled understanding of liberal nationalism. Precisely because the Jews have suffered such a long history of unjust persecution, they are

> the toughest of all the white elements that have been poured into the American crucible, the race having, by its unique experience of several thousand years of exposure to alien majorities, developed a salamandrine power of survival.[30]

The very power of that kind of historically rooted sense of identity makes the resulting sense of multicultural identity a powerful resource in the internal criticism of defects in American liberal nationalism (for example, its anti-Semitism). The Jewish experience with the promises and betrayals of liberal nationalism in Europe made Jews more exacting critics of the comparable promises and betrayals they encountered in American liberal nationalism, allowing them to bring to bear on their American experience demands for equal respect that were, properly

---

[30] See ibid., 204.

understood, constitutionally enforceable demands. In subjecting American culture and law to such reasonable demands, American Jews not only preserved and elaborated the best elements of the Jewish tradition but helped realize and extend the best values of the American constitutional tradition, as well. The aims of multicultural and American identity were, as Louis Brandeis urged, mutually complementary.

Zangwill's reference to "the white elements," however, drew a self-consciously unstable line between the claims by and on behalf of the multicultural identity of the new European immigrants and that of African Americans. On the one hand, Zangwill pandered to racist stereotypes: "This is not to deny that the prognathous face is an ugly and undesirable type of countenance or that it connotes a lower average of intellect and ethics, or that white and black are as yet too far apart for profitable fusion."[31] But, on the other hand, Zangwill rather anxiously questioned many dominant racist stereotypes of the day, describing much racial prejudice as just that, "negrophobia . . . not likely to remain eternally at its present barbarous pitch,"[32] based, as it is, on "largely panic-born myths."[33] Zangwill even suggested that "the 'Melting Pot' of American will not fail to act in a measure it has acted on the Red Indian, who has found it almost as facile to mate with his white neighbours as with his black"[34] and pointed, remarkably for his period, to the growing impact of African American culture on American culture as a desirable "spiritual miscegenation."[35]

Zangwill's argument shows the difficulty that even a morally independent multicultural critic had in dealing with the burden that American racism had imposed on the late-nineteenth-century immigrants as nonvisible blacks; the impulse was, of course, to distinguish one's own case from that of African Americans or even to acquiesce in the racialization of other immigrant groups (as Zangwill did about "the dark-white races on the northern shore of the Mediterranean—the Spaniards, Sicilians, etc.—who have already been crossed with the sons of Ham from its southern shore").[36] In an era when the unjust cultural

---

[31] See ibid., 206.
[32] See ibid., 204.
[33] See ibid., 205.
[34] See ibid.
[35] See ibid., 207.
[36] See ibid., 205.

construction of American racism was still so little publicly acknowledged or even understood, it is difficult to blame any of the recent
immigrants (or other immigrants, like the Irish Americans, before
them)[37] for not seeing the continuity of their own case with that of
African Americans (or, conversely, to blame African Americans who
during this period and earlier stigmatized recent immigrants as inferior).[38] What is striking in Zangwill's argument, against this background, is that his sense of multicultural identity led him at least to
raise reasonable doubts about the racist subjugation of African Americans. Other American Jews, like Boas, aggressively raised even more
profoundly subversive doubts.

It is, I believe, the very possibility of raising such doubts (either in
theory or practice) that made the new immigrants such a threat to
American racism, indeed (incomprehensibly to them), increasingly
attracted racism.[39] American cultural racism arose, as we have seen
(chapter 4), from a long-standing abridgment of the basic human rights
of a class of persons and the rationalization of their corresponding
servile status in terms of dehumanizing stereotypes whose force
depended on limiting persons and issues to discourse consistent with
the abridgment. This cultural racism could be extended to the new
immigrants because they came from European cultures in which many
of them had endured a similar cultural injustice (European anti-Semitism in the case of the Jews—the Jew as the slave of the Christian [see
chapter 3], and the racism directed at Southern Italians). Two factors,
however, made the newcomers a particular threat to the public consensus supportive of American racism. First, American racism drew its
force from the confusion of nature and culture, crucially suppressing
any suggestion that racism was culturally constructed. But, as Henry
James clearly saw in the case of the Italian Americans, the Italians he
had known in Italy were transformed by America; this could not be
attributed to racial differences (there were none either in Italy or here)
but was clearly due to culture. The same could be reasonably suggested
about other immigrants. If so, American racism would have to face its

---

[37] See, in general, Ignatiev, *How the Irish Became White*.

[38] See, on this point, Douglas, *Terrible Honesty*, 307–8; for the animus against the
Irish during the earlier period of their massive immigration to the United States, see
Takaki, *A Different Mirror*, at 154.

[39] See, for a good discussion of this process, Douglas, *Terrible Honesty*, 303–307.

dirty secret, its unjust cultural construction. Second, the force of American racism importantly depended on the unjust repression of both speakers and views that might challenge its authority; indeed, consistent with the paradox of intolerance, it was most likely to scapegoat such dissent precisely when dissent was most reasonably needed or likely. But, the recent immigrants were often not culturally attuned, as a matter of practice or theory, to the terms of American racism; Italian Americans, as we saw, were both less anti-Semitic and racist than mainstream Americans, even doing business with African Americans in ways that shocked other Americans. The force of American racism fell with all its accustomed ferocity on the recent immigrants, making them ideological scapegoats, because they might and, indeed, as we saw, did raise reasonable doubts about American racism that Americans wanted not to hear. Both the excesses of the Palmer raids (which led to the deportation of politically dissident immigrants) and the unfair terms of the trial of Sacco and Vanzetti made clear to Italian Americans that any ideologically dissident questioning (like advocacy of anarchism) would not be tolerated.[40] It is in this spirit that, in Zangwill's play, the blueblood Quincy dismisses David Mendel's attack on American anti-Semitism as socialism. Such massive ideological repression made clear that the American public mind was not open to any serious challenge to its cultural racism and, in particular, to a challenge from recent immigrants and that the 100 percent Americanization of such immigrants rapidly became an overwrought crusade to repress any serious multicultural examination of the defects in American liberal nationalism.[41]

America was, in the wake of the Civil War, more constitutionally committed to liberal nationalism than it had ever been.[42] Yet, in this period, as we have seen, American racism was, in flagrant violation of these liberal guarantees, entrenched in the public and private life of the nation by the judicial legitimation of both racial segregationist and antimiscegenationist laws. The immigrants who came from Europe between 1880 and 1920 were importantly shaped by their own cultural experiences of the promises and betrayals of liberal nationalism in Europe. When they found American racism so aggressively targeted at

---

[40] See DeConde, *Half Bitter, Half Sweet*, 164–8; Gambino, *Blood of My Blood*, 108–12.

[41] See, on this point, Higham, *Strangers in the Land*, at 234–63.

[42] See, on this point, Richards, *Conscience and the Constitution*.

them, they faced hard choices. Some chose, as Italian Americans largely did, to privatize their multicultural identity, largely accepting their stigmatized public status as nonvisible blacks by withdrawing into private life and not engaging in a public discourse, based on their multicultural identity, that would protest that status; other groups, as we have seen, often engaged in multicultural protest, finding common grounds with African Americans in increasingly successful forms of antiracist dissent. In light of these successes and the availability of the principles of public law (including both principles of free speech and antiracist principles), I have argued that Italian Americans increasingly define and should define a public identity as Italian Americans that, properly understood, brings their multicultural identity powerfully to bear on the understanding and elaboration of basic issues of human rights, their own and others'.

The growing importance of a sense of ethnic identity is, from the perspective developed in this book, not a matter of optional cultural aesthetics, let alone a matter of regret,[43] but a consequence of an emerging theory and practice that harness multicultural identity to the protest of the terms of one's unjustly stigmatized identity (what I have called moral slavery). If I am right about this, multicultural identity is an important cultural resource that can empower morally independent voices and the reasonable public discourse they make possible about the promises and betrayals of liberal nationalism, here and abroad. It can also, properly understood, critically address the continuing political force of American racism.

Racism could not continue to have the force it has if more Americans critically recognized how significantly it had unjustly affected their own lives. My focus in this book on Italian American identity arises, in part, from this concern. The privatization of Italian American identity depended on a collective loss of memory about the racist indignities endured by the people of the South in Italy and in America, as if that were a reasonable condition for one's Americanization. But

---

[43] See, for arguments of this sort, J. Harvie Wilkinson III, *One Nation Indivisible: How Ethnic Separatism Threatens America* (Reading, Mass.: Addison-Wesley, 1997); Peter D. Salins, *Assimilation American Style* (New York: HarperCollins, 1997); Arthur M. Schlesinger, Jr., *The Disuniting of America: Reflections on a Multicultural Society* (New York: W. W. Norton, 1992). But cf. Nathan Glazer, *We Are All Multiculturalists Now* (Cambridge, Mass.: Harvard University Press, 1997).

failures to make sense of important cultural memories cut one off from a continuing sense of the human struggles against injustice fought by one's parents and grandparents and thus deprive one of the resources better to understand and give effect to one's sense of ethical responsibility to refuse complicity with comparable injustices today. American racism could not reasonably be regarded as limited to African Americans or Asian Americans if the argument of this book has force. Yet it is often so regarded when the shape of one's identity as nonvisibly black is no longer critically understood or acknowledged, let alone protested.

Multicultural identity, as I have defended it, makes such discourse more available and thus enlarges the range of public intelligence about the sources of the remarkable durability and political power of the pervasive evil of American racism and empowers a more expansive sense of responsibility to combat it. It critically confronts how American cultural racism has sustained itself by imposing its terms on new immigrants, themselves often regarded as nonvisibly black (in effect, as white skins wearing black masks), as the condition of their Americanization. Correspondingly, it suggests a new public space, based on a growing sense of the indignity of this pervasive injustice, for protests that might be the basis for larger political coalitions that might better address and remedy such defects in American liberal nationalism.

I do not believe that, if such a sense of multicultural identity were more broadly cultivated, either the American people or the judiciary could take the view they currently do take against forms of affirmative action as a reasonable remedy for racism.[44] It is, in my view, quite ideologically natural that critical attacks on the emerging discourse of ethnic identity often relate their worries to the legitimation of affirmative action, suggesting that the two issues move in tandem.[45] Indeed they do, but not in the way such critics of both polyethnicity and affirmative action suppose; rather, multicultural discourse, properly understood and developed, does not balkanize but better reveals the pervasive extent of the evils of American cultural racism and the role reasonable programs of affirmative action might play in addressing and remedying them.

[44] See, for an important judicial endorsement of this view, *Adarand Constructors, Inc. v. Pena*, 115 S. Ct. 2097 (1995).

[45] See, for example, Wilkinson, *One National Indivisible.*

Nothing in the reasonable understanding of the basis for the scrutiny extended to invidious racial discrimination requires, as the judiciary now supposes, that it be extended to all racial classifications. It is not a reasonably defensible constitutional principle that all classifications, such as race, that turn on immutable and salient characteristics must be forbidden, for many such classifications are uncontroversially just.[46] It is reasonable to condemn expressions through law of irrationalist prejudice that expresses a history and culture of what I earlier called moral slavery (chapter 4), but that principle condemns only laws that expressed such prejudice, not laws that use classifications directed at remedying the evil inflicted by such prejudice. Nonetheless, both many Americans and the judiciary irresponsibly condemn, as a matter of principle, affirmative actions plans that are reasonably necessary to address the cultural evils inflicted by moral slavery. Such views fail to take seriously either the depth of the racism inflicted on African Americans or the extent of racism inflicted on others. A public discourse based on multicultural identity would address this problem for two reasons.

First, American racism not only targeted, for reasons earlier discussed, the new immigrants but also, for the same reasons, importantly divided them from African Americans.[47] If a conventionally accepted ground for superior status in America was conferred by racial privilege, the new Americans—as part of their Americanization—absorbed this sense of the invisible privilege of whiteness.[48] There was thus every reason, particularly during a period when the unjust cultural construction of racism was so little understood, let alone discussed, uncritically to acquiesce in these American assumptions, indeed, to profit from them to the extent that at least the worst ravages of racism might be directed away from oneself and one's family. If close interpretive study of one's ethnic identity should critically reveal unacceptable acquiescence in the terms of American racism, affirmative action programs that ostensibly impose costs on oneself might be acceptable as a reasonable remedy for those cultural groups who unjustly bore the brunt of one's unfair advantage.

[46] See, on this point, Richards, *Conscience and the Constitution*, 170–76.

[47] See, on this point, Douglas, *Terrible Honesty*, 303–9.

[48] See Flagg, *Was Blind, But Now I See*; Lopez, *White by Law*; Roediger, *The Wages of Whiteness*.

Second, a more critical interpretive understanding of the degree to which American racism in fact targeted one's own ethnic identity may enlarge reasonable public understanding of how affirmative action programs might be better designed and implemented to take such pervasive racism into account. Programs of affirmative action should be reasonably designed to address and remedy the cultural construction of American racism, including the role that racism played in the unjust distribution of educational opportunity broadly understood. If I am correct, for example, that the racialization of Italian American identity was uncritically sustained by unjust circumstances that limited the scope of educational opportunities (in particular, higher education) available to Italian Americans as a group, that enduring unjust cultural legacy might reasonably be addressed by appropriately designed affirmative action admissions programs that give weight to remedying this injustice, among, of course, many other factors.

The perspective on ethnic identity here proposed may also advance our general critical understanding of the role immigrants play and continue to play in the progressive development of American liberal nationalism. If I am right, immigrants' multicultural identity, properly understood and elaborated, is an important part of what they contribute or could contribute to a more critically impartial, morally independent ongoing evaluation of the promises and betrayals of liberal nationalism, at home and abroad. Such an identity should on these grounds be encouraged, not stigmatized. For example, life in America requires immigrants to become English-language literate, and steps must accordingly be taken reasonably to achieve this end. But, multicultural identity is, as I have argued, also an important value, and reasonable steps to preserve this sense of identity may include retention of literacy in the language of one's country of origin. Certainly, if the only ground for requiring exclusively English-language literacy as public policy were racist, such a policy would be wholly unacceptable.[49] Indeed, if the pressures to conform to dominant American practices and values are as strong as they appear to be, the better balance of government policy might be to err on the side of preserving multicultural identity in order to reasonably support and sustain the political values of this identity.

---

[49] See, on this point, Kymlicka, *Multicultural Citizenship*, at 97.

Nothing in the account I have offered gives support to the claim that multicultural identity, at least of the sort I defend, is tribalizing and separatist.[50] Claims for ethnic identity have been advanced in such terms, as by Horace M. Kallen,[51] but my account is decidedly not of this sort; indeed, the formation of such tribal identities, when self-consciously hostile to the human rights of what Carl Schmitt called enemies (chapter 2), is at the heart of the twentieth century's moral heart of darkness. My account underscores the importance of rights-based public discourse on multicultural identity in general and on Italian American identity in particular; such reasonable discourse may, if anything, unsettle tribal understandings by questioning the results of the largely uncritical ways that, for example, a privatized sense of Italian American identity has been generationally transmitted. The cultural resources of multicultural identity are much too important to the integrity of democratic public discourse to be kept under tribally self-protective wraps. Only reasonable public discourse of the sort earlier suggested can express, explore, and elaborate the Italian American experience with the promises and betrayals of liberal nationalism in Italy and in the United States, a narrative from which Italian Americans and all Americans have much to learn. As I remarked in chapter 1, the stories of all American ethnic groups must be told with comparable attention to their interpretive depth and complexity so that we may better understand both the differences and the similarities in our struggles for an equal place in a coherent understanding of liberal nationalism. In this way, we may better understand and acknowledge one another as persons, not as stereotypes imposed by the structural injustice of American racism. The resulting sense of ethnic identity in general is a matter not of tribal ascription but of self-reflective moral choice based on a common experience of injustice that groups discover they share, on grounds of principle, with other groups. Reasonable discourse depends upon the existence of moral and cultural pluralism under conditions of freedom, including fruitful comparisons among various multicultural traditions, so that groups may better understand and protest the injustices to which these traditions have been subject. The discourse of ethnic identity is thus not a zero-sum game but a com-

---

[50] See, for example, Wilkinson, *One Nation Indivisible*.

[51] See Horace M. Kallen, "Democracy versus the Melting-Pot: A Study of American Nationality (1915)," in Sollors, *Theories of Ethnicity: A Classical Reader*, 67–92.

mon humane enterprise of moral and constitutional struggle against injustice. The exploration of multicultural identity thus rediscovers and elaborates for Italian Americans what the America of their grandparents' dreams has made possible for their grandchildren if they will choose, as ethically responsible agents, to take advantage of it, namely, a democratic basis for the defensible ethical and cultural values of Italian culture, a humane cosmopolitanism.[52]

The gains to the culture at large from such discourse should by now be obvious. American liberal nationalism has, from its founding, been haunted by its self-blinding, unjust cultural entrenchment of the institutions of moral slavery. This theme has haunted the nation's history throughout; the periods of greatest triumph for liberal nationalism (the Civil War and the Reconstruction Amendments) have been followed by its most reactionary publicly aggressive racism.[53] Injustice has been most easily imposed on the most vulnerable, namely, new immigrants, by writing into the script of Americanization the acceptance of the terms of American racism. Multicultural public discourse, like related forms of rights-based claims of identity, affords a valuable form of rights-based protest against the terms of entrenched moral slavery by exposing to public discussion the dimensions of the promises and betrayals of liberal nationalism, both in America and abroad. It thus offers critically impartial discourse, in terms of which we may use our collective experience as a union of diverse peoples to be more worthy of our moral ideals; these ideals are the property of no ethnicity or race or gender or sexual preference but are the common heritage of humankind struggling for a politics of equal respect for all. Immigrants have played an important role in the progressive moral development of American national identity when they have critically brought to bear on American life their multicultural insights into this heritage and how it might better be realized.

But Italian Americans, a politically skeptical and demanding people, will ask: What are the gains of such discourse for ourselves? As the people of the South would have put the point in one of their characteristic proverbs that I earlier quoted: *Chi lascia la via vecchia e piglia la via nuova, sa quello che lascia me non sa quello che trova* (He who leaves the old way for

<hr>

[52] Cf. Randolph S. Bourne, "Trans-National America (1916)," in Sollors, *Theories of Ethnicity: A Classical Reader*, at 93–108.

[53] See, in general, Smith, *Civic Ideals*.

the new knows what he leaves but knows not what he will find).[54] Perhaps the reason that will be most moving to Italian Americans is the motive that led me to undertake this study, the sense that our privatized Italian American identity has cut us off from understanding and honoring the ethical struggles of our families, not only against such proverbial Southern conservative wisdom but against both Italian and American racism. The journey I have taken in this book has helped me, for example, to understand things about my parents and grandparents I had never previously understood. They were passionately familial and tenderly loving in private life and rigidly ethical and demanding in their work lives, and they kept the two always in exquisitely compartmentalized balance; they valued equally love in private and respect in public life. They were religiously devout Catholics but, in their own morally independent and tolerant ways, often surprisingly liberal, even secular, in their views on both public and private life. They loved the cosmopolitanism they found in New York City, which was, for them, a Naples with a public culture of art and theatre and opera made in the American image, democratically available to all. In everything connected to family life, they loved laughter and music and the good things in life and abundantly had, in James's terms, "colour"; in public life, they wore masks—rigidly focused on work and routine, guarded, circumspect, and skeptical (when, as a young lawyer, I commuted with my father from New Jersey to lower Manhattan, I was shocked to find him, in his work life, literally a different person). I now understand my shock. I also better understand and value what was unusual in my parents as Italian Americans, the weight they placed on the challenge of the best higher education America could offer their children. My journey into the interpretive roots of my Italian American identity has enabled me better to understand what moved them about America and how much that was framed by what had disappointed their parents in Italy and to realize that America had exacted from them and their parents a sacrifice of self they should not, as a matter of justice, have been asked to pay.

My journey has also enabled me better to understand myself and my sense of ethical responsibility, formed by a family tradition that seems to me now neither insular nor parochial but based on the reasonable search and struggle, against a background of injustice in both

---

[54] See Covello, *The Social Background of the Italo-American Child*, 257.

Italy and America, for a life lived on the basis of humane cosmopolitan values (including liberal nationalism) available democratically to all on terms of equal respect for human dignity. America has grown morally in the coherence of its liberal nationalism since the great immigration of Southern Italians of 1890–1920, and that growth (for example, in our constitutional understanding and condemnation of our cultural racism) supplies a new context of choice. We now better understand the unjust terms of the Faustian bargain and that challenging these terms is not only much less demanding than it once was but much more beneficial, both personally and socially. We better understand what our moral roots are in a unjustly stigmatized tradition whose resources sustained our forebears' intelligence and courage in the face of such injustice and can sustain us as well if we can live in the truth and value of our multicultural identity. Our lives may thus be richer because more grounded in an appropriate self-respect and a sense of enduring humane values. Such sacrifices for such benefits makes more reasonable, on balance, the exercise and elaboration of multicultural identity as a cultural resource for rights-based protest and discourse that also better realizes America's enduring moral values. We may now both better understand and respect the choices our parents and grandparents made and, on the basis of a critical understanding of our different context of choice, recognize that our ethical responsibilities must, in light of their and our values of liberal nationalism, be different. The people of the South who critically rejected such a weight of culture and history for a new life lived under a better form of liberal nationalism would have expected, indeed, demanded, of their grandchildren no less in the quest for human dignity. We do better justice to them and to ourselves when we live more truthfully from a reflective sense of their search for enduring values, realized in the creative tensions among our multicultural identities.

I have offered both an interpretive and a critical account of Italian American identity, but, if I am right, the account offers a methodology that might be fruitful as well in the study of other forms of ethnic identity. Perhaps, in light of this study's fairly extensive discussions of both African American and Jewish American identity, this will be obvious. But, as I remarked in my opening discussion of the ambitions of this book (chapter 1), even the best recent work in ethnic studies notably has omitted any sustained discussion of Italian Americans, as if, contrary to fact, any discussion of non-Anglo immigrant experience could reasonably omit them.[55] To avoid such lapses, we need a better theorized sense of how American cultural racism was constructed and sustained and the role of the nonvisibly black in this process. My aim has been to show in some detail how such cultural racism impacted Italian American identity, thus bringing to the surface issues about American racism that are not, in my judgment, sufficiently well understood or discussed. Only such a way of theorizing or modeling American racism can ensure that the study of American ethnic groups will not itself enforce the racist script of silencing dissent that such study certainly means both to identity and to criticize. The larger interest of my investigation of the Italian Americans is to interpret their experience, as well as the experience of other ethnic groups, in terms of such a model.

We need, of course, analogous narratives that try to do interpretive justice to both poles of all multicultural identities as an invaluable resource for the progressive critical understanding of the legitimate normative demands of our constitutional union of diverse peoples and cultures, but we need, too, narratives appropriately informed by an understanding of the pervasive cultural roots of American racism and the general role that immigrants have played in sustaining its injustice. Only such narratives enable ethnic groups better to understand the circumstances of injustice that have shaped them, both in their countries of origin and in the United States, and appropriately to resist the privilege of whiteness that has often rationalized this injustice. In fact, Italian Americans were themselves victimized by racism, both in Italy and in the United States, and have good reasons, in contemporary circumstances, to refuse a continuing cultural acquiescence in an American cultural racism that is as unjustly stigmatizing of them as it is of Americans of color. The Italian American story has its own interpretive integrity, which has been obscured and deformed by the demands of Americanization under circumstances of injustice. My argument has been that it is no longer an acceptable basis for any people's Americanization that they subscribe to the terms of American cultural racism. Our racism is our national scandal and shame, certainly no longer anything we would be prepared publicly to acknowledge as a legitimate basis of our liberal nationalism; yet, if I am right, the American sense of ethnic iden-

---

[55] See, for example, Takaki, *A Different Mirror*.

tity remains, in light of the history I have set out, deeply implicated in this scandal and shame.

Historical narratives of the sort developed here are urgently needed to make clear what the distinctive cultural experience of various ethnic groups has been, both in their countries of origin and in the United States. Such a sense of distinctive cultural experience enables members of ethnic groups better to understand who they are, recovering the sense of historical memory that American cultural racism has suppressed (inventing and imposing, in its stead, an ahistorically hegemonic privilege of whiteness). Such memory was suppressed, for example, by the terms of the privatization of Italian American identity, already discussed at some length. The withdrawal of Italian American identity into the private sphere was made possible, indeed, was required, by a public sphere in which Italian American protest against the unjust stigma of their multicultural identity was silenced. The grandparents and parents, who had experienced the brunt of the worst injustices of American cultural racism, refused to speak of their experience, let alone to explore the burdens racism had unjustly imposed on their sense of themselves, including their ambitions and aspirations. Their grandchildren, in consequence, know little of this history and thus cannot bring it to bear in protest of its unjust suppression. But, a life thus emptied of such memories becomes a victim of the false memories constitutive of the privilege of whiteness; Italian Americans, rooted in richly humane traditions, disown the best in their multicultural traditions and, for this reason, betray as well the best in American constitutional traditions. The resistance to such politically powerful stereotypes of racial difference requires an alternative interpretive standpoint of the sort I have urged. Such an interpretation insists that attention be paid to struggles for dignity under circumstances of injustice, that the complexities of different ethnic experiences be carefully understood and weighed, and that the stereotypical simplification of these moral complexities be resisted as the root of the power and durability of the profound injustice of American racism.

If immigrants have borne too heavy a burden of perpetuating this injustice, they have the means at hand to help end it. Fortunately, in releasing themselves from this unjust burden on their sense of themselves, they not only better achieve their own moral and constitutional rights but renew the moral sense of what often attracted immigrants to

America. We saw this sense of moral promise in the deliberations of the Italian immigrant that concluded chapter 3:

> Why to live always in the memory of past grandeur? They were only men. I am a man, and my son will be a man. Why not live to be somebody ourselves, in a nation more great than any nation before, and my son perhaps the greatest of any great man?
>
> And I see that big work to build the future. I see the necessity to learn the English, to become the citizen, to take part in the political life, to work to create the better understanding between the races that they come to love each another, to work for better conditions in industry. For health and safety and prosperity, to work for the progress in science, for the better government, and for the higher morality—and it become more pleasure to work than to take the leisure. Suddenly it looks to me like that is the American, that is what the American is always to do, always to work for the achievement. It come to me, like I am born—I am American![56]

Being reborn in that sense of moral promise was the meaning of America to many immigrants, including Italian Americans. Their story is a tribute to our moral powers to reinvent our identities on terms more adequate to our convictions of justice. The challenge of American multicultural identity is to keep that story truthfully alive in all its moral and human complexity; better understanding our past enables us better to understand our contemporary moral freedom and responsibility. We should be thankful that we stand on the shoulders of free men and women who have shown us what can and must be done.

---

[56] Quoted in Lopreato, *Italian Americans*, 173–4.

Bibliography

CASES

Adarand Constructors, Inc. v. Pena, 115 S. Ct. 2097 (1995).
Bowers v. Hardwick, 478 U.S. 186 (1986).
Brown v. Board of Education, 347 U.S. 483 (1954).
Civil Rights Cases, 109 U.S. 3 (1883).
Craig v. Boren, 429 U.S. 190 (1976).
Dred Scott v. Sanford, 19 How. 393 (1857).
Frontiero v. Richardson, 411 U.S. 677 (1973).
Gitlow v. New York, 268 U.S. 652 (1925).
Loving v. Virginia, 388 U.S. 1 (1967).
McLaughlin v. Florida, 379 U.S. 184 (1964).
Meyer v. Nebraska, 262 U.S. 390 (1923).
Pace v. Alabama, 106 U.S. 583 (1863).
Palmore v. Sidoti, 466 U.S. 429, 434 (1984).
People v. Liberta, 64 N.Y.2d 152, 474 N.E.2d 567 (N.Y. Ct. App. 1984).
Pierce v. Society of Sisters, 268 U.S. 510 (1925).
Plessy v. Ferguson, 163 U.S. 537 (1896).
Reed v. Reed, 404 U.S. 71 (1971).
Romer v. Evans, 116 S.Ct. 1620 (1996).
Slaughter-House Cases, 16 Wall. 36 (1873).
United States R.R. Retirement Bd. v. Fritz, 449 U.S. 166 (1980).
United States v. Virginia, 116 S.Ct. 2264 (1996).
Williamson v. Lee Optical, 348 U.S. 483, 488 (1965).

BOOKS AND ARTICLES

Acton, Harold. *The Bourbons of Naples 1734–1825.* London: Methuen, 1956.
———. *The Last Bourbons of Naples (1825–1861).* New York: St. Martin's Press, 1961.
Ackerman, Bruce. "Beyond *Carolene Products.*" 98 *Harv. L. Rev.* 713 (1985).
Adams, Charles Francis, ed. *Works of John Adams.* Vols. 3–6. Boston: Little, Brown, 1851.

Adams, Henry. *Henry Adams.* Ed. Ernest Samuels and Jayne N. Samuels. New York: The Library of America, 1983.

Adams, Julian, David A. Lam, Albert I. Hermalin, and Peter E. Smouse. *Convergent Issues in Genetics and Demography.* New York: Oxford University Press, 1990.

Allum, P. A. *Politics and Society in Post-War Naples.* Cambridge: Cambridge University Press, 1973.

Amsterdam, Anthony G. "Thurgood Marshall's Image of the Blue-Eyed Child in *Brown.*" 68 *N.Y.U. L. Rev.* 226 (1993).

Arendt, Hannah. *On Revolution.* Harmondsworth: Penguin, 1973.

———. *The Origins of Totalitarianism.* New York: Harcourt Brace Jovanovich, 1973.

Ashbrook, William. *Donizetti and His Operas.* Cambridge: Cambridge University Press, 1982.

Baldwin, James. *No Name in the Street.* New York: Dell, 1972.

———. *The Price of the Ticket: Collected Nonfiction, 1948–1985.* New York: St. Martin's Press, 1985.

Banfield, Edward C. *The Moral Basis of a Backward Society.* New York: Free Press, 1958.

Barkan, Elazar. *The Retreat of Scientific Racism: Changing Concepts of Race in Britain and the United States Between the World Wars.* Cambridge: Cambridge University Press, 1992.

Barzini, Luigi. *The Italians.* New York: Atheneum 1965.

Basic Law of the Federal Republic of Germany. Bonn: Press and Information Office of the Federal Government, 1987.

Beard, Charles A. *An Economic Interpretation of the Constitution of the United States.* New York: Free Press, 1941.

Beattie, James. *Elements of Moral Science.* Delmar, N.Y.: Scholars' Facsimiles & Reprints, 1976.

———. *An Essay on the Nature and Immutability of Truth.* New York: Garland Publishing, Inc. 1983.

Beeman, Richard et al., eds. *Beyond Confederation: Origins of the Constitution and American National Identity.* Chapel Hill: University of North Carolina Press, 1987.

Bendersky, Joseph W. *Carl Schmitt: Theorist for the Reich.* Princeton: Princeton University Press, 1983.

Benedict, Michael Les. *A Compromise of Principle: Congressional Republicans and Reconstruction 1863–1869.* New York: W. W. Norton, 1974.

Benedict, Ruth. *Race: Science and Politics.* New York: The Viking Press, 1945.

Berlin, Ira. *Slaves without Masters: The Free Negro in the Antebellum South.* New York: Pantheon Books, 1974.

Berlin, Isaiah. *Vico and Herder: Two Studies in the History of Ideas*. London: Hogarth Press, 1976.

Berman, Paul, ed. *Blacks and Jews: Alliances and Arguments*. New York: Delacorte Press, 1994.

Bigsby, Christopher, ed. *The Cambridge Companion to Arthur Miller*. Cambridge: Cambridge University Press, 1997.

Blassingame, John W. *The Slave Community: Plantation Life in the Antebellum South*. Rev. ed. New York: Oxford University Press, 1979.

Blum, Carol. *Rousseau and the Republic of Virtue: The Language of Politics in the French Revolution*. Ithaca: Cornell University Press, 1986.

Boas, Franz. *The Mind of Primitive Man*. Rev. ed. 1911; Westport, Conn.: Greenwood Press, 1983.

Bobbio, Norberto. *The Age of Rights*. Trans. Allan Cameron. Cambridge: Polity, 1996.

———. *The Future of Democracy: A Defence of the Rules of the Game*. Trans. Roger Griffin. Minneapolis: University of Minnesota Press, 1987.

———. *Ideological Profile of Twentieth-Century Italy*. Trans. Lydia G. Cochrane. Princeton: Princeton University Press, 1995.

———. *Liberalism and Democracy*. Trans. Martin Ryle and Kate Soper. London: Verso, 1990.

Bourdieu, Pierre. *The Political Ontology of Martin Heidegger*. Trans. Peter Collier. Cambridge: Polity Press, 1991.

Bouwsma, William J. *Venice and the Defense of Republican Liberty*. Berkeley: University of California Press, 1968.

Branch, Taylor. *Parting the Waters: Martin Luther King and the Civil Rights Movement, 1954–63*. London: Papermac, 1990.

Brand, Peter, and Lino Pertile, eds. *The Cambridge History of Italian Literature*. Cambridge: Cambridge University Press, 1996.

Braudel, Fernand. *Out of Italy: 1450–1650*. Trans. Sian Reynolds. Tours: Flammarion, 1991.

Brooke, James. "After Silence, Italians Recall the Internment." *New York Times*, August 11, 1997, A10.

Brubaker, Rogers. *Citizenship and Nationhood in France and Germany*. Cambridge, Mass.: Harvard University Press, 1992.

Budden, Julian. *The Operas of Verdi*. 3 vols. New York: Oxford University Press, vol. 1, 1973; vol. 2, 1978; vols. 3, 1981.

Burckhardt, Jacob. *The Civilization of the Renaissance in Italy*. Trans. S. G. C. Middlemore. London: Penguin, 1990.

Burke, Edmund. *The Works of Edmund Burke*. 6th ed. Vol. 2. Boston: Little, Brown, 1880.

Burke, Peter. *Vico*. Oxford: Oxford University Press, 1985.

Bynum, Caroline Walker. *Fragmentation and Redemption: Essays on Gender and the Human Body in Medieval Religion*. New York: Zone Books, 1991.

——. *Holy Feast and Holy Fast: The Religious Significance of Food to Medieval Women*. Berkeley and Los Angeles: University of California Press, 1987.

——. *Jesus as Mother: Studies in the Spirituality of the High Middle Ages*. Berkeley and Los Angeles: University of California Press, 1982.

Calhoun, John C. *A Disquisition on Government*. Ed. Richard K. Cralle. Orig. pub., 1853; repr. ed., New York: Peter Smith, 1943.

Campbell, R. H. and Andrew S. Skinner. *The Origins and Nature of the Scottish Enlightenment*. Edinburgh: John Donald Publishers, 1982.

Carr, Herbert Wildon. *The Philosophy of Benedetto Croce: The Problem of Art and History*. London: Macmillan, 1917.

Casale, Giuseppe. *Benedetto Croce between Naples and Europe*. New York: Peter Lang, 1994.

Caserta, Ernesto G. *Croce and Marxism: From the Years of Revisionism to the Last Postwar Period*. Napoli: Morano Editore, 1987.

Cash, W. J. *The Mind of the South*. New York: Vintage Books, 1941.

Cassirer, Ernst. *The Question of Jean-Jacques Rousseau*. Trans. Peter Gay. New Haven: Yale University Press, 1989.

Castiglione, Baldesar. *The Courtier*. Trans. George Bull. London: Penguin, 1967.

Catherine of Siena. *The Dialogue of the Seraphic Virgin*. Trans. Algar Thorold. Rockford, Illinois: Tan Books and Publishers, Inc., 1974.

Cavalli-Sforza, L. Luca, Paolo Menozzi, and Alberto Piazza. *The History and Geography of Human Genes*. Princeton: Princeton University Press, 1994.

Chafe, William H. *Women and Equality: Changing Patterns in American Culture*. New York: Oxford University Press, 1977.

Chamberlain, Houston Stewart. *The Foundations of the Nineteenth Century*. Trans. John Lees. 2 vols. London: John Lane, 1911.

Chase, Salmon Portland and Charles Dexter Cleveland. *Anti-Slavery Addresses of 1844 and 1845*. New York: Negro Universities Press, 1867.

Child, L. Maria. *An Appeal in Favor of Americans Called Africans*. Orig. pub., 1833; repr. ed., New York: Arno Press and New York Times, 1968.

Cobb, Thomas R. R. *An Inquiry into the Law of Negro Slavery in the United States of America*. Orig. pub., 1858; repr. ed., New York: Negro Universities Press, 1968.

Cobban, Alfred. *A History of Modern France*, 3 vols. Harmondsworth, Middlesex: Penguin, vol. 1, 1963; vol. 2, 1965; vol. 3; 1965.

Cohen, Jane Maslow. "Regimes of Private Tyranny: What Do They Mean to Morality and for the Criminal Law?" 57 *U. Pitt. L. Rev.* 757 (1996).

Collingwood, R. G. *The Idea of History*. Rev. ed. Ed. Jan Van Der Dussen. Oxford: Oxford University Press, 1994.

Commager, Henry Steele. *Theodore Parker*. Boston: Little, Brown, 1936.

Cooke, Jacob E., ed. *The Federalist.* Middletown, Conn.: Wesleyan University Press, 1961.

Covello, Leonard. *The Social Background of the Italo-American School Child: A Study of the Southern Italian Family Mores and Their Effect on the School Situation in Italy and America.* Leiden: E. J. Brill, 1967.

Cox, LaWanda. *Lincoln and Black Freedom.* Urbana: University of Illinois Press, 1985.

Cralle, Richard K., ed. *The Words of John C. Calhoun,* vol. 4. New York: D. Appleton, 1861.

Crespi, Angelo. *Contemporary Thought of Italy.* New York: Alfred A. Knopf, 1926.

Crimp, Douglas. *Cultural Analysis/Cultural Activism.* Cambridge: MIT Press, 1988.

Croce, Benedetto. *Aesthetic As Science of Expression and General Linguistic.* Trans. Douglas Ainslie. New Brunswick: Transaction, 1995.

———. *History: Its Theory and Practice.* Trans. Douglas Ainslie. New York: Harcourt, Brace, and Co., 1923.

———. *History of Europe in the Nineteenth Century.* Trans. Henry Furst. London: George, Allen & Unwin, 1953.

———. *A History of Italy 1871-1915.* Trans. Cecila M. Ady. New York: Russell & Russell, 1929.

———. *History of the Kingdom of Naples.* Trans. Frances Frenaye. Chicago: University of Chicago Press, 1970.

———. *History as the Story of Liberty.* Trans. Sylvia Sprigge. New York: W. W. Norton, 1941.

———. *Logic as the Science of the Pure Concept.* Trans. Douglas Ainslie. London: St. Martin's Press, 1917.

———. *Philosophy of the Practical: Economic and Ethic.* Trans. Douglas Ainslie. London: St. Martin's, 1913.

———. *Politics and Morals.* Trans. Salvatore J. Castiglione. New York: Philosophical Library, 1945.

Dahl, Robert A. *Democracy and Its Critics.* New Haven: Yale University Press, 1989.

Davis, David Brion. *The Problem of Slavery in Western Culture.* Ithaca: Cornell University Press, 1967.

———. *The Slave Power Conspiracy and the Paranoid Style.* Baton Rouge: Louisiana State University Press, 1969.

Davis, F. James. *Who Is Black?: One Nation's Definition.* University Park: Pennsylvania State University Press, 1991.

Deak, Istvan. *The Lawful Revolution: Louis Kossuth and the Hungarians, 1848–1849.* New York: Columbia University Press, 1979.

Deane, Seamus. *The French Revolution and Enlightenment in England 1789–1832.* Cambridge, Mass.: Harvard University Press, 1988.

DeConde, Alexander. *Half Bitter, Half Sweet: An Excursion into Italian-American History.* New York: Charles Scribner's Sons, 1971.

De Gennaro, Angelo A. *The Philosophy of Benedetto Croce: An Introduction.* New York: Greenwood Press, 1968.

Degler, Carl N. *In Search of Human Nature: The Decline and Revival of Darwinism in American Social Thought.* New York: Oxford University Press, 1991.

———. *Neither Black Nor White: Slavery and Race Relations in Brazil and the United States.* Madison: University of Wisconsin Press, 1986.

Donald, David. *Charles Sumner and the Coming of the Civil War.* New York: Alfred A. Knopf, 1960.

———. *Charles Sumner and the Rights of Man.* New York: Alfred A. Knopf, 1970.

Douglas, Ann. *Terrible Honesty: Mongrel Manhattan in the 1920s.* New York: Farrar, Straus and Giroux, 1995.

Donato, Pietro di. *Christ in Concrete.* Indianapolis: Bobbs-Merrill, 1939.

Doyle, William. *Oxford History of the French Revolution.* Oxford: Clarendon Press, 1989.

Dreyfus, Hubert L. *Being-in-the-World: A Commentary on Heidegger's Being and Time, Division I.* Cambridge, Mass.: MIT Press, 1991.

Duberman, Martin, ed. *The Antislavery Vanguard: New Essays on the Abolitionists.* Princeton: Princeton University Press, 1965.

Du Bois, W. E. B. *Black Reconstruction in America, 1860–1880.* Orig. pub., 1935; New York: Atheneum, 1969.

———. *W. E. B. Du Bois.* Ed. Nathan Huggins. Orig. pub., 1896; New York: Library of America, 1986.

Dudziak, Mary L. "Desegregation as a Cold War Imperative." 41 *Stan. L. Rev.* 41 (1988).

Dunn, John. *Modern Revolutions: An Introduction to the Analysis of a Political Phenomenon.* 2d ed. Cambridge: Cambridge University Press, 1989.

Dworkin, Ronald. *A Bill of Rights for Britain.* London: Chatto & Windus, 1990.

———. *Law's Empire.* Cambridge, Mass.: Harvard University Press, 1986.

Elkins, Stanley M. *Slavery: A Problem in American Institutional and Intellectual Life.* 3d ed. Chicago: University of Chicago Press, 1976.

Ely, John Hart. *Democracy and Distrust: A Theory of Judicial Review.* Cambridge, Mass.: Harvard University Press, 1980.

Evans, Sarah. *Personal Politics: The Roots of Women's Liberation in the Civil Rights Movement and the New Left.* New York: Vintage Books, 1979.

Fanon, Frantz. *Black Skin, White Masks.* Trans. Charles Lam Markmann. New York: Grove Weidenfeld, 1967.

Farias, Victor. *Heideigger and Nazism.* Philadelphia: Temple University Press, 1989.

Farrand, Max, ed. *The Records of the Federal Convention of 1787.* Vol. 1. New Haven: Yale University Press, 1966.

Fehrenbacher, Don E. *Abraham Lincoln: Speeches and Writings 1832–1858* New York: The Library of America, 1989.

———. *The Dred Scott Case: Its Significance in American Law and Politics*. New York: Oxford University Press, 1978.

Femia, Joseph V. *Gramsci's Political Thought: Hegemony, Consciousness, and the Revolutionary Process*. Oxford: Clarendon Press, 1987.

Ficino, Marsilio. *Commentary on Plato's Symposium*. Trans. and intro. Sears Reynolds Jayne. Columbia: University of Missouri, 1944.

Finkelman, Paul. "Prelude to the Fourteenth Amendment: Black Legal Rights in the Antebellum North." 17 *Rutgers L. J.* 415 (1986).

Flagg, Barbara J. *Was Blind, But Now I See: White Race Consciousness and the Law*. New York: New York University Press, 1998.

Foerster, Robert F. *The Italian Emigration of Our Times*. New York: Arno Press and New York Times, 1969.

Foner, Eric. *Reconstruction: America's Unfinished Revolution 1863–1877*. New York: Harper & Row, 1988.

Foner, Philip S., ed. *The Life and Writings of Frederick Douglass*. 5 vols. New York: International Publishers, 1975).

Fontana, Biancamaria, ed. *Constant: Political Writings*. Cambridge: Cambridge University Press, 1988.

Fralin, Richard. *Rousseau and Representation*. New York: Columbia University Press, 1978.

Franklin, John Hope. *The Militant South, 1800–1861*. Cambridge, Mass.: Belknap Press of Harvard University Press, 1956.

Fredrickson, George M. *The Black Image in the White Mind: The Debate on Afro-American Character and Destiny, 1817–1914*. Middletown, Conn.: Wesleyan University Press, 1971.

———. *White Supremacy: A Comparative Study in American and South African History*. Oxford: Oxford University Press, 1981.

Friedan, Betty. *The Feminine Mystique*. Orig. pub., 1963; repr. ed., London: Penguin, 1982.

Friedrich, Carl J. "Rebuilding the German Constitution," 43 *Am. Pol. Sci. Rev.* 461-82, 705-20 (1949).

Furet, Francois. *Revolutionary France 1770–1880* Trans. Antonia Nevill. Oxford: Blackwell, 1992.

Furet, Francois, and Mona Ozouf, eds. *A Critical Dictionary of the French Revolution*. Trans. Arthur Goldhammer. Cambridge, Mass.: Belknap Press of Harvard University Press, 1989.

Gallie, W. B. *Philosophy and the Historical Understanding*. 2d ed. New York: Schocken Books, 1968.

Gambino, Richard. *Blood of My Blood : The Dilemma of the Italian-Americans*. Garden City, N.Y.: Doubleday, 1974.

Garrison, William Lloyd. *Selections from the Writings and Speeches of William Lloyd Garrison.* Boston: R. F. Wallcut, 1852.

Genovese, Eugene D. *Roll, Jordan, Roll: The World the Slaves Made.* New York: Vintage Books, 1974.

———. *The World the Slaveholders Made: Two Essays in Interpretation.* Middletown, Conn.: Wesleyan University Press, 1988.

Gerard, Kent, and Gert Hekma. *The Pursuit of Sodomy: Male Homosexuality in Renaissance and Enlightenment Europe.* New York: Harrington Park Press, 1989.

Gilman, Sander L. *Jewish Self-Hatred: Anti-Semitism and the Hidden Language of the Jews.* Baltimore: Johns Hopkins University Press, 1986.

Glanz, Rudolf. *Jew and Italian: Historic Group Relations and the New Immigration (1881–1924)* New York: Shulsinger Bros., 1970.

Glazer, Nathan. *We Are All Multiculturalists Now.* Cambridge, Mass.: Harvard University Press, 1997.

Glazer, Nathan, and Daniel P. Moynihan. *Beyond the Melting Pot: The Negroes, Puerto Ricans, Jews, Italians, and Irish of New York City.* Cambridge, Mass.: MIT Press, 1970.

Goffen, Rona. *Titian's Women.* New Haven: Yale University Press, 1997.

Golay, John Ford. *The Founding of the Federal Republic of Germany.* Chicago: University of Chicago Press, 1958.

Goodell, William. *Views of American Constitutional Law in its Bearing Upon American Slavery.* Orig. pub., 1845; repr. ed., Freeport, N.Y.: Books for Libraries Press, 1971.

Gossett, Philip et al. *The New Grove: Masters of Italian Opera.* New York: W. W. Norton, 1983.

Gossett, Thomas F. *Race: The History of an Idea in America.* New York: Schocken Books, 1965.

Gould, Stephen Jay. *The Mismeasure of Man.* New York: W. W. Norton, 1981.

Grant, Madison. *The Passing of the Great Race or the Racial Basis of European History.* New York: Charles Scribner's Sons, 1919.

Gramsci, Antonio. *Selections from the Prison Notebooks.* Ed. and trans. Quintin Hoare and Geoffrey Nowell Smith. New York: International Publishers, 1971.

Greenberg, Jack. *Crusaders in the Courts: How a Dedicated Band of Lawyers Fought for the Civil Rights Revolution.* New York: Basic Books, 1994.

Greenfeld, Liah. *Nationalism: Five Roads to Modernity.* Cambridge, Mass.: Harvard University Press, 1992.

Gutman, Herbert G. *The Black Family in Slavery and Freedom 1750–1925* New York: Vintage Books, 1976.

Hacker, Andrew. *Two Nations: Black and White, Separate, Hostile, Unequal.* New York: Charles Scribner's Sons, 1992.

Haller, John S., Jr. *Outcasts from Evolution: Scientific Attitudes of Racial Inferiority, 1859–1900* New York: McGraw-Hill Book Company, 1971.

Hampson, Norman. *Will and Circumstance: Montesquieu, Rousseau and the French Revolution.* Norman: University of Oklahoma Press, 1983.

Haraszti, Zoltan. *John Adams and the Prophets of Progress.* Cambridge, Mass.: Harvard University Press, 1952.

Heimert, Alan. *Religion and the American Mind: From the Great Awakening to the Revolution.* Cambridge, Mass.: Harvard University Press, 1966.

Hendin, Josephine Gattuso. *The Right Thing to Do.* Boston: David R. Godine, 1988.

Hertzberg, Arthur. *The French Enlightenment and the Jews.* New York: Columbia University Press, 1990.

Hertzberg, Arthur, ed. *The Zionist Idea: A Historical Analysis and Reader.* New York: Atheneum, 1959.

Herzl, Theodor. *The Jewish State.* Trans. Sylvie d'Avigdor. New York: Dover, 1988.

Higham, John. *Strangers in the Land: Patterns of American Nativism 1860–1925.* New Brunswick: Rutgers University Press, 1988.

Higonnet, Patrice. *Sister Republics: The Origins of French and American Republicanism.* Cambridge, Mass.: Harvard University Press, 1988.

Hilberg, Raul. *The Destruction of the European Jews.* 3 vols. New York: Holmes & Meier, 1985.

Hiscocks, Richard. *Democracy in Western Germany.* London: Oxford University Press, 1957.

Hoffman, Ross J. S., and Paul Levack, eds. *Burke's Politics.* New York: Alfred A. Knopf, 1959.

Holmes, George, ed. *The Oxford History of Italy.* New York: Oxford University Press, 1997.

Hont, Istvan, and Michael Ignatieff, eds. *Wealth and Virtue: The Shaping of Political Economy in the Scottish Enlightenment.* Cambridge: Cambridge University Press, 1983.

Horsman, Reginald. *Race and Manifest Destiny: The Origins of American Racial Anglo-Saxonism.* Cambridge, Mass.: Harvard University Press, 1981.

Horwitz, Robert H., ed. *The Moral Foundations of the American Republic.* 3d ed. Charlottesville: University Press of Virginia, 1986.

Howe, Daniel Walker. "Henry David Thoreau on the Duty of Civil Disobedience," an Inaugural Lecture delivered before the University of Oxford on 21 May 1990. Oxford: Clarendon Press, 1990.

Hucko, E. M. *The Democratic Tradition: Four German Constitutions.* Leamington Spa, U.K.: Berg, 1987.

Hughes, H. Stuart. *The United States and Italy.* 3d ed. Cambridge, Mass.: Harvard University Press, 1979.

Hulliung, Mark. *Citizen Machiavelli*. Princeton: Princeton University Press, 1983.

Hume, David. *Essays, Moral, Political, and Literary*. Indianapolis: LibertyClassics, 1987.

———. *Essays Moral, Political, and Literary*. Oxford: Oxford University Press, 1963.

Hutchinson, George. *The Harlem Renaissance in Black and White*. Cambridge, Mass.: Harvard University Press, 1995.

Ignatiev, Noel. *How the Irish Became White*. New York: Routledge, 1995.

Jacobitti, Edmund E. *Revolutionary Humanism and Historicism in Modern Italy*. New Haven: Yale University Press, 1981.

Jacoff, Rachel, ed. *The Cambridge Companion to Dante*. Cambridge: Cambridge University Press, 1993.

James, Henry. *Collected Travel Writings: Great Britain and America*. New York: Library of America, 1993.

Janis, Mark W., and Richard S. Kay. *European Human Rights Law*. University of Connecticut Law School Foundation, 1990.

Jefferson, Thomas. *Notes on the State of Virginia*. Ed. William Peden. New York: W. W. Norton, 1954.

Johannsen, Robert W., ed. *The Lincoln-Douglas Debates*. New York: Oxford University Press, 1865.

Jones, Philip. *The Italian City-State: From Commune to Signoria*. Oxford: Clarendon Press, 1997.

Jordan, Winthrop D. *White over Black: American Attitudes Toward the Negro, 1550–1812*. New York: W. W. Norton, 1977.

Judt, Tony. "Betrayal in France," *New York Review of Books*, 40, no. 14 (August 12, 1993), at 31–34.

———. *Past Imperfect: French Intellectuals, 1944–1956*. Berkeley: University of California Press, 1992.

———. "Rights in France: Reflections on the Etiolation of a Political Language," *Toqueville Review* 14, no. 1, (1993).

Kalven, Harry, Jr. *The Negro and the First Amendment*. Chicago: University of Chicago Press, 1965.

Katz, Jacob. *From Prejudice to Destruction*. Cambridge, Mass.: Harvard University Press, 1980.

King, Martin Luther. *A Testament of Hope: The Essential Writings of Martin Luther King, Jr.* Ed. James Melvin Washington. Orig. pub., 1963; repr. ed., New York: Harper & Row, 1986.

Klein, Herbert S. *Slavery in the Americas: A Comparative Study of Virginia and Cuba*. Chicago: Elephant Paperbacks, 1989.

Klineberg, Otto. *Race Differences*. New York: Harper & Brothers, 1935.

Koch, H. W. *A Constitutional History of Germany*. London: Longman, 1984.

Kommers, Donald P. *The Constitutional Jurisprudence of the Federal Republic of Germany.* Durham: Duke University Press, 1989.

Kymlicka, Will. *Liberalism, Community, and Culture.* Oxford: Clarendon Press, 1989.

———. *Multicultural Citizenship: A Liberal Theory of Minority Rights.* Oxford: Clarendon Press, 1995.

Kymlicka, Will, ed. *The Rights of Minority Cultures.* New York: Oxford University Press, 1995.

Lane, Ann J., ed. *The Debate Over Slavery: Stanley Elkins and His Critics.* Urbana: University of Illinois Press, 1971.

Langmuir, Gavin I. *History, Religion, and Antisemitism.* Berkeley and Los Angeles: University of California Press, 1990.

Leeming, David. *James Baldwin.* New York: Alfred A. Knopf, 1994.

Lerner, Michael. *The Socialism of Fools: Anti-Semitism on the Left.* Oakland, Cal.: Tikkun Books, 1992.

Levi, Carlo. *Christ Stopped at Eboli.* Trans. Frances Frenaye. New York: Farrar, Straus and Giroux, 1963.

Lewis, David Levering. *W. E. B. Du Bois: Biography of a Race, 1868–1919* New York: Henry Holt, 1993.

Lilla, Mark. *G. B. Vico: The Making of an Anti-Modern.* Cambridge, Mass.: Harvard University Press, 1993.

Lindemann, Albert S. *Esau's Tears: Modern Anti-Semitism and the Rise of the Jews.* Cambridge: Cambridge University Press, 1997.

Litchfield, E. H., ed. *Governing Postwar Germany.* Ithaca: Cornell University Press, 1953.

Litwack, Leon F. *Been in the Storm So Long: The Aftermath of Slavery.* New York: Vintage Books, 1979.

———. *North of Slavery: The Negro in the Free States 1790–1860.* Chicago: University of Chicago Press, 1961.

Lofgren, Charles A. *The Plessy Case.* New York: Oxford University Press, 1987.

Lopez, Ian F. Haney. *White by Law: The Legal Construction of Race.* New York: New York University Press, 1996.

Lopreato, Joseph. *Italian Americans.* New York: Random House, 1970.

Lumley, Robert, and Jonathan Morris, eds. *The New History of the Italian South: The Mezzogiorno Revisited.* Exeter: University of Exeter Press, 1997.

Lyotard, Jean-Francois. *Heidegger and "the jews."* Trans. Andreas Michel and Mark Roberts. Minneapolis: University of Minnesota Press, 1990.

Lyttelton, Adrian. "The First *Duce*." *Times Literary Supplement,* July 24, 1998.

Machiavelli, Niccolò. *The Discourses.* Ed. Bernard Crick; Trans. Leslie J. Walker. Harmondsworth: Penguin, 1970.

———. *The Prince and Discourses.* Ed. Max Lerner. New York: Modern Library, 1950.

Mangione, Jerre, and Ben Morreale. *La Storia: Five Centuries of Italian American Experience.* New York: HarperCollins, 1992.

Manzoni, Alessandro. *The Betrothed.* Trans. Bruce Penman. London: Penguin, 1972.

Marx, Karl. *Karl Marx: Early Writings.* Trans. T. B. Bottomore. London: C. A. Watts, 1963.

Massey, Douglas S., and Nancy A. Denton. *American Apartheid: Segregation and the Making of the Underclass.* Cambridge, Mass.: Harvard University Press, 1993.

Masters, Roger D. *The Political Philosophy of Rousseau.* Princeton: Princeton University Press, 1968.

Mazzini, Joseph. *The Duties of Man and Other Essays.* London: J. M. Dent & Co., 1860.

McCaffrey, Lawrence J. *The Irish Catholic Diaspora in America.* Washington, D.C.: Catholic University of America Press, 1997.

McKitrick, Eric L. *Andrew Johnson and Reconstruction.* New York: Oxford University Press, 1960.

McNeil, Genna Rae. *Groundwork: Charles Hamilton Houston and the Struggle for Civil Rights.* Philadelphia: University of Pennsylvania Press, 1983.

McPherson, James M. *Battle Cry of Freedom: The Civil War Era.* New York: Ballantine Books, 1988.

———. *The Struggle for Equality: Abolitionists and the Negro in the Civil War and Reconstruction.* Princeton: Princeton University Press, 1964.

Meek, Ronald L. *Social Science and the Ignoble Savage.* Cambridge: Cambridge University Press, 1976.

Michaelis, Meir. *Mussolini and the Jews: German-Italian Relations and the Jewish Question in Italy, 1922–1945.* Oxford: Clarendon Press, 1978.

Miller, Arthur. *A View from the Bridge.* New York: Penguin, 1977.

Miller, David. *Philosophy and Ideology in Hume's Political Thought.* Oxford: Clarendon Press, 1981.

Miller, James. *Rousseau: Dreamer of Demcracy.* New Haven: Yale University Press, 1984.

Miller, William Lee. *Arguing About Slavery: The Great Battle in the United States Congress.* New York: Alfred A. Knopf, 1996.

Minow, Martha. *Not Only for Myself: Identity, Politics and the Law.* New York: New Press, 1997.

Mirandola, Giovanni Pico Della. *Oration on the Dignity of Man.* Trans. A. Robert Caponigri. Chicago: Henry Regnery Co., 1956.

Morgan, Edmund S. *American Slavery American Freedom: The Ordeal of Colonial Virginia.* New York: W. W. Norton, 1975.

Myrdal, Gunnar. *An American Dilemma: The Negro Problem and Modern Democracy.* 2 vols. Orig. pub., 1944; repr. ed., New York: Pantheon Books, 1972.

O'Driscoll, Mary, O. P. *Catherine of Siena: Passion for the Truth Compassion for Humanity: Selected Spiritual Writings.* Hyde Park, N.Y.: New City Press, 1993.

Orsini, Gian N. G. *Benedetto Croce: Philosopher of Art and Literary Critic.* Carbondale: Southern Illinois University Press, 1961.

Pagels, Elaine. *Adam, Eve, and the Serpent.* New York: Random House, 1988.

Paglia, Camille. "At Home With: Mario Puzo; It all Comes Back to Family." *New York Times,* May 8, 1997, section C, p. 1, col. 1.

———. "Questions for: Mario Puzo," *New York Times Magazine,* Sunday, March 30, 1997, section 6, p. 15.

———. *Sexual Personae: Art and Decadence from Nefertiti to Emily Dickinson.* New York: Vintage, 1991.

Paine, Thomas. *Rights of Man.* Ed. Henry Collins. Harmondsworth, Middlesex: Penguin, 1969.

Palmer, R. R. *The Age of the Democratic Revolution.* Vol. 1. Princeton: Princeton University Press, 1959.

Pangle, Thomas L. *Montesquieu's Philosophy of Liberalism.* Chicago: University of Chicago Press, 1973.

Patterson, Orlando. *The Ordeal of Integration: Progress and Resentment in America's "Racial Crisis."* Washington, D.C.: Civitas, 1997.

———. *Slavery and Social Death.* Cambridge, Mass.: Harvard University Press, 1982.

Paz, Octavio. *The Labyrinth of Solitude.* Trans. Lysander Kemp, Yaro Milos, and Rachel Phillips Belash. New York: Grove Press, 1985.

Pelikan, Jaroslav. *Mary through the Centuries: Her Place in the History of Culture.* New Haven: Yale University Press, 1996.

Perry, Michael J. "Modern Equal Protection: A Conceptualization and Appraisal." 79 *Colum. L. Rev.* 1023 (1979).

Phillips, Wendell. *Can Abolitionists Vote or Take Office Under the United States Constitution?* New York: American Anti-Slavery Society, 1845.

———. *The Constitution: a Pro-Slavery Compact.* Orig. pub., 1844; repr. ed., New York: Negro Universities Press, 1969.

Phillips-Matz, Mary Jane. *Verdi: A Biography.* New York: Oxford University Press, 1993.

Plato. *Collected Dialogues of Plato.* Ed. Edith Hamilton and Huntington Cairns. New York: Pantheon, 1961.

———. *Gorgias.* Trans. Walter Hamilton. Harmondsworth: Penguin, 1973.

Poliakov, Leon. *The Aryan Myth: A History of Racist and Nationalist Ideas in Europe.* Trans. Edmund Howard. London: Sussex University Press, 1971.

———. *The History of Anti-Semitism.* Vol. 3. Trans. Miriam Kochan. New York: Vanguard Press, 1975.

Pompa, Leon. *Vico: A Study of the "New Science."* 2d ed. Cambridge: Cambridge University Press, 1990.

Potter, David M. *The Impending Crisis 1848–1861*. New York: Harper & Row, 1976.

Pulzer, Peter. *The Rise of Political Anti-Semitism in Germany and Austria*, rev. ed. Cambridge, Mass.: Harvard University Press, 1988.

Putnam, Robert D. *Making Democracy Work: Civil Traditions in Modern Italy*. Princeton: Princeton University Press, 1993.

Puzo, Mario. *The Fortunate Pilgrim*. London: Heinemann, 1965.

———. *The Godfather*. New York: Signet, 1969.

———. *The Last Don*. New York: Ballantine Books, 1996.

Rakove, Jack N. *The Beginnings of National Politics*. Baltimore: Johns Hopkins University Press, 1979.

Rawls, John. *A Theory of Justice*. Cambridge, Mass.: Harvard University Press, 1971.

Reed, Adolph L., Jr. *W. E. B. Du Bois and American Political Thought: Fabianism and the Color Line*. New York: Oxford University Press, 1997.

Reiss, Hans, ed. *Kant's Political Writings*. Cambridge: Cambridge University Press, 1970.

Rhea, Joseph Tilden. *Race Pride and the American Identity*. Cambridge, Mass.: Harvard University Press, 1997.

Richards, David A. J. "Commercial Sex and the Rights of the Person: A Moral Argument for the Decriminalization of Prostitution." 127 *U. Penn. L. Rev.* 1195 (1979).

———. "Comparative Revolutionary Constitutionalism: A Research Agenda for Comparative Law." 26 *N.Y.U. Jl. Int'l Law and Pol.* 1 (1993).

———. *Conscience and the Constitution: History, Theory, and Law of the Reconstruction Amendments*. Princeton: Princeton University Press, 1993.

———. *Foundations of American Constitutionalism*. New York: Oxford University Press, 1989.

———. "Free Speech and Obscenity Law: Toward a Moral Theory of the First Amendment." 123 *U. Penn. L. Rev.* 45 (1974).

———. *Sex, Drugs, Death and the Law: An Essay on Human Rights and Overcriminalization*. Totowa, N.J.: Rowman and Littlefield, 1982.

———. *Toleration and the Constitution*. New York: Oxford University Press, 1986.

———. *Women, Gays, and the Constitution: The Grounds for Feminism and Gay Rights in Culture and Law*. Chicago: University of Chicago Press, 1998.

Riley, Patrick. *Kant's Political Philosophy*. Totowa, N.J.: Rowman & Littlefield, 1983.

Roberts, David D. *Benedetto Croce and the Uses of Historicism*. Berkeley: University of California Press, 1987.

Roediger, David R. *The Wages of Whiteness: Race and the Making of the American Working Class*. London: Verso, 1991.

Rosselli, Carlo. *Liberal Socialism.* Trans. William McCuaig. Princeton, N.J.: Princeton University Press, 1994.

Rotello, Gabriel. *Sexual Ecology: AIDS and the Destiny of Gay Men.* New York: Dutton, 1997.

Roth, Henry. *Call It Sleep.* Orig. pub., 1934; repr. ed., New York: The Noonday Press, 1991.

Rousseau, Jean-Jacques. *The Confessions.* Ed. Lester G. Crocker New York: Pocket Books, 1956.

———. *Emile.* Trans. Barbara Foxley. London: J. M. Dent & Sons, 1961.

———. *La Nouvelle Heloise.* Trans. Judith H. McDowell. University Park: Pennsylvania State University Press, 1968.

———. *The Social Contract and Discourses.* Trans. G. D. H. Cole. New York: Dutton, 1950.

Ruggiero, Guido de. *The History of European Liberalism.* Trans. R. G. Collingwood. Boston: Beacon Press, 1964.

Rutland, Robert A., ed. *Papers of James Madison.* Vol. 8. Chicago: University of Chicago Press, 1973.

Rutland, Robert A. et al., eds. *The Papers of James Madison, 1786–1787.* Vol. 9. Chicago: University of Chicago Press, 1975.

———. *The Papers of James Madison, 1787–1788.* Vol. 10. Chicago: University of Chicago Press, 1977.

———. *The Papers of James Madison, 1791–1793.* Vol. 14. Charlottesville: University Press of Virginia, 1983.

Said, Edward W. *Culture and Imperialism.* New York: Alfred A. Knopf, 1993.

———. *Orientalism.* Vintage: New York, 1978.

Salins, Peter D. *Assimilation American Style.* New York: HarperCollins, 1997.

Sarti, Roland. *Mazzini: A Life for the Religion of Politics.* Westport, Conn.: Praeger, 1997.

Schama, Simon. *Citizens: A Chronicle of the French Revolution.* New York: Alfred A. Knopf, 1989.

Schlesinger, Arthur M., Jr. *The Disuniting of America: Reflections on a Multicultural Society.* New York: W. W. Norton, 1992.

Schmitt, Carl. *The Concept of the Political.* Trans. George Schwab. New Brunswick: Rutgers University Press, 1976.

———. *The Crisis of Parliamentary Democracy.* Trans. Ellen Kennedy. Cambridge, Mass.: The MIT Press, 1985.

———. *Political Romanticism.* Trans. Guy Oakes. Cambridge, Mass.: MIT Press, 1986.

———. *Political Theology.* Trans. George Schwab. Cambridge, Mass.: Harvard University Press, 1985.

Schmitt, Charles B., and Quentin Skinner, eds. *The Cambridge History of Renaissance Philosophy.* Cambridge: Cambridge University Press, 1988.

Schumann, Reinhold. *Italy in the Last Fifteen Hundred Years: A Concise History.* Lanham, Md.: University Press of America, 1986.

Seligman, Edwin R. A., ed. *Encyclopaedia of the Social Sciences.* Vol. 7. New York: Macmillan, 1937.

Sewell, Richard H. *Ballots for Freedom: Antislavery Politics in the United States 1837–1860.* New York: Oxford University Press, 1976.

Sharratt, Michael. *Galileo: Decisive Innovator.* Cambridge: Cambridge University Press, 1994.

Shklar, Judith N. *Men and Citizens: A Study of Rousseau's Social Theory.* Cambridge: Cambridge University Press, 1985.

———. *Montesquieu.* New York: Oxford University Press, 1987.

Sièyes, Emmanuel. *Qu'est-ce que le Tiers Etat?* Paris: Press Universitaires de France, 1982.

Signorile, Michelangelo. *Queer in America: Sex, the Media, and the Closets of Power.* New York: Random House, 1993.

Smith, Denis Mack. *Cavour.* New York: Knopf, 1985.

———. *Cavour and Garibaldi 1860: A Study in Political Conflict.* Cambridge: Cambridge University Press, 1954.

———. *Italy: A Modern History.* Ann Arbor: University of Michigan Press, 1969.

———. *Italy and its Monarchy.* New Haven: Yale University Press, 1989.

———. *Mazzini.* New Haven: Yale University Press, 1994.

———. *Modern Italy: A Political History.* Ann Arbor: University of Michigan Press, 1997.

———. *Mussolini: A Biography.* New York: Vintage, 1983.

———. *Victor Emanuel, Cavour, and the Risorgimento.* London: Oxford University Press, 1971.

Smith, Denis Mack, ed. *The Making of Italy 1796–1870.* New York: Walker and Company, 1968.

Smith, Rogers M. *Civic Ideals: Conflicting Visions of Citizenship in U.S. History.* New Haven: Yale University Press, 1997.

Sollors, Werner, ed. *Theories of Ethnicity: A Classical Reader.* London: Macmillan, 1996.

Southern, David W. *Gunnar Myrdal and Black-White Relations: The Use and Abuse of an American Dilemma, 1944–1969.* Baton Rouge: Louisiana State University Press, 1987.

Sowell, Thomas. *Migrations and Cultures: A World View.* New York: Basic Books, 1996.

Spain, August O. *The Political Theory of John C. Calhoun.* New York: Bookman Associates, 1951.

Spooner, Lysander. *The Unconstitutionality of Slavery,* in two parts. New York: Burt Franklin, 1860.

Sprigge, Cecil. *Benedetto Croce: Man and Thinker*. Cambridge: Bowes & Bowes, 1952.

Spurlin, Paul Merrill. *Rousseau in America 1760–1809*. University: University of Alabama Press, 1969.

Stampp, Kenneth M. *The Peculiar Institution: Slavery in the Ante-Bellum South*. New York: Vintage Books, 1956.

Stanton, William. *The Leopard's Spots: Scientific Attitudes toward Race in America, 1815–59*. Chicago: University of Chicago Press, 1960.

Starobinski, Jean. *1789: The Emblems of Reason*. Trans. Barbara Bray. Charlottesville: University Press of Virginia, 1982.

Steinberg, Jonathan. *All or Nothing: The Axis and the Holocaust, 1941–1943*. London: Routledge, 1990.

Sternhell, Zeev. *The Birth of Fascist Ideology: From Cultural Rebellion to Political Revolution*. Princeton: Princeton University Press, 1994.

————. *The Founding Myths of Israel*. Trans. David Maisel. Princeton: Princeton University Press, 1998.

Stille, Alexander. "The Candidate of Beauty." *London Review of Books*, July 2, 1998.

Stocking, George W., Jr. *Race, Culture, and Evolution: Essays in the History of Anthropology*. New York: The Free Press, 1968.

Stocking, George W., Jr., ed. *A Franz Boas Reader: The Shaping of American Anthropology, 1883–1911* Chicago: University of Chicago Press, 1974.

Sumner, Charles. *His Complete Works*. 20 vols. New York: Negro Universities Press, 1969.

Sundquist, Eric J. *To Wake the Nations: Race in the Making of American Literature*. Cambridge, Mass.: Belknap Press of Harvard University Press, 1993.

Takaki, Ronald. *A Different Mirror: A History of Multicultural America*. Boston: Little, Brown, 1993.

————. *Iron Cages: Race and Culture in 19th-Century America*. New York: Oxford University Press, 1990.

————. *Strangers from a Distant Shore*. New York: Penguin, 1989.

Tal, Uriel. *Christians and Jews in Germany*. Trans. Noah Jonathan Jacobs. Ithaca: Cornell University Press, 1975.

Talmon, J. L. *The Origins of Totalitarian Democracy*. Harmondsworth, Middlesex: Penguin, 1952.

Tamir, Yael. *Liberal Nationalism*. Princeton: Princeton University Press, 1993.

Taylor, John. *Construction Construed and Constitutions Vindicated*. Orig. pub., 1820; repr. ed., New York: Da Capo Press, 1970.

————. *New Views of the Constitution of the United States*. Orig. pub., 1823; repr. ed., New York: Da Capo Press, 1971.

tenBroek, Jacobus. *Equal under Law*. New York: Collier, 1969.

Thernstrom, Stephan, ed. *Harvard Encyclopedia of American Ethnic Groups*. Cambridge, Mass.: Belknap Press of Harvard University Press, 1980.

Thom, Martin. "More Than a Lombard Patriot.", Times Literary Supplement. July 3, 1998.

Thorpe, Francis Newton. *The Federal and State Constitutions.* Vol. 7. Washington, D.C.: Government Printing Office, 1909.

Tiffany, Joel. *A Treatise on the Unconstitutionality of American Slavery.* Orig. pub., 1849; repr. ed., Miami, Fla.: Mnemosyne Publishing Co., 1969.

Tocqueville, Alexis de. *The Old Regime and the French Revolution* Trans. Stuart Gilbert. Garden City, N.Y.: Doubleday Anchor, 1955.

Tomasi, Lydio F., Piero Gastaldo, and Thomas Row. *The Columbus People: Perspectives in Italian Immigration to the Americas and Australia.* New York: Center for Migration Studies, 1994.

Tushnet, Mark V. *Making Civil Rights Law: Thurgood Marshall and the Supreme Court, 1956–1961.* New York: Oxford University Press, 1994.

———. *The NAACP's Legal Strategy against Segregated Education, 1925–1950.* Chapel Hill: University of North Carolina Press, 1987.

Tussman, Joseph, and Jacobus tenBroek. "The Equal Protection of the Laws." 37 *Calif. L. Rev.* 341 (1949).

Vico, Giambattista. *The Autobiography of Giambattista Vico.* Trans. Max Harold Fisch and Thomas Goddard Bergin. Ithaca: Cornell University Press, 1944.

———. *The New Science of Giambattista Vico.* Ed. Thomas Goddard Bergin and Max Harold Fisch. Ithaca: Cornell University Press, 1948.

Viscusi, Robert. *Astoria.* Toronto: Guernica, 1995.

Vlastos, Gregory. *Platonic Studies.* Princeton: Princeton University Press, 1973.

Voegeli, V. Jacque. *Free but Not Equal: The Midwest and the Negro during the Civil War.* Chicago: University of Chicago Press, 1967.

Walker, Frank. *The Man Verdi.* London: J. M. Dent, 1962.

Ward, David. *Antifascisms: Cultural Politics in Italy, 1943–46: Benedetto Croce and the Liberals, Carlo Levi and the "Actionists."* Madison, N.J.: Fairleigh Dickinson University Press, 1996.

Warner, Marina. *Alone of All Her Sex: The Myth and Cult of the Virgin Mary.* London: Picador, 1990.

Watkins, F. M., ed. *Rousseau: Political Writings.* Edinburgh: Thomas Nelson, 1953.

Wheatcroft, Geoffrey. *The Controversy of Zion: Jewish Nationalism, the Jewish State, and the Unresolved Jewish Dilemma.* Reading, Mass.: Addison-Wesley, 1996.

White, Morton. *Philosophy, The Federalist, and the Constitution.* New York: Oxford University Press, 1987.

Wilkinson, J. Harvie, III. *One Nation Indivisible: How Ethnic Separatism Threatens America.* Reading, Mass.: Addison-Wesley, 1997.

Wilson, Representative Henry. *Congressional Globe.* 38th Congress, 1st Sess., March 19, 1864.

Wolin, Richard. *The Politics of Being: The Political Thought of Martin Heidegger.* New York: Columbia University Press, 1990.

Woodhouse, John. *Gabriele D'Annunzio: Defiant Archangel.* Oxford: Oxford University Press, 1998.

Woodward, C. Vann. *The Future of the Past.* New York: Oxford University Press, 1989.

———. *Origins of the New South 1877–1913.* Baton Rouge: Louisiana State University Press, 1971.

———. *Reunion and Reaction: The Compromise of 1877 and the End of Reconstruction.* New York: Oxford University Press, 1966.

———. *The Strange Career of Jim Crow.* 3d rev. ed. New York: Oxford University Press, 1974.

Zangwill, Israel. *The Melting-Pot.* New York: Macmillan, 1922.

Zuccotti, Susan. *The Italians and the Holocaust: Persecution, Rescue, Survival.* New York: Basic Books, 1987).

Index

abolitionists: on argument for toleration, 130, 131, 138; on colonization movement, 109, 161; on Constitution's toleration of slavery, 29; on corruption of conscience in proslavery defenses, 136; on equal protection theory, 159; ethical transformation as aim of, 162–63; on full citizenship for blacks, 35, 161–62; on nonviolence, 162; the radical antislavery position, 30–38

absolute monarchy, 40, 41, 47, 90, 91, 94

Ackerman, Bruce, 120

Adams, Charles Francis, Jr., 170–71

Adams, Henry, 183, 210, 211

Adams, John: on British Constitution, 16, 88; on constitutionalism, 14–15; on fame, 17; on French constitutionalism, 42–43; Massachusetts Constitution, 14, 25; on popular sovereignty, 46; revolutionary constitutionalism of, 10

affirmative action, 229–31

African Americans: affirmative action for, 230; alleged incapacities of, 160–61; alliance with Jews, 194; Black Codes, 165; the colonization movement for, 109, 161; double-consciousness under racism, 7, 125–26, 131, 154, 183; Du Bois on reconstructing identity of, 126, 132, 146, 148–49, 151, 183, free blacks discriminated against, 161, 161n.144; freedmen, 163, 164, 166, 167; Harlem Renaissance, 192, 215; Irish immigrants' racism toward, 4; Italian Americans treating as equals, 173, 227; at mercy of Southern state governments, 170, 176; multicultural identity of, 215; Myrdal on, 138; "one drop" rule, 123; passing for white, 123, 184, 185, 197; political powerlessness of, 120; racial apartheid of, 148; recent

immigrants stigmatized by, 226; Reconstruction Amendments on inclusion of, 168; rights-based protest of structural injustice, 127, 146, 194, 214–15; as scapegoats, 131–32, 173; servile sphere for, 158; and Southern cultural unity, 66, 167; stereotypes of, 138–39, 154–55; in World Wars, 140. *See also* civil rights movement; slavery

alternative cultural traditions, 187, 216

America. *See* United States

American Dilemma, An (Myrdal), 138

American ethnic identity: doing justice to both components of, 6; Du Bois's struggle to redefine African American, 126, 132, 146, 148–49, 151, 183; as implicated in racism, 236–37; Italian American identity and racism, 12, 118, 181–212; revival of, 213–14, 217, 228; as tribalizing, 232. *See also* multicultural identity

Americanization: accepting racism as condition of, 229, 230, 233, 236; challenging injustice precluded by, 186, 187, 197, 227; cultural differences rejected by, 173; as Faustian bargain, 190; immigrant culture rejected by, 177; Miller's depiction of effects of, 206–7; and privatization, 193

American liberal nationalism: cosmopolitanism in, 200–201; growth of, 235; immigrants in development of, 231; Italian Americans choosing over Italian, 198, 200, 201; and the Italian emigration, 116–212; Italian liberal nationalism compared with, 5, 12; racism legitimated in, 172; rights-based protest making progress in, 217; self-doubt about, 173; structural injustice conflicting with, 186; as structurally flawed, 159, 233; treatment of immigrants as test of, 223–24

expansion of American revolutionary constitutionalism, 1. *See also* rights-based protest

politics of loyalty, 129

polygenetic theories of human origin, 134

popular sovereignty: Catholic interpretation of, 47–48; as contestable normative concept, 46; in French revolutionary constitutionalism, 44–63; in Italian constitutionalism, 91, 92; legitimating unconstitutional uses of power in France, 62; Parisian mobs as expression of, 54–55; Protestant interpretation of, 46–47; republican constitutionalism resting on, 45–46; Rousseau on, 48–52, 62; and Schmitt's positivist interpretation of legitimacy, 68–69; Sièyes on, 52–53

positivism, 68, 106, 200, 203

power, political. *See* political power

privatization: as condition of structural injustice, 191; defined, 5; as Italian American response to racism, 12, 191–94, 197, 201, 204, 211, 219, 228, 237; Jewish Americans rejecting, 195

Privileges and Immunities Clause (Fourteenth Amendment), 167

Progressive Era, 170, 186

protest. *See* rights-based protest

Protestantism: critical inquiry encouraged by, 128; ethics of self-government supplied by, 57; Gramsci on, 84–85, 201; interpretation of popular sovereignty, 46–47; nativism among Protestants, 171; right to conscience emphasized in, 16, 47

public opinion: in democratic resolution of differences, 60; in Madison's theory of faction, 21; moral revolution in Northern, 163–64; shift in American after Radical Republicans, 170–71

public/private distinction, 155, 157–58

public reason, racism as corrupting, 162

Puzo, Mario, 192n.273, 205–6

Qu'est-ce que le Tiers Etat (Sièyes), 52

race: Boas on racial explanations, 136–37; interpretive status of, 123–24; Montesquieu and Hume on differences of,

133–34; nineteenth-century scientific theories of, 134–36, 169; objectifying stereotypes based on, 154; racialization of European immigrants and Jews, 172; as suspect classification, 123, 147. *See also* racism

racial discrimination: affirmative action for redressing, 230; antimiscegenation laws, 142–43, 150, 155, 176; Black Codes, 165; in cultural construction of racism, 166; against free blacks, 161, 161n.144; *Plessy v. Ferguson* upholding, 169; state-sponsored racial segregation, 140, 167–68, 176

racism: anti-Semitism compared with, 124, 139, 185, 219; cultural entrenchment of, 105; culture confused with nature in, 174, 175, 226; as European problem, 219–20; and imperialism, 109, 171; Madison on, 35n.83; as moral slavery, 3, 147, 151; religious intolerance compared with, 185; scientific justification of, 106, 134–36, 169, 200, 203; sexism compared with, 147. *See also* American racism; anti-Semitism; Italian racism; racial discrimination

recent immigrants. *See* new immigrants

Reconstruction Amendments: as addressing defect in the Constitution, 26; and ethical transformation of public opinion, 163; ethical vision of national identity in, 164; as expression of American revolutionary constitutionalism, 27–39; federal failure to enforce, 166–67; Fifteenth Amendment, 38, 170; human rights enforced by, 65; inclusion of black Americans as mission of, 168; interpretation after Civil War, 118–19, 141; negative and positive features of, 38; as preserving legitimacy of American revolutionary constitutionalism, 38; Thirteenth Amendment, 38, 39, 147; and universalism, 3. *See also* Fourteenth Amendment (U.S. Constitution)

religion: in American constitutionalism, 56–59; church and state, 58–59; civil religion, 51, 57, 58; in French revolutionary constitutionalism, 59–60. *See also* Christianity

About the Author

David A. J. Richards is currently Edwin D. Webb Professor of Law and Director, Program for the Study of Law, Philosophy, and Social Theory, at the New York University School of Law, where he teaches Criminal Law and Constitutional Law. A third-generation Italian American, his family immigrated to the United States from the hill towns near Naples in the 1890s. Having attended public elementary and secondary schools in Orange, New Jersey, he graduated magna cum laude from Harvard College (studying with John Rawls) in 1966, received his D. Phil. in philosophy from Oxford University (supervised by H. L. A. Hart and G. J. Warnock) in 1970 and his J.D. cum laude from Harvard Law School in 1971. His doctoral dissertation was published as *A Theory of Reasons for Action* by Oxford University Press in 1971. After practicing law for three years with a Wall Street firm, he taught for three years at Fordham Law School. Joining the faculty at New York University School of Law in 1977, he was named Edwin D. Webb Professor of Law in 1994.

His subsequent books include *The Moral Criticism of Law* (Dickenson-Wadsworth, 1977), *Sex, Drugs, Death, and the Law: An Essay on Human Rights and Overcriminalization* (Rowman & Littlefield, 1982) (named best book in criminal justice ethics, Institute of Criminal Justice Ethics, John Jay college), *Toleration and the Constitution* (Oxford University Press, 1986), *Foundations of American Constitutionalism* (Oxford University Oress, 1989) (named one of the best academic books of the year, *Choice* magazine), *Conscience and the Constitution: History, Theory, and Law of the Reconstruction Amendments* (Princeton University Press, 1993), and *Women, Gays, and the Constitution: The Grounds for Feminism and Gay Rights in Culture and Law* (University of Chicago Press, 1998). A book, entitled *Identity and the Case for Gay Rights: Race, Gender, Religion as Analogies,* based on the Shikes lecture in civil liberties he delivered in April 1998 at Harvard Law School, is forthcoming from the University of Chicago Press.